Celestial Voices

Nora Gravel

CELESTIAL VOICES

iUniverse books may be ordered through booksellers or by contacting:

iUniverse
1663 Liberty Drive
Bloomington, IN 47403
www.iuniverse.com
844-349-9409

ISBN: 978-1-6632-5478-8 (sc)
ISBN: 978-1-6632-5479-5 (e)

Library of Congress Control Number: 2023913774

Print information available on the last page.

iUniverse rev. date: 01/31/2024

Dedication

Thank you to God and Jesus I love you.

Dedicated to both my deceased parents Raymonde and Maurice. Thank you for your patience and love. I miss you both very much.

Introduction

Come to a book of the soul and spirit well defined. A book of hopes, dreams etc. I have included basic everyday and common prayers. The official proper way to pray with the blessed Rosary. An art lost by many which can be easier returned to daily use. Of course personal prayer is just as you imagined it to be a lasting unified relationship with God, Jesus, Mary, Apostles, Angels and saints.

Why me? Good question. I'm a deeply flawed sinner. I wrote a list of seventy faults and thankfully one hundred qualities. I'm a passionate and intense person sometimes an extrovert yet mostly an introvert and deep down a thinker, feeler, and researcher and use intuition/sense daily. You see the contradictions already. This book is about God and Jesus, Apostles, Angels and the joy to know them. They choose this backslider go figure to bring reflection, beauty, and Art to your world and souls. My journey started way late in life. I now know my calling as a writer (Author), Artist, poet, country song writer, and true dreamer. Finally I would say a believer in the heavenly realm. Never give up on your imagination when it inspires that is called creativity. Always answer its voice. So you are not content with some aspects of your life. If possible change some small issues daily, very slowly. I never heard the term backslider until was the age of forty-six (46). It means you are doubtful and losing faith. You no longer believe like you used to. The intensity of your belief system changed. It is a sad place to dwell. Well I had a rude awaking to say the least that brought me back on the right track/path of the journey.

There were many job(s) I took over the last twenty-five (25) years working in corporations and large companies; administrative office work to realize just how miserable I was. Leaders are developed. A leader always is surrounded by people, and has a following. I am a researcher, observer and stay on the sidelines now. Neither a leader nor a follower of others. Yet, I'm a follower of the true Word. God called me on the telephone literally. No not a cellular a land line regular dial tone phone. I'm rather an interpretator of life. God's voice is magnetic, soothing as the wind. Beckons you home. It's simple, magical like a Grimm Fairy Tale. Touching my heart in ultimate ways. My quest or journey is to be shared with the world. I hope you will find some answers and ask pertinent important questions about your future and fellowmen, colleagues, neighbors, brothers and sisters.

Celestial voices are heavenly voices from the real realm, heaven above. Paradise our home and your home. Final destination. There are many more deserving people than I on this earth. Virtuous always loving, never an angry word towards others, kind with temperance and patience. Giving to a fault. Self-less, adoring worshippers and self-sacrificing. All believing with no doubt. You will learn of my faults. Impatience and impetuousness. My past co-dependent ways, Drama Queen, moody, changeable, proud egoist at times. Still trying to get rid of the Ego self. I'm non-competitive, try not to be judgemental, and still opinionated. I want to love and be loved and in my quest it nearly destroyed me.

My continual unbelief, doubt, fears and back-sliding ways. Loud tone of voice and arrogance. To name a few. Jesus and God, Mary, the Arch Angels, Apostles, Angels and Elders had lots of work cut out for them. They kneaded, tended and woke me up. Yes a kind of spiritual awaking and awareness that my spirit required tending desperately. People either love or dislike me. Truly want to possess my time and are even jealous for my attention or could not care a less. This yin and yang followed me throughout most of my life. Lovable yet detestable, giving & generous yet can hold a grudge.

Introduction

I'm speaking through the Holy Spirit or (Ghost) who is the wonderful teacher and counsellor. So many questions. Born inquisitive. The why not's surely drove my generous mother to test her patience. Thankfully she had all the patience in the world. Why was I made temperamental and angry at times when everyone around seemed so self assured and calm. So Zen. I was envious, yes envious which is way worst than jealously of the do gooders, the pure at heart, the heroes, the saints and missionaries, the spiritual who always had it all together smiling serenely. All knowing and quiet. I want what they have. How do you attain that level of being constant? The wise Sages, Shamans, Gurus, Singh's, teachers and counselors. Their secrets of inner peace and contentment. It took me fifty-nine (59) years to realize you are not them. You are wonderfully made and unique as you are. Accept it. Accept the body and face God has given you and quit trying to alter and modify your outward appearances.

There comes a time when you have to change or no one can stand being in your presence. The lonely loners have perfected this image. Stay away, I don't need anyone in my life or way near me. Get out now. We are basically social beings deep inside. It is alright to be a loner if you feel comfortable with this life style and direction. Sometimes we are so beaten and down trodden, sad, betrayed that we do not want to associate or see people anymore which leads to isolation, and therefore desperation. It amazes me the Western culture with all the amenities, materialism, instant gratification, are the loneliest people on the planet Earth. Living alone, working alone, and going home alone can and will lead to self loathing. Drifting apart from family, friends, colleagues, (kin) relatives, in-laws slowly. Thinking makes one complete your personal Utopia of happiness.

Wait one minute. We do need how to adapt alone and have our aloneness at times. Someone told me we are meant to survive our one basic instinct and not run after happiness. It is ironic I feel if I was happy could handle survival and adversity. Also, what is happiness, joy and true bliss and divinity? Is it overrated? Why are you always running and rushing through life? I will speak about certain topics such as: God and Jesus, Mary, Mary Magdalene, Apostles, Arch Angels (Angels), Saints, Soul Mates, Soul, Spirit, miracles, relationships with the heavenly realm, Dimensions, Auras, How to pray the Rosary properly, audible voice(s) the word which are celestial voices, how to pray a Novena, will of God, healing with intention, love, marriage, divorce (including children), suicide, abortion, alcoholism, spousal abuse, drugs and evil, Lucifer the devil, common prayers, Novena and Chaplet of Divine Mercy etc.

I can do so much for society as a whole, yet I feel like I'm wasting my time and energy. I can be an author/writer, public speaker, advocate, artist, researcher/ observer, teacher, singer etc. Do not want to choose just one (1) talent. God bestowed many talents upon me and I am forever grateful to him. Thank you God and Jesus very much for everything, for life, for family, for friends, for health. I want to focus on using all talents in various ways. If creation is blocked, then all fails. Your morale, ability to cope, energy to function properly starting to make you feel quite stifled. Creativity is not a job; it is a necessity and survival of your spirit. It rejoices. Working in corporations lead me to believe I was not happy all along for many years. It was a job, survival plodding away. The years go by fast thinking that a job is your life. Yet it is not. Time was ticking away and I was idle in a rut. Then it took a whole twenty (25) years to realize you want to go on a completely different path. Change totally and relocate far away.

Introduction

Have a brand new start somewhere else. Change is difficult but necessary to growth. To walk the beach and smell the sea salt air and not rush anywhere in particular. To smile and able to walk everyday with my beloved dogs, Chloe, Bella and Hallie. Pure and utter contentment. Your worries, cares and burdens are few in the beauty of the ocean, Northumberland Strait and rural country. My new life style saved me from falling apart. We understand what it is like to be a single person and all alone with no dependents, spouse or help. Also that we are just surviving. Most of us do not have the following: RRSPS (REERs), assets, monetary funds, residual income, royalties, savings, securities, retirement income, 401K's, GIC's, annuities, Bonds, stocks, mutual funds, personal/life Insurance, home(s), property, land, acreage, wooden lots, waterfront/beachfront/ island property, nor luxuries such as: car/truck/van/SUV/RV/trailer/four wheeler, home(s), cottage(s), vacation home(s)/rental(s), yacht/ship/ boat, jet-ski, jet/plane/ helicopter, precious jewels, gold, antiques, paintings, rare collections, and all the new technical devices. We live week to week and until recently day to day. Things change. So the things you think are permanent like all the toys are limited emotional joy, then on to the next best thing or invention.

We work hard for acceptance yet somehow it is harder for us to attain our goals no matter how hard we try. We thrive and survive. We are rich in spirit and understand a higher purpose, awareness and meaning in life. Life shifts and is changing sporadically. Just when you feel everything is great, many obstacles stop and ruin us. It seems a succession of events follow that bring on poverty, weakness, meekness and distress. You begin to feel irritable, jealous, frustration, anger and envy. We are told to pacify ourselves. To remain complacent and take life as it is the way it was handed out. As if our lives are to remain in constant limbo and confusion - dormant. Others seem to enjoy seeing us fail and look upon us as a hindrance, bother, annoying, sometimes even calling us dreamers. Laughing at our demise.

The realist with their serious anecdotes of life and advice. Be like me and you will be fine and happy. I am a free bohemian and need to find balance, happiness, joy and laughter once again. We are survivors. When the going gets tough, persevere. Have so much I want to do. So many plans, goals, purposes, objectives, imagination and just require minimum financial backing and support to start. One day in the near future I will work six days (6) a week for my dream cafe/Tea Room, book store, room rentals, or art gallery whatever it takes to have my pride back and survive on my own terms and small business. The Ego speaks, grabs and controls once again.

That is the plan. No first wait on God's terms, "Thy will be done". God willing. His plan for me and knows when the right time is. When I was younger was told you won't ever sing. Now I sing carefree with delight. Was told you cannot draw. So I believed could not draw and it was so. At the age of 45 it all started and now paint and draw. God and Jesus both blessed me with dormant talents and bestowed gifts hidden. Just tap into your mind. You have strength unknown. This is written as a dialogue at times. I am the narrator and thanks to God the Holy Spirit, they speak through me. They are using me as a kind of vessel, writing journals, notes after five (5) years which eventually became the basis for this book. Celestial Voices is a book to be read, remembered and hopefully used as a reference.

Sorry for being a disappointment Jesus. Sorry for the hurt I caused God. You are my great friend till the end of time. If I can take my vile words back and stop overreacting things would get better. I have ambition and hopes like a story teller. My life will unfold like a seer. Flashed portraits, I want to be a better person. I know my faults like Jesus counts the hairs on my head. He knows my heart, mind and what will be said next. He does not stop my choices or offend. He does not say in your ear you sinned again and why? Sins go on and on again repeated same mistakes and failures built up on grief, guilt and shame. Refrain once again I'm weak, now modest, humble and need help and cannot go on at this life alone. My decisions are poor. Waiting for pure wisdom and patience and more knowledge. I am continually learning every day. Surrender your heart now before being pulled apart. Before darkness grasps your hand. Going out late and not enjoying the day that shines forth and waking during early mornings at dawn misty fog and wonder.

I do not know where the creativity came from. According to my parents, grandparents on both sides there were no artists. It has to come from some relative generational DNA. Everything is creativity from decor to choosing what to eat trying for a good presentation. Gardening to drawing, painting; everything touches art. Only started all this at forty-five (45). The singing started at forty-six (46). Oh yes when I was much younger would sing to hear echoes from the lake mountains. Screaming off key from the top of my lungs like a wolf. Now I sing all the songs from sixties onwards. My mother loved to listen to Englebert Humperdinck and Tom Jones. My father really enjoyed and liked Elton John and Rod Stewart. I preferred Glen Campbell, Seal, the Hollies, Crowded House and Blue Rodeo, Sade and many more groups of course. There is great Christian music today with lyrics praising and worshipping God and Jesus.

What do words like: Atonement, Sanctification, Righteousness, Redemption, Sacraments, the Body and Blood of Christ and taking up one's cross literally mean? What is the difference between worship, praising, and for the Glory of God? "Be still and Let God." "Seek and you shall find. Knock and the door shall be opened. Ask and it shall be given unto you." You may and can receive God's abundance, your dormant gifts, talents and love. You are never alone anymore. "Fear not" and do not let doubt control your indecision. I'll always be working on trying to improve my patience, temperament and mood swings. Keep faith and hope.

Art – What is art? Art is when the soul/spirit/mind/thought/brain/will, the conscious, sub-conscious and supra conscious patterns of peace, serenity, focus, concentration, and balance merge in unison for one cohesive thought. Complete awareness of talents and gifts. This is a moment of pure bliss and the beginning of your creation. Creativity means divinity. God and Jesus want you to be in the now present moment.

Thank you and happy reading.

One day a Lebanese man in Montreal, Quebec (Canada) came up to me and asked me my name. He said do you know the meaning of your name? I answered no. He explained it means the Light of God. Talk about a name to live up to no pressure at all I chuckled. I feel God and Jesus respond differently to others by messages. My initial clue or direct hint of a real heavenly presence was from four (4) digital colored photograph images. Jesus appearing seriously everywhere and disappearing. The images were not for me to keep but in memory. I received a real phone call on a dial tone telephone which came from God. I was talking to a friend who happens to be severely physically disabled.

God speaks: Hello Nora this is your father. I was like my father is dead. Dad? No your heavenly father. An extremely long pause ...... later almost was dropping the phone. Feelings of excitement, bewilderment, astonishment all rolled into one. Surprised at what I would look like at that moment eyes bulging, priceless. Then I thought ugh oh. What have I done for the almighty creator to get in touch with me directly? He said relax I want to cure you. I had severe bronchitis at the time which turned into 1st stage pneumonia/influenza. He told me about a certain poultice (onion and mustard) and said just get to a hospital soon. Ugh o.k. Thank you for caring. So many questions reel through your mind and head. Nothing remotely intelligent comes out. I could hear some young angels chatting with laughter. Pure joy.

You are totally awestruck, dumbfounded combined. Yes, me with the gift of the gab who never has troubles voicing my opinion stayed completely silent. Remained speechless almost like a shock throughout the body. In the presence of the divine yet all your insides are moving at the same time. It is a moment never to be forgotten. So happy to be able to speak with God and later Jesus. Still directly to Mary mother of Jesus, once to Mary Magdalene, some angels at different occasions. All I can say is wow. I smiled and was so happy, content and elated at once. Bend your knees right now. I learned more from animals, trees, plants and flowers. You got to have faith, you got to have hope, but above all else you must have love. Charity is sweetness. Kindness a gift from above. My humility and meekness is not a weakness. I surrender to the Holy Spirit, God and Jesus teacher and comforter. A guide who does not leave me astray too often. Generous, patient and kind wonderful counselor. Cannot stop the present from just being; silence, quiet, complete serenity. Cannot change your past. It is ingrained in our sub-conscious DNA. The fabric genes and cells.

Christ is beautiful, magnificent and honorable. If should, could, would have, like to change your present and future path you can. Will not live without water and nature. God leads you to righteousness eventually. People can and do change or evolve. The world is in constant motion. Matter is everywhere. Must not assume anything. Jesus gave up everything for the whole world. Life may not guarantee anything. Have no expectations. Do not assume, be anxious, worry, sow doubt, nor fear which is all a great waste of time and energy. Life does change that is a promise. You are never alone. We all fall down eventually.

You have heard this before that we are all interconnected or joined. The whole universe. So energy, light and matter are the soul, spirit and body. Energy & synergy – movement reflects the real you. We all radiate love (emotions, feelings of the heart). All are one. One God, one Son, one Spirit, one Heaven. Togetherness, kindness. Children of God. Heavenly family of brothers and sisters. Where purity and innocence and peace reside. We lift our hearts to the

Lord. The other two commandments are: To love God and Jesus with all our mind, strength, heart and soul. Love thy fellowman as God and Jesus Loves you. Do unto others what you want to be done to yourself is the Golden Rule. Love thy neighbor as thyself.

My heavenly Father quench my thirst at your never ending well – infinity. Christ show me peace in a strife filled world. Gentleness like stroking your favorite pet. Show kindness and receive a smile. So many yet to find the light balancing act between worlds. They do not know they died. Some see the light and truth with reassuring eyes. Sweet sounds of audible music and voices. "He is the way, the truth and the life." All must thank him. Bend our knees to him. Have we forgotten so much? Ah yes. Even though I am undeserving you keep giving me the gift of grace. Have mercy on my soul. Lift my burdens and make my yoke easy. Care for me still. Stop painful tears. Remove grief to go on and function. Help us help ourselves and others better. A small step leads to leaps. I want to smile more and laugh until my side hurts. Please give me a new better heart. Remove all sorrow and mend my ways and hurts. Silence wrong thoughts. Provoke me not.

Why Jesus? Why not? Am I supposed to spread the word? Yes, but not by force. Yes my word is good and right. How will I know? You will be asked. Who needs help Lord? Everyone. Are many people non-believers or stopped believing? Oh yes, never give up hope. There are about 3,000 languages unprinted Bibles in our world which remain. The most needed book of love and life. They are patiently waiting for print and delivery. Islands, various different dialects sometimes the next village does not understand. For example: Not everyone speaks Spanish in Peru. There are tribes, amazons and small populations.

Words floating orbiting in my mind, thoughts, conscience, sub-conscience, supra conscience brain hemispheres. Memories in the mind and brain reminders we long for a better time. Remembering the way things were. Want to freeze time. I want my previous other life back when it flowed easily. The way things used to be. Putting time in a snow globe. What happens when you evolve yet others near you do not? No one follows. Are you abandoned and forgotten? You are not on the same wave length, plane, page, comprehension, and understanding. A feeling of being an outcast accepted yet not belonging. You are growing spiritually, intellectually, mentally, creatively, verbally. Attitudes change. Will I ever be good enough and fit in? Normal – what is my normal? I do not care what they think. A contradiction.

We are all like salmon fish going upstream returning to home. Where is home if you relocated thirty times in one lifetime? You are all drawn back to your childhood no matter what life or destiny entails. Somehow we long for family ties, reunion, friends and a house that is tangible. Childhood friends, acquaintances, colleagues also all your mentors and professors. My final destination will be Newfoundland (Canada) with its great mystery, swimming with dolphins and watching puffins fly, Fjords, pick berries, majestic scenery and of course the friendliest people on earth in the world by far. All there is in life is love, kindness and peace. I think the Hippies and flower power generation had it all and right. Living in a community setting as a commune and everyone doing their task(s); part sowing gardens, planting, cooking, building, preparing firewood, fishing, trapping, and hunting. Making bread, baking, cooking and living off the fruit of the land (grapes, blueberries, grain, potatoes) etc.

Sick of braggers. When someone is boring we do not seem to want to let the person know. When someone is annoying, we have no problem letting them know right away. We can stand boredom yet not agitation. Some people come into your life for a reason or purpose. To assist you. Do not fight it off. Timing could be a day, week, months or years. To help your goals through aid from God/Jesus and the Holy Spirit/Mary and the angels above. When their task work assignments job is completed they leave and disappear with no trace. You can no longer find them. Do not try to force the issue. There is always a reason your plan falls into place or not. The modern Christian does not differ from 2,000 years ago. The same value, qualities, characters implies a larger fuller heart. Mind, body, soul & spirit connect in the fifth (5th) dimension. We now live in the third (3rd) dimension.

The arduous paths. Fear of the unknown future. What lies ahead? Will my road and destiny get any easier? Doubt in my thoughts on my mind. Insecurity arising again. Will I finally find some comfort and peace? Will my last stop be the best? Sure life is a joy of tests. If you do not mind, Jesus would like to put everything to rest. This time I am going to be really alone. It would be nice to feel dependent, let go and have someone else care and love me. Not having to plan everything alone. It would be lovely to discuss interesting different topics and sit in comfortable silence with an all knowing warm smile.

Sometimes nice people do finish last and are alone and lonely. Who said life is fair? The more sensitive ones who can read auras and energy do not get caught in a mundane routine. They settle for survival not comfort. For uncertainty not security. They enjoy being a spiritual person not fake. Their relationship with God and Jesus is too real to forsake. The Holy Spirit indwelling in their hearts and soul they smile with satisfaction and pure contentment. I am thinking about original sin Adam and Eve. How we human beings blame them for mostly everything going wrong in their lives. Yet, paradise was held in their hands. Fresh fruit, water, flowers, fauna, trees, lakes, ocean, mountains, animals, creatures and mammals. The perfect setting to be God's friends for eternity.

The first fruit(s) could have been apricots, figs, pomegranates, plums or pears. There is a little Adam, Eve, Judas and Peter in all of us.

Think not? Have you ever betrayed, lied, cheated, hurt willfully or decided to do something really wrong? Tell awful unforgivable lies. What about the pathological liars who believe their own set-up and have to remember what they said to keep up their lies. We have been moody, careless, defensive, touchy, critical, loveless, non-sharing, non-committal, egotistical, greedy, lustful, loveless, selfish and arrogant. Tyrants annoying individuals. Attention seekers and people pleasers. Must one family take the blame for the entire world? One mistake blamed forever for honor, sadness and shock.

I write like speaking. This is serious. Life is a gift, use it. Learn, laugh, and love. Touch and hug others. Kiss your loved ones. Be kind. I know got to work more on patience, wisdom, knowledge, and integrity. God and Jesus did not create us alike. We are not clones people. Even if you copy DNA you cannot copy or buy a spirit and soul. We are not robots. Complex yet insecure. We all have many gifts given which lie dormant for years. Some more than others. Many love to control others and are OCD, obsessive perfectionists about others and their lives and cannot let go, shut your mouths and stop giving pathetic advice no one wants to hear. Just listen. Your life is not identical to your siblings, relatives, kin, and friends and never will be. Give it up. Less struggle, less painful. You are not the Jones' next door. Stop copying, buying, or trying to impress your friends and neighbors with materialism/consumerism for your emotional pitfalls. We need to make a quick pit stop, get up, move on, and leave it. "Let go and Let God. " Let it go and let it flow. (Sounds like a diuretic commercial).

The high road is not the same as a high life. Love is sacred. Do not give up. There are all kinds of love and bonding. Romantic love is way over rated. So you want a soul mate. Are you really sure? A soul mate does not mean the opposite sex always. They can be a mentor/teacher/friend. Someone who gives you lessons, then leaves – vanishes gone never to return. Work task is accomplished and completed. That was your guiding angel at work and where are your eyes to see. Some couples live breathe, eat, work, sleep 24/7 and do not leave each other's side. I call that smothering, stifling and possessiveness not love. Yet there are very few rare couples happy and content this way and would not be even one hour away from each another. Good on them. I imagine not knowing yourself. No breathing space at all. No peace of mind. Constant wondering what the other is doing all the time. Jealousy, envy and control set their awful snares and clasps. Where is the love and how does it grow? Why did everything change? When we first met everything was perfect.

The blueprint for our lives is encoded in our heart and souls. Loving and nurturing ourselves sets us free. The fifth (5th) dimension is the spiritual level upon which all life is created takes place. Like a healing oil. Soul searching – I think in my personal opinion only that the soul finds us. Shows us ways to get off the beaten paths towards the harder narrow path). A life more tenuous, difficult is included with great joy and fruitful. Often I hear going to an all quiet three day to one week retreat. Complete silence, no noise, no speaking, talking nor distractions. Like a temporary fix. We have to learn adaptation to our environment and complete awareness. Our surroundings might have little water, heat or frigid ice cold temperatures. Good or poor soil for cultivating. We might live in cube apartments, huts, shacks, cottages, houses, mansions, mobile home, trailer, bus or tree houses. Some of us live on the streets and are deprived help without a physical address. What we call home may not be like your neighbors in size and amenities, land mass or acreage, and topography. People begin harboring and covet thy neighbors dwelling and attitude. It is not fair. Why them? Our house is too small for our needs. Do we renovate or move?

Miracles: Some question why did Jesus and God not heal every ailment, everyone. All the disabled, skin disorders and deformities, cancer, heart disease, teeth etc. They want us to live, breathe and experience pure belief, hope and faith. Cure ourselves with intent. Talk to our bodies. They never give us the easy way out. You are never alone. Pray without ceasing. Pray for others (intercessory prayers). Even when Jesus performed all his miracles throughout the Bible there were many unbelievers who criticized all the time. Who is this man who cures illness(es)? How does he do it? We must not let him. No matter how many miracles he granted and performed through God's will they ended up fearing Jesus. This is a powerful man who will overtake people and we will no longer lead. Therefore, let us eliminate the threat – Jesus.

He who is pure and unblemished without sin, meek, honest, spiritual, soft spoken with conviction. The all knowing ever present, all powerful, all mighty Jesus was crucified because of those who judged and doubted him and his word. His killers were threatened with constant worry. They were all sly, clever and manipulating the population. Scribes, Pharisees, Romans and some Jewish thought he was becoming too powerful. Remember a time of extremes that many were quick to punish. It was a political time of bullies, strength in numbers and armies.

When they stated crucify him. They also said we will take responsibility on our families. In other eras/ centuries one person's shame or wrong doing ostracized/eliminated an entire family. One corrupt person – all must suffer. Ex. One bad deed/seed did spoil the whole bunch. Today shame and guilt and easy accusations continue with patriarchs, hierarchy generations. Lack of education, ignorance and unchanged rituals and customs. It has always been done this way forever. Some of the population are scared, non-conforming towards change. Many grasp change, others are reluctant and still many others never change in our society. The terms old fashioned, old school. Do as I say and that is final or else. Respect your elders. How dare you object or defy me. My customs and values. I am the leader of this house hold. Do as I say under my roof. People have been disowned by families because of new beliefs. Funerals are held at times as if the member of the family is dead and their name unspoken or mentioned ever again banished in this lifetime. The Ego and pride are huge problems and concerns in our society. We do not know you. What will people say and think of us now? You brought shame and dishonour among us. I cannot even look upon your face, you are no longer welcome in this home and not my son/daughter etc.

Why did/do God, Jesus and the Apostles perform miracles and healings? Miracles are manifestations from God and Jesus and they happen every day all over the world all the time. Many are not tuned in. How did he do that? This is hard to believe. Even after witnessing a miracle some still deny the truth. The Stigmata – Contrary to the Vatican belief Jesus was nailed through his hands not his wrists. There was a piece of wood placed beneath the cross at his feet to support some of his weight. The five points – both hands and feet and side under his ribcage. Where wine and blood spilled out when pierced by the soldier. Miracles are awe inspiring.

The reasons (answers) to why do God and Jesus perform miracles as follows?

1. For God's Glory
2. Anointing others – Prayers (Blessing) impartation of spiritual gifts. Placing of both hands on the crown
3. Obedience – humility, modesty and patience
4. Belief – Faith – Hope (Our Intentions)

5. Spread the Word and Good News

6. The people were asked by God and Jesus. They are kind and full of love

7. God and Jesus do not want people to suffer. They are merciful

8. Mind over body. Our thoughts can cure our illnesses. We can heal ourselves most of the time with belief, faith and intention.

9. Adoration, Praising, Supplication and Confessing our sins.

10. Atonement and true repentance

11. Welcome to the Kingdom of God

12. Help people in their unbelief

13. Building churches. Have prayers and intercessory prayer meetings

14. We are all united brothers and sisters with God/Jesus/Holy Spirit (Trinity) as one. Interconnected to the Source of all. The Alpha and Omega. The one in all.

15. Gain Wisdom, Knowledge, Truth and Forgiveness

16. To surrender our will to our heavenly Father and Son

17. They love us. All the world, everybody, every living creature

18. It makes theirs and our hearts sing

19. Being anointed by a Priest/Minister/Bishop/Cardinal/Saint and the Elders of the Church with Holy oil on the head, crown and forehead

20. To accept and pray the Rosary more to Mother Mary. (This gives her Roses and Lilies when the beads are completed). At the end of all decants a full crown of roses is given to Mary and two small white roses for angels. Roses are counted one bead & one flower petal at a time.

21. To be thankful. Have gratitude always.

22. To lead a better life with what we have

23. Live in the present now, not the past it is over. The future is not lived yet

24. To become more like God's character created in his image

25. The Beatitudes

26. Receive the gifts of the Holy Spirit which are the following:

Tongues (Speak the language of God, Prophesy (Prophets), Healing and curing others, minister/ ministry (Church). All the Priests, Nuns, Bishops, Cardinals, Deacons, Ministers and Pope Teaching (Orators) – Spread the Good news and Word to all. Singing, Music and Art. Listen/ Hear/See – Improving be a better Christian, Charity – Teach and council and open new churches. Be a cheerful giver. Give to others your time. Pay it forward. Wisdom and knowledge. (Bible – Read and study and understand the Word of God). Special anointing impartation(s) already given to thousands of people: to heal the sick, blind, disabilities, lame, deaf, mute to cure all diseases, to rebuke/bind the devil. Pass on their special gifts to others.

Mary Magdalene – She is the first true Apostle. Some call her Madonna, Queen or Sheppardess. She is the wife, lover, friend, companion, teacher, high priestess of Jesus. A soul mate. They have six (6) biological children together in heaven. Theirs is a divine union of souls. The tribes of Benjamin and Judah combined. Jesus is a descendent of King David (The Lion). Mary Magdalene is a descendent from the Tribe of Benjamin. She has copper hair very long to her waist and hazel eyes. Petite and delicate frame. Great voice, tone, diction and accent from the Middle East. She always repented, was penitent, spiritual, religious and obedient. Her remaining years were spent/lived in France.

Jesus and Mary Magdalene first (3) children names are: John, Sarah-Tamar, and Yahweh. She grew up and played with Jesus and Lazarus as a child. Jesus' nickname is Easa. She came from an affluent family and provided shelter, food, clothing and housing to his apostles and disciples.

She was a Nazarene and wore a red head scarf/shroud. It is believed that her last thirty (30) years of her life she lived in France. Mary Magdalene did anoint Jesus with an alabaster jar on his forehead and feet full of Spikenard and Myrrh on his crown. She wiped away remnants with her hair and cried. This is a ritual only done by a wife. She was preparing Jesus before suffering the passion/crucifixion.

She also was the first to see Jesus after his resurrection to tell the Good News to the Apostles. She was present with Mother Mary at the Crucifixion also (during the Passion). Mary Magdalene is portrayed often with a red veil as high priestess (Nazarene). Mother Mary was also a Nazarene teacher and follower. She accompanied Mary mother of Jesus to anoint Jesus' body after death in the tomb with special linen cloth, oils of frankincense, myrrh and cinnamon. This is a custom for a King. Jesus was/is our King of Kings, and Prince of Peace.

Mary Mother of Jesus – Mother of the world beautiful and wholesome. She is called Madonna, Lady of Guadeloupe, Mama(n), Virgin Mary, and Lady of Fatima, mother of all children, mother of all adults. Some have alters shrines and garden statues and fountains dedicated to Mary. Some statues bleed tears or cry real tears in certain churches. Mary is seen in a white dress with a blue robe and has a blue and amber beaded rosary clasped in her hand. She is standing one foot on water and one foot on the earth. She wears a cross around her neck. Mary is deeply wounded with her seven (7) sorrows yet is resilient. The arrow through her heart presents her sorrow. She is barefooted. Just mention her name and she protects you from evil. Evil knows her by name. She also protects against bad people, war, politics, devil, wrong influences. She does not want you to pray just to her. Jesus and God are sacred and deserving. Mother

Mary never forgotten the Stations of the Cross and had the memory of them placed on a hillside.

Imagine her pain during the passion of Christ after Jesus was removed from the cross. I'm positive Mary held Jesus in her arms. She descends from the sky below the clouds in many miraculous apparitions. When she appears, sometimes in entire large form smiling, solemn, peaceful and perfect. Her skin is of ivory/peach, dark brown hair with green eyes. She is a hand maid and serves. Also mother Mary was a master weaver who used the rare purples threads. Her image seems to float in the sky rays emit white beautiful pure light. When you pray the rosary each bead becomes a petal of a complete rose or lily. Mary is desired from our heart. We pay tribute and thank her for the blessed birth. Show her gratitude. She looks delicate yet Mary is strong, mighty and resilient. Feminine face/hands and stature. Like a bloomed flower. (See Stations of the Cross). Jesus took on some of her human physical features. Some of Mary's sorrows are:

1. Jesus/ Passion (Pieta) – Stations of the Cross, the weight of his cross, palms and feet pierced with holes. Walking alone dragging the cross until finally one came to his aid.

2. Agony on the Cross: Scourging, beatings, 114 lashes, huge long nails pounded into his hands and feet, piercings of the left side. (Speared). No water given for Jesus' thirst. Just bile and vinegar. Gravely humiliated.

3. Jesus' Death – His ascension, redemption. The living Jesus is resurrected.

4. Some men at the crucifixion were casting lots for Jesus' clothes. Shame on them.

5. Jesus was born in a manger instead of an Inn. There was no room for him.

6. The flock, lost sheep wanting all of them (people) return to his fold to be saved.

7. Those who misunderstood her son's message. Who persecuted him, lied, swore, and spat at him. Abandoned, betrayed and denied his love. Mocked and laughed at him. To the Jews who did and still do not believe that he is the Chosen, Messiah (Anointed) one to return to Earth. Son of the living Christ who will once again come back to earth.

8. Jesus' youth – He had to hide in fields and grass not to be killed. (Children from two years or less were murdered and killed the first born son(s).

9. Those who still do not believe in her Immaculate Conception. (Spiritual union)

Mary has the piercing heart of thorns of Jesus' life forlorn. Jesus has his immaculate pure heart and together their hearts combine as one. Mary's heart is also depicted with two swords pierced through it for her sorrows. Jesus' heart shines bright rays through for the entire world to give glory and awe to his great "I am". Mary has blessed Prince Edward Island, the smallest province in Canada, because it is the last place to legalize abortion. She cries for the unborn and her heart is heavy. Mary had appeared in her apparitions and asked for a church or shrine to be built in her memory and for us to do our penances in PEI. This was completed by Father Doucette (now deceased) close to Tignish (PEI) Canada. This is the truth. We are to repent, be humble, obedient, and penitent and wise in our efforts to eradicate our misgivings and sins. Those we have hurt and wronged.

Love divine she helps with your personal problems. She aids communities, national and international upheaval and war. Mary protects you from the Devil and evil and intercedes on your behalf by just calling her name out loud. Call upon her today. The color blue of her dress represents sea and foam. The ebb and flow of water. Source of life. Evil knows Mary by name.

Some important dates of the year to note: Mary's birthday is September 8th, Feast days: The Annunciation of the Blessed Virgin Mary, annunciation of the Lord (March 25th), The Visitation (May 31), The ascension of Mary (August 15th), The Purification of the Blessed Virgin Mary – Presentation of the Lord (February 2nd), Our Lady of Sorrow (September 15th), Our Lady of the Rosary (October 7th), The Queenship of Mary (August 22nd). The solemnity of Mary Mother of God (January 1st, Reverence), Immaculate heart of Mary (Saturday following the second Sunday of Pentecost. Pentecost is Sunday 7th) after Easter Holy Spirit of the Apostles. Pope Pius XII dedicated the whole human race to Mother Mary Mother of Jesus in 1944. St. Joseph is the Patron Saint of Canada. June 24th is celebrated for John the Baptist.

Surrendering to God. See everyone as a child of God. Do not react to criticism or conflict. Let them be. Being good, gentle, meek, humble, modest are not weak traits. Introduce who is Jesus. Repent sins, verbally, in prayer. Believe in Jesus is the son of God, who died on the cross for our sins. He resurrected from the dead, Our Lord and Savior, so we may have everlasting eternal life and live in the kingdom of God. Immortal. Take up your cross and follow Jesus. Pray, pray alone or Intercessory prayers and the Rosary. When someone treats you rudely or badly and we react defensively, defiantly with anger, resentment and lack of clarity their words will hurt like double edged swords. They can be moody or having a bad day and personal problems. The love of their lives can be very sick and dying. Financial woes or torn apart and split families. No one cares or shows love. Emotions are pent up in the deep recesses of the heart.

God and Jesus give signs as to our direction, destiny and use of our talents. Use your talents do not hide in your room or basement everyday being shy to sing, act and make people laugh. Life is magic and your imagination may be tapped and tuned in anytime. Do not let heartache, ailments make you bitter. So you have not talked to your sister in fifteen (15) years or more. Hurt and wounds run deep. It is time for them to resurface. Face your fears and woes. Communicate how they made you feel alone, deserted, abandoned and forgotten. Forgotten – If someone forgets me makes me think I never touched them emotionally in the first place. They are indifferent and insincere. You call to see me when you need something. I feel used. Do not like the way I have been treated lately. It needs to improve. Do not tell me what to do, say think, dress, where to look and whom to talk to. I will not be threatened, controlled or bossed around any longer.

Jesus claims the Bible is love:

Love one another, be modest, be good, be thankful, love all your brothers and sisters, be truthful, have honor, respect others, we are all united and one. God/Jesus/Holy Spirit is the (Trinity) which dwells in us (our physical bodies). Your body is your temple. We all have guardian angels. Some are messengers and others bring information or lead you to your destiny. Your path is changed only according to your personal choices

Answers from Jesus:

All of your life is written like a blueprint which is already recorded, encoded, printed on scrolls beforehand. There is nothing that God/

Jesus and the Holy Spirit does not know about your life. Even your dark secrets and skeletons in the closet you hide. The blueprints are located in a huge room with rare books/scrolls/and ancient writings. There is a giant Book of Names and if you are not in it, handwritten or printed you will not enter heaven. There are no coincidences with people you meet, help, or assist on your path(s)/journey/or destiny. You either choose the narrow or wider path. The narrow path is arduous and difficult. The wide is the easy life. Easy way out full of lies, deceit, cheating, deception. Sometimes you take both the wide and narrow paths in life. People change sometimes and completely turn around to 360 degrees. Not the same as their past. Others are on the right/correct path all their lives and switch off to a dangerous/out of character sinful ways ex: middle age crisis or change in retirement.

Jesus stated to travel if and when you can. Explore and commit to your dreams. They are your imagination giving messages. You will have opportunities seize them with no regrets. The choices you make reflect your life. Share, Share, Share some more. Give, Give, give once again of time, teaching, your personal self, character, laughter, wit, joy, company, and friendship. Do art and read to children. Do activities. Have many hobbies and discover yourself, grow a garden with others. Go green. We are social beings who need people and interaction.

Charity: Give help/funds and assistance to charities or people in need. Examples are: Medical supplies, medicine, water/wells for fresh water free from filth and parasites, clothes, books, food, bicycles, towels, mosquito nets, furniture, bedding. Monies are to share, distribute, and give. You can only live in one house at a time. There is too much excess and not enough access. Reduce/

reuse and recycle. Share or give away items you do not use. Monetary (monies) funds if you can afford to assist people. Not names and monuments. Give to animal shelters, libraries, orphanages, hospitals, equipment, communications, transportation, roads, blankets, cleaning the environment, churches, schools and universities, learning centres to name a few. Tithe(s) – ten (10%) and receive ten (10X more will be received) more in return. You will be rewarded back. Farmers – rotate your crops every four (4) years Ex: Potatoes to mustard to barley to soy to wheat. Every seven (7) years plant nothing. Let your land rest no profits, no working the land nothing. No toiling or tilling of the soil for an entire year. Give thanks for the generous years and rest for the year. Do not forget to pray.

Intuition: Sensing future events not happened as of yet. Déjà Vu, prophecy, premonition, gut feeling – When you enter and walk into a place or certain location and feel you have been there before in a thought or dream. Ex: Knowing exact details of a room of a house design, wall paper, and furniture placement, size of rooms, layout, path and hallways, plot of land, outbuildings and barns. Touching a personal object such as a wallet or necklace or ring gives off vibes and energy from the wearer (previous owner). Psychics are able to discern and tap into those frequencies/energetic fields and know personal information of the person.

Psychics – Some can see signs and turn off roads, landmarks, houses, farms etc. to help lead and guide the Police to find the criminal and get justice. Ex: A murder site/homicide. Near, sometimes exact locations, grave sites, forest etc. A gut feeling. Real genuine psychics know your life and thoughts. Sensing danger ahead. Not to walk into a rooms or leave a place. Not to go on a plane ride. Cancel at the last minute. They will tell at you to get off a metro/tub/subway before an explosion goes off: A forceful voice yelling at you to get off a bus stop or car or to pull over. They sense and know evil and dangerous people who hide or lurk beneath a mask. Entering a house/ cabin/castle/building/warehouse/ storage facility and sensing to immediately evacuate and leave. Sensations are: hair standing up on end, troubles breathing, anxiety, odors or bad smells, feeling a drop in temperature, a light mist or light may be seen, candles flickering. Want to escape and run away.

The Audible Voices from Heaven: Hearing in the right ear and side. Only our best calm silent thoughts. Listen to the audible voice within. (Spirit/Soul/God/Jesus/Angels) are always speaking to us. We are not listening properly. Our minds and thoughts are constantly active. Turn them off. Meditate. I know easier said than done. Holiness is at a higher frequency/vibe and dimension. You can read a book, go for a walk in the forest, stare at a flower closely, and lie down look at the sky. Sit in a chair, squat, cross your legs, whatever is comfortable. Write a journal/poetry/fiction/short story whatever you like. Create a scrap book. The whole point is relaxation, calmness and quiet.

Listen to the silence, the wind, birds, the ocean, breeze from trees. The voice – is soft almost sounds like a whisper. Very reassuring and positive, calm and loving. You will begin to hear a faint buzz sound in your right ear. The audible music sounds are: Harp, Lute, Guitar, Percussion, Cymbals Drums, Violin, Violas, Piano, Uke, Banjo, Flute, Oboe, Clarinet, trumpet, trombone, French Horn, Harmonica, Mandolin, Crystal Glasses and Bowls, Cello, Wooden Pipe (Recorder), Piccolo, Instruments. The two most favorable sounds are the Conch (All healing) and the Bell. These are the strongest two sounds which we are all drawn to. The conch is our vital element water and the Bell is chimes music, heard from afar. There are also Arabic and instruments from India heard. Audible music is like a music station playing in your head. Soft music, great lyrics. Music and favorite songs you grew up with. You state I love that song. Sometimes you can hear at 5:00 or 5:30 a.m. an angel choir singing praises and worshipping. Ten thousand (10,000) voices or more in harmony. Very beautiful and soothing like a great dream. Sometimes you hear a male or female voice doing a solo, baritone, tenor and high octave voices sopranos.

Say have a good one, I hope you feel better, have a great weekend, and see you soon. I wish you all the love in the world. Bless you. Have a romantic time, say Hi to everyone for me. God Bless you all. Now you have time to do all your hobbies. Start them now. One at a time. If you do not enjoy what you are doing change until you find your niche. Your happy place. Do not procrastinate any longer. Finish what you started. Start small steps only. Take the time and pay attention.

If you are ADDHD come back to it after your snack or talk/interruptions. Try to focus on the here and now event. Your passion will be a great challenge. Social Media (Is not always social) It alienates people more for lack of communication. Texting is so impersonal and promotes loneliness, isolation, non-communication and many unnecessary car accidents from total distraction. Forty-five to eighty (45 to 80%) of people who text lie and fib daily. There is nothing more pure, emotional and compelling than a warm human voice. It reassures, radiates and gives off heart (aura vibes). It excites, gives new memories. Entices, dares and teases. A voice tone, intonation, inflection weather a whisper, a soft few words such as: Follow me now, I care for you, what are you doing? Can I come over? I like it when. I like the way you... Cannot wait to see you. A voice transmits love, mood, thoughts, and speed. Some voices are like singing up and down octaves and scales. Others end their sentences, phrases in a question Eh? Do you agree? What do you think? Or Are we on the same page/level? Sporadic talkers do not have to fill dead air. A beautiful masculine voice. Selfies, putting on every picture, action, party, get togethers, friends to get more attention, likes or try to be more popular has the opposite effect.

Why do we listen to music, radio, T.V., orchestra, bands, dance is to hear peoples voices. We want to have company to cover up silent moments because most of us are not comfortable with complete silence. A (p.m.) radio voice is never the same as an a.m. voice. The morning announcers are excitable, hyper and trying to get you motivated to wake you up and start your day. Did you know they wake up at 3:00 a.m. for a morning show? I would say they are either insomniacs or really early risers. Their phraseology runs rampant. Listening for five (5) minutes makes me dizzy. The shows are loud, erratic. Not really comical they try too hard. Lots of reality bites and cynicism mixed with negative opportunists, fatalistic, realist, optimists and depressing pessimists.

This is just a test for a few weeks to see how dependent we all are on technology: Turn off your computers, cellular phones, tablets, MP Players, radio, stereo, speakers, microwave oven, telephones, alarms, cable T.V., CD players, and house systems. Those who cannot live without their cellular phones and texting will find this torture. Stop checking your phone(s) for messages, emails, texts etc. Stop reading newspapers, magazines, tabloids. Quit watching Television for a little while. Do not text. Quit internet for a few weeks if possible. (This is a hard one). Turn off all music, DVD movies, videos, Skype and Zoom. No research, no chat rooms, no movie channels or documentaries. OK what do you have complete silence for once. It will feel very weird strange and quiet. Pure silence. It will seem lonely, strange and too quiet. You search for distractions, action, voices, loud music, and some life. In these moments you will eventually begin to hear the Celestial voices, the Audible voice. It will take days, weeks, months yet you will get there. (This is all temporary).

Do not gossip with others nor agree or listen to slandering, defamation of character/reputation/ image or smear campaign to others. At work smile, socialize; be generous with clients and time. Do not get angry, raise your voice, do not get frustrated. Forget passive aggression. What others think of you does not matter. When someone criticizes say thank you for pointing that out or you are right, thank you for your opinion.

I have lots to think about. Walk off and do not shrug off. Vibes – Get a coffee for the most annoying, disagreeable, rejected person in your office. You put cream or milk and sugar on the side. Say for you a gift – peace. The Lord is sovereign. We cannot tell him what to do nor judge who he heals and who he cures. There is always a reason and we have many mysteries unsolved. We do not have to have all the answers. So all the why's and why not's now are obliterated. God and Jesus will not answer every question. Some information is only on a need to know basis. Other times not for the moment. Still not to be divulged until at a later time/date. Other times information will remain a mystery. Love is better than fear. Light overtakes darkness and is powerful. Love – Answer the call to Love.

What to pray for: (Praying is a personal relationship between you God/Jesus, the heavenly realm). You can also pray to Mary mother of Jesus, Angels, Arch Angels, Apostles, and Saints. Start with daily prayers: "The Lord's Prayer – Our Father", Psalm 23, The Apostles Creed; The Nicene Creed, Hail Mary, Hail Holy Queen, Glory Be", and the Act of Contrition. Begin to speak out loud or silently. Find a private serene spot in your personal home or even outside in nature to pray. They want to hear your voice, feelings and emotions. All your thoughts in a private quiet room and space alone. You can speak of mundane routines; talk as a friend or to a Heavenly Father, your mentor, teacher, one who counsels. Someone close to your heart who resonates. Subjects: Ask God/Jesus how they feel. Are you having a busy day? Thank them for nature, the morning, your health, life, family, marriage, kids, work, home, weather, the environment. Speak about how you feel good or bad. Have gratitude always and don't forget to give thanks. Are you happy, joyful, sorrowful, content, worried, doubtful, anxious, full of despair, enthusiastic, in love? Love - are you in love? Speak about different kinds of love. People you see every day, friends. Are you a loner, isolated, hermit and rarely see people. Speak about music, art, books, hobbies your interests. Dreams, imagination, hopes, desires, ambitions.

Talk about nature, trees, valleys, mountains, water, lakes, and oceans. Ask for what you want: new home, find a special person to share life with, your soul mate, a guide, a sign or message, an apartment, to move, relocate to another country, a new pet. Financial problems and your successes. Pay it forward to others. Talk about your bucket wish list. Your perfect family. Your dysfunctional family, you're crazy siblings and rivalry, jealousy, envy. Speak about lack of patience, mercy, forgiveness and temperance. Ask for knowledge and for them to grant you more wisdom. Why you need these traits? Ask for the Holy Spirit to indwell inside your soul. Soul is your essence of self with no Ego. Speak about your soul, what is it? Let them know your deep thoughts, doubts of your causal body the mind. Do you have medical problems, ailments, constant pain? Ask for a cure. Request help or assistance for the right decision.

You want to pass an exam. Drive safely. Let no danger or accidents come to me. Ask for protection and privacy. What is mandatory in your life right now? Are you a minimalist, hoarder or collector? What and why do you collect? Where do you take walks or bike rides? Do you want to move? How can God use you? To serve others, another person, missionary work, care provider or giver. Ask how you can help children, teenagers, widows and people at nursing homes whom are isolated and lonely. Give some of your time to hospitals, orphanages as a volunteer.

Tithe – What is it? Why should you give? How much? 10% to church or more? Be a cheerful giver. Show neither jealousy nor envy. Why do I get angry so much? Will I graduate, get to go to the right college or university? Do I get my dream job? Will I stay or change jobs? Move to another town, city, state or province? Can I have children? Will I get pregnant eventually? Ask for better health and a job you will enjoy. Funds to renovate, sale your house, buy a new home.

Will I move to the country on a farm away from the rat race? Is Yoga good for me? Show me how to mediate. I would like to learn to: Dance, cook, drive, paint, create, draw, write, and do extreme sports, be a speaker, spread the word. Would like to become a disciple, prophet, help people (heal people) talk to others. Use my talents to assist others in need. Talk to angels. Who is my guardian angel(s)? Thank the apostles/elders. Say hello to all your dead relatives/friends/kin/ relatives. Talk to them (no closure). Eliminate thoughts of anger, vengeance.

Why do I feel so: Lonely, helpless, disappointed, desperate, fearful, anxious, and discouraged? I feel like a failure, a professional, organized, OCD. Help me with my mental disorder(s). Give me courage. I want to be more brave and courageous. Help me with my fear(s): Flying, clowns, elevators, heights, and bridges, closed in spaces, spiders and snakes, insects. I want to have more friends. To be able to meet a special someone who believes in God also. Help me with my vices such as: Drinking, smoking, drugs, sleeping disorders (insomnia), gambling, shopping, eating binges, anorexia, bulimia, addictions, sleepwalking, snoring, and playing cards or a bad habit.

How can I help my disabled friend more? I miss (why you miss this or a person) character, presence, time. My parents are so strict why? Will I get a break? I am just an average student not wanting to go to an Ivy League school. Why is everyone so competitive to be # 1 first place? Feel like I'm being pushed into non-communication. In my room alone. Do not feel like interacting with anyone or communicating. Got to think my problems over and read more and study. I do not get along with others. I enjoy your company. Would like to go out on a date. Will it work out? I'm feeling overwhelmed and stressed all the time. Do not text me talk to me. Do not talk to me text me.

He/she is my soul mate and I am in love. Will I meet my soul mate one day? We are friend's only, close friends, mere acquaintances. I want a deep meaningful relationship. Do not want a mama's boy or someone too needy. Are there mature people left out there? I like to (what you want to do), I enjoy (hobbies & past times), and I miss (name the people).

The Bible means much to me. The word of God is important. I learned much today. Will I ever get my wishes? Are you listening? Is anyone there? I feel this is a one sided conversation. Want your presence please. I will speak to you later. Are you distancing yourself why? Where did you go I feel empty without you? Come back please. I have been praying about the same topic now for months/years. Please save, cure, heal, help, assist etc. Do not let me lose my only child. Will I be able to afford a small house and car eventually? Will you grant me my dream wedding? I foresee a bright future. I love you God, Jesus, Apostles, Angels, Arch Angels, Elders, Disciples, prophets, saints because (state why you love and whom).

The following are examples of small thoughtful Prays: (Blessings before a meal)

Thank you God and Jesus for the food we are about to receive. It is made with love. Bless my family and friends who are about to indulge in your bounty.

Thank you for your abundance our Lord. There is always enough. Thank you for the roof over our heads, our warm home, heat and this lovely prepared meal.

Bread is life. Thank you for your generosity and providing everyday for our family no matter what.

Lord God I live alone and thank you for the food, bread and wine/drink. Although I do not enjoy eating alone I know the Holy Spirit will join with me sharing my meal today. Bless all the children of the entire earth who have short supply or next to no food. Feed them our Lord this day forth. Amen.

Bless the food we are about to receive. There is always bounty. Please see my grateful heart God and Jesus. I love you all. I also know you will feed the world. God Bless.

We are all gathered here for Thanksgiving. A time of sharing, caring and grace. Where we traded with our brothers and sisters for centuries. Healing salves for our ills and herbs, teas, and fruit from plants from Mother Nature earth saved our lives and health. All of us would have perished without their help. Thank you kindly for saving my sons and daughters from starvation and strife. I bless this feast in your name. I am forever grateful. Thank you graciously. Amen.

Thank you our Lord for the bread (your body) the holy Eucharist and the wine (your blood) received at church services. We eat and drink in memory of you. There is always a way. We are never ever alone. Amen.

Save me, Oh Lord, protect me and my family from any accidents. Let us all be safe and healthy. Amen.

Before Driving:

I ask the angel of protection to guide me on my journey during this North Eastern storm. I'm concerned and fear yes. Yet now my life is in your hands. Let me get there on a safe peaceful journey. The weather is nasty yet please spread your bright light on the road ahead and lead the way safely. Bless you the almighty arch angel of protection. Amen.

Mother Mary help me now and protect me from Satan's wrath, his deceit and his lies. Come right away. I await you. I love you and I am also your child. Amen.

Today I'm not going to die. It is neither my time nor destiny as of yet. I have every intention of getting through this situation by abiding in God's love to live. Thank you very much. Sincerely in advance.

I am humbled and surrender to your direction, trust and love. Show me the way Lord Jesus. Blessed be.

Jesus I'm knocking on your door to assist me immediately. This is an urgent matter. I feel my life is in jeopardy. Many thanks in advance. I await your help now. I now feel in great peril and danger.

God our Father creator above cure my aches and pains. I no longer want to suffer. These physical ailments (Name them). Release my burden. Your yoke is easy and my burden is great. I appreciate you. Arch Angel Raphael please spread you jade green light or evergreen light all over my body and heal my ailments. (Name them one by one). Thank your bright healing lights Arch Angel Raphael for curing me completely of all my illnesses/ailments/aches and pain. Amen. (Repeat 4 to 6 times a day when sick/ill, or in the hospital recuperating, critically ill, in intensive care/palliative care)

Sweet Jesus save my precious child as I know already how innocent and lovely he/she is. I do not want to lose my child. I do not know if I have the strength to bear waiting and the patience. Grant me strength, heal my angel of life. I cannot thank you enough. I love you. Amen.

Dear Jesus I'm relocating to a new town/city/country/continent and very anxious and worried to be accepted and belong in the new life and community. Grant me your blessing and assistance for a safe favorable journey. Take away my feelings of loneliness/isolation and apprehension. In Jesus' name. Amen.

Please let me get to said destination (name location/place) by car/plane/ ferry/boat/cruise/jet ski/truck/van/ SUV/RV/kayak/canoe/row boat/dog sled on time with no interruptions or delays if possible. Thy will be done. My family is awaiting my safe arrival. (Safe Journey home) Bless you all. Amen.

Suicide:

Dear God/Jesus save my (son/daughter and person's name) from attempting suicide. I have noticed he/she is very depressed, worried, anxious, discouraged lately, and full of despair. They doubt your abilities. I'm praying an intercessory prayer for he/she is no longer full of life. Free from any hurt or disappointment Holy Spirit wonderful counsellor also help and assist said person (name). Thank you very much from the bottom of my heart.

Dear Lord, help them through this bleak despairing burden for this time/ situation/problem. A thousand thanks in advance. I praise and worship and give you all the glory. Amen.

Prisoners:

Inmate(s)/prisoners. Dear Jesus hear my pray and plea in advance. State the (person's/inmate/ prisoner's full name) has been incarcerated for the last (State how many years). I feel he/she is losing hope and their grip on life and is giving up. Losing their faith in humanity. Praying for your bright white light to shine upon him/her. Make (person's name) known that they are loved and not forgotten.

For not every prisoner is guilty Lord. Many are framed or take on another's blame/burden and have been falsely accused and victimized. Please strengthen them my Lord. Their lives have not been fair with many lost quality years gone already. In the name of Jesus I pray for their healing and prompt release.

Depression: (Intercessory Prayer – Praying for others) Even though (person's name) soul/spirit is lost for the moment search their hearts Lord for you see everything. You can heal wrong/bad thoughts, the mind and brain. Show (person's full name) how to love once again. To not lose faith for their life is a gift bestowed from God. Not all is as bleak as it seems at this moment. You are the righteous way and driving force in our lives. Grant them more energy and motivation please. Thank you.

What are your likes and dislikes and opinions? Why are my prayers not answered? No need to want for want (there is abundance which exists already). It leaves a question of limit, not enough. Therefore will not receive what you want because you believe the lack thereof. Belief + Faith + all knowing + Intent = Equals (Receiving). By repeating I want, I need that is what you get. The lack of, without. Lack – not what you mention. It is difficult to comprehend. God provides everything: Your talents, time frame, connections, right place, right people to communicate with, answer the door, the knocking, the asking, you're seeking. Until you find, receive or create. Coincidence or luck – everything is planned and happens for a reason. Everything is solved sequentially like a puzzle. Piece by piece, steps are taken exactly in place beginning to end results and completion. Accomplishment – success. Be thankful and have gratitude always.

Arch Angel Michael (Protector of homes and accidents)

Please protect my home/room from attack, robbery, theft, vandalism and fire. Please guard each corner of my property North, South, East, and West with Guardian angels wearing the armor of God and let no harm come to my personal space home/ranch/land/property/cottage/vacation property/ farm/ barn/ animals/business/or office. Let us rest in peace at night and every night this day forward and be able to sleep soundly with no worries. I am forever grateful for your help. Thank you.

Arch Angel Raphael (Healer):

Please provide your bright jade green or evergreen light all over my entire body. Heal the life threatening disease that has consumed my body. Make my body, sound, strong and vigilant against all aggressive tumors and multiplying cells. (Example: Cancer, Leukemia and Septicemia). Cure and help me immediately. I ask that your green gracious healing light surround my entire being and I will no longer suffer any ailments whatsoever. Thank you very much God and Jesus in advance. I love you too. I'm now cured, healthy and my body functions normally. Let all my body systems work synergistically and well. May God bless you for your assistance. I would like to live a healthy life full of vigor and enthusiasm. (Continually repeat 4 to 6 times a day or more when sick/critically ill).

Evil (Casting out demons)

In Jesus' name I rebuke you (Evil). Come out of his/her (state full name) body immediately. In the name of the son of God our redeemer Jesus, son of the living God and healer who has sacrificed his life for all by his crucifixion. Christ who has lived, died and yet to come again. Our resurrected Saviour. You may have heard evil must be binded (tied up).

The devil, demons, Lucifer, Legion are all evil and wish to destroy, steal, corrupt, harm and eventually kill/murder people. Evil once called out of someone's body would like to inhabit another body as soon as possible preferably someone at their weakest moment.

Past Lives:

Yes we do have past lives some had two to thirty-five (2-35) past lives or more. Tendrils: We are all part of the infinite life and interconnected. When a group prays and another group prays elsewhere it gives off good vibrations of hope, belief and clarity. God and Jesus hear all group prayers (2) two or more people. We are therefore awakened. Aware of nature and the energy (auras) around us. This field of matter. Rocks, trees everything has an energy field (matter). The soul could take up the same body and relive to correct previous errors/mistakes for growth. They can also choose another new body entirely. The Soul goes where it wants to and decides for itself what is best. There is no pressure tactics. Our spirit does leave the body as well as our souls when we die go to heaven. Your body is your temple.

God/Jesus and Holy Spirit and soul Purgatory. Suicide victims need to amend choices. Have a choice to choose heaven – once again. Jesus and God know we are weak yet do not want us to take our lives. God states I give you life for a reason and purpose to experience its process. Some suffer more ailments, some are fortunate, some are mentally ill, some are givers and generous, some are takers stingy, some are needy, and everything balances itself out. Yes, we can leave our bodies to travel (astral travelling) and go through the sky, sun, moon, planets, galaxies, earth, the world and return back into your physical body.

Divorce:

Your children will later blame and resent you even if you say it is not their fault and are loved. Divorce is not smooth sailing. It is like a death seeing a ghost reappear time and again. There is a long period of bereavement. Some cannot fathom the indignity. The person who asks for the divorce moves on quickly. The other holds the pieces of the puzzle and family together. All the problems, emotions, panic, anxiety and tears. Especially in a strong marriage with no signs coming right out of left field.

Many want their spouse(s) back again and regret their decisions. Reasons for divorce are many. Violence, abuse physical/psychological/mental. Unfit parents, substance abuse, addictions. Indifference, apathy – no communication. Indifference – no more love. Cheating on either spouse. Sometimes the one who cheats wants his spouse back. The one cheated on is too stubborn to forgive and holds an eternal/internal grudge. Their ex goes on to be happy with a widow with children. You are sitting alone and miserable because he/she tried to get you back for years and you said no to the reconciliation. No children. Spending monies you do not have (Financial), irreconcilable differences, arguing, fighting, tension, lack of communication. Bitterness, resentment, relationship falls apart, drifting apart. Sickness and health. Jealousy, possessiveness, control is out of hand. Selfish behavior and makes no sacrifices. Mental illness is (hereditary DNA). Greed and spending too much (money you do not have in advance leads to financial ruin). There are many other reasons. You did not realize until many years later that you were married to a psychopath, sociopath, needy, or extremely controlling individual.

Never bash the person you had children with. Love consecrated your children. Have some respect. Do not use your children as pawns nor tug of war in a divorce. Do not play one parent against the other or make your children hate one parent over the other because you do. Your children can feel emotions/wrath and what is meant between the silence. They sense both your animosity, resentment, hurt and this is why kids blame themselves. Before having an affair, try rekindling the romance in your present/current life with your spouse. Do nothing in haste. There will be shock, denial, unbelief hope of a reunion, reuniting, reality and moving on. The children will try to act nice hoping the parents will rekindle their romance and bring them back together once again.

Do not call your ex spouse all the time to disrupt their lives if they found someone new to love. You have to accept that they are in new relationships. You will only feel more hurt and neglected if you decide to nag/bother them. Rejection is part of break ups. Do not harass and give guilt or shame trips. Phone only to meet with the children and their time. Parents have to allow each other cellular phone time/E-mail/Text/Zoom/Skype for their children. Adults do not act like children. It is my time, my turn, no you cannot do that. Schedules get interrupted for reasons, accidents do happen. Life moves on and changes happen constantly. Sometimes there are delays and accidents. Do not jump the gun and accuse each other bickering and fighting.

Psalm 112:9:

"He hath dispersed abroad. He hath given to the poor. His righteousness remaineth forever". In the psalm this is part of the description of a man whom god blesses in many ways. Now he that ministereth seed to the sower both minister bread for your food, and multiply your seed sown and increase the fruits of your righteousness. In King James Version this is Paul's prayer that God will provide ample income for the Corinthians so that they can sow more of it into the offering for the poor and reap a greater benefit. Some translations follow other manuscripts that make this a promise rather than a prayer.

Now he who supplies seed to the sower and bread for food will also supply and increase your store of used seed and will enlarge the harvest of your righteousness. That is, God will increase your income so that you can give more and bring about increased benefits. Being enriched in everything to all thankfulness.

Change belief(s) you change behaviour. Change behaviour you can change belief(s) also. The first statement is true. I do not know about the second it has never succeeded yet. All problems of the world stem from obstinacy, corruptible belief systems and conformists. Fundamentalists (Who is right and wrong) (I am better) (Do it my way or the highway) Example: Change your religion and convert to ours or else. Using fear and corruption as a sense of power. There is power in being a non-powerless conformist. Not everyone are leaders. There are some followers, some counsel, some are logical, some advise, some give advice, some examine, some research and study. You always hear about people in the background without accolades who do not get rewards and (ministries and philanthropists) admiration for what they do.

They are appreciated by few and are not in the public eye. They prefer to observe and are deep thinkers and writers. Not the kind of personalities with full egos and can let others shine in the bright vibrant limelight with no regrets, envy nor jealousy. The strong silent type's introverts are ever silently present.

They are content to contribute. Smile on others successes and are happy to teach others to learn. They are selfless and givers of themselves, personal time, energy. They give more. Put their heart/soul and spirit in assisting and aiding others to achieve greatness and success. Instead of up front on stage they are more on the sidelines, standing in the background forever encouraging others. Ex: Lighting and studio set up stages, props and producers. There is a need of people everywhere in different jobs/tasks/passions and hobbies. Some prefer delegating people. Others are people motivators with enthusiasm. Again another is a gifted speaker while he reads a speech prepared and written by another who is hidden. The loners and the group workers. We all have gifts and are all meant to be used for the positive outcome. To make the world a better place. To assist, help and aid all you can one person at a time. Small miracles happen every day and the larger miracles happen every day also. We notice only what we see and what is proven. They are happy in your accomplishments and sad in your demise.

Meditate for audio – hear, see visualize. Smell scents flowers, perfume, powder, pine, forest, fresh linen. You are a total of your thoughts and they do affect/effect your life. Avoid negative, depression, gossip, idleness, despair, hopelessness, feelings of abandonment, forgotten, loneliness, envy, jealousy, greed, lust, vengeance. Listen to your heart it never fails you. Live in the present moment now. Manifest only love all the time, all your life to all people in all your endeavors. Really try. You must fail to succeed.

You see, feel and hear God with your 6th sense (Psychic – intuition which is called ESP – Extra Sensory Perception). Gut feeling, knowing, and hunch. When your heart is open then God and Jesus reveal their true selves. Ex: Déjà Vu, Past Lives, Reincarnation, Prediction, Future. Ex: Look at your eyes and face in the mirror straight for at least one minute. Your reflection of inner self.

The outer of self – out of Body experience is your real self – soul. Not the Ego. Say hello to your real self soul and God. There will be two identical looking bodies like a twin. One is your soul the other is your body. One body can move while the other remains still and vice versa. The eyes are the windows of the soul for real. You can see Jesus and God in the eyes and pupils in Spirit form (light green pupil color).

When you look into the eyes of one whom you love (soul mate) you can feel God's presence and love. You feel relaxed and beautiful. Knowing someone cares and it is a mutual feeling – reciprocal. Hold hands, pray together, stay together. Live life and be thankful together. Deep-meaning, closeness. You are in your own world and it is lovely. Never give up. Take a chance on true love. Do not let the feeling pass you by. It does not happen every day. Some wait a lifetime. What is home to you? The final destination. Neither more moves nor insecurity. A smile and relief and feeling of excitement. That rush and flushed feeling. Meeting everyone passed on and lost. How do I get there before death is it possible? God's eye color is light olive green when he enters and indwells in your body. You can see his divinity in others. Conversations with God and Jesus: Oh yes it is – absolutely nothing is impossible with God and Jesus on your side. Lifting your spirit, removing your pride. There is always a way. It is all inner go inner. But how do I? With help my child, there is help yet few choose this path of enlightenment. Fear of the present and future events. Fear what will be felt true emotions. Will I die of amazement? Is it just too much to take in at once?

What if we get lost and cannot find our way back? Just floating around till someone leads me home and back. So many questions and so little time. Time is temporal. I hear voices, music constantly playing soft and very low. The good voices my dear there is no fear. What do these sounds and voices want?

To be closer, near you. Sometimes cannot turn it off. Oh, it is consistent 24/7. It is just you do not listen most times. I am hearing musical instruments and singing. Now isn't that something. Yes. If I tell other people they will think I have truly lost it. Do you always worry what others think? They are not too concerned about you right now. That is funny. I always knew you had a sense of humour. Is this craziness? Oh no for heaven's sake literally. What have you learned? That there is an a.m. radio playing in my head constantly. Yes, what else? I like these sounds and music. They make me calmer. It is like the flow of water and sea. Some whistles and drums. Someone is strumming their guitar.

The alto, soprano, and tenor voices, songs are heard. Faint harps, flutes and lutes. Yes. Yes true. A trumpet call? Oh no not yet. You will know the difference. This is as soothing as a lullaby. Is that a piccolo? Maybe indeed. Now the oboe and Tuba. Wow, where are the violins and cello and piano? Oh they are complete instruments. Do I get electric and bass guitars? Yes, when the radio is on it plays any music you like. We select good songs. Sax and clarinet, harmonica and accordion, cymbals, percussion. What do you think this is a Brass band? Flamenco guitar. I like the sound very much. Go near the bell/chiming sound and gradually toward the conch tone sound. Word of God – The Audible Sound Stream, Ocean melody's, voice of God, vibration and tuning in, deep meditation, energy movement and life, life stream, melody, sweet music, angelic. There is absolutely no stress.

Clear your mind void of all thoughts and incoming – 3rd eye. Peace calm, stillness. Focus concentrate. Pick a position a small room which is inviting warm can hear 24/7 audible. The sound is situated in the heart and rises up to the throat and lowers down to the naval area during REM sleep. Deep sleep is the unconscious state. I love you with all my heart and soul.

Meditation sounds:

Right eye – listen to – Yes Positive. Left Eyes – Avoid no – negative.

The sound comes from the eye center (Third Eye Chakra) all Seeing Eye. There are a total of fourteen (14) dimensions. The 3rd dimension present is light. The 4th is Time and Space. The 5th dimension is spiritual awakening. There are (3) perishable worlds: (3) Bodies (1) Physical (2) Astral (3) Causal (the mind)

They live and thrive in true inner beauty with calmness and peace which would be admired for seekers of God and Jesus. True serenity, always smiling and not having to prove their personal worth. Truly magnificent and beautiful. Stripped of excess, materialism and ask nothing. They are our teachers. Guru – Master (Teacher) Leaders help you attain your goal(s). You must practice deep meditation every day for 1.5 to 3 hours per day. Do not open the 3rd Eye (Chakra) alone/on your own. You require guidance to the realms. Conscious – Awake, Sub-conscious – sleep state, deep sleep (REM) – unconscious, super conscious – deep meditative state. Meditation – Means going inner inside. Die every day to oneself the body (Paul). Step out of the body to visit realms and dimensions. Unlock the (3) outer worlds bodies. One by one at appropriate phase. Know oneself and let go of I/me/mine and Ego. Time and Space are not thought of. The body is not part of the soul and spirit. It contains them until both spirit and soul are released. We are not our bodies yet have to remain healthy. The soul and spirit can be merged together.

What is the purpose of life? To attain the heavenly kingdom of God. To see, touch, hear Jesus and God. To visit heaven. Ultimately clean up all the bad Karma before we die. To daily visit the various realms/dimensions/upper realms. Destiny fate is predicated and foretold already known and written on a scroll in heaven. Yes there is a huge book of Names. To be like a good sheep and follower of Jesus. Listen, be obedient. Serve, observe, learn and attain wisdom and understanding. Manage to learn and maintain with action characteristics of God and Jesus and the Apostles. Not just doing – but by performing actions but being in the now. To become more Christ like in his image such as a disciple or prophet. Faithful and forever present. Select choose the more difficult straight and narrow path. Take up one's cross and produce good fruit.

To worship and listen to the voice within. The source of all creation and creative power. To receive the key to the gate(s) 10th gate. (Jesus is the Master and he holds the key only). To seek the truth of life. Meet a master, Guide, Guru, Mahatma, and Singh, Spiritual leader, Shaman etc. or other who is really alive lives and resides presently on earth. "Seek and you shall find. Knock and the door shall be opened to you. Ask and it shall be given." The kingdom of God resides within you. To work hard continually and receive gifts of God like qualities. Elements: "Essence" – Love, and Soul (Earth/Water/Air/Fire/Ether). Yoga – Union, spiritually. The soul becomes one with God.

Happiness – is pure Joy. It is impossible to be happy without smiling outward or inward. Happiness is contagious. You do not care to act like a fool and be yourself. Act weird, nutty a little bit crazy out of the ordinary. Not like others you are unique special an individual. Happiness & caring are holding hands. I will be happy after some rest and relaxation vacation. Too busy taking care of others. How can I be happy with a sick child or children or parent? I lost my husband and literally rebuilding a life. A house. Happiness is being around like minded people. Animals are guaranteed to make one happy. Happiness in creating true independence without forgetting about your loved one. I am told by others happiness is a state of mind. Control your thoughts from negative to positive equal's happiness. Be happy with what you now have. Do not expect. No expectations.

You cannot always get what you want. Happy people are not complicated, demanding. They are simple to please and live simply. Thinking simply without contradictions. To be happy is quite complex in North American western society. You cannot run after happiness it finds you all of a sudden. Everything is going right. Life is predictable, comforting, calm right now. I want to remain in this state. Only one problem life continually moves, shifts and changes, grows and evolves. Happiness is being totally free. Also finally being able to laugh at one self with others. You will not be happy if you state the following: I will be happy when, I need, I want, I desire, I deserve, It's about time, Got to attain (Goals, objectives, dreams, ambitions, desires, purpose, path). Happiness is being happy with what you presently have. Need and desire what you already got.

God and Jesus are present for every birth, death and miscarriage of all people, and animals. Yes, animals do go to heaven and will meet you at the pearly gates. (All of your beloved pets during your lifetime). What's mine is yours is never ours but God's. He is in control of the shore and our destiny. All knowing and true to rescue you from falling off a cliff or a bridge, do not jump. Just think for once. My land, no his. He created the world and the word. We are only temporary stewards of his land. Is it his voice which lingers but where? Audible everywhere. Sounds, music, lyrics. Like a radio station tuned in.

Bigotry, racism, hatred, evil does not start in the womb. It is taught by our parents, relatives, siblings, school mates, colleagues and ancestors. What makes you different from others? Nothing. We all bleed red. You see kids are wonderful at impersonating and mimicking, interpretation, comprehension and imitating. They learn from you more by your actions and what is not said. Kids feel with their emotions and even though they do not understand they will soon. Experts at body language and tone of voices. So do not ruin their childhood and dreams. Teach them to believe in themselves. Listen and really care. Stop using passive aggression. They want responsibility and enlightenment and relish your presence. Just looking at you they know your moods and if you are irritated. Do no shatter their fragile hearts.

Children are impressionable and can figure out puzzles too. Even though not advanced in years, mature, not learned nor schooled. Teach those values and their worth. To love themselves and others more. Teach about abandonment, playing, feeling free with no restrictions, and no rules. Teach them about generosity and helping others. There will be plenty in the future. Show the weak people need encouragement too. Help them up, lift their spirits. Show them life is not always fair yet it is beautiful. Not all people are like you. Respect their differences and cultures; other religions and beliefs. Change their beliefs, and then behaviour can change.

Love and accept each other. It is that simple. We are forever all one with God and all humanity connected with the environment, with the galaxies and dimensions. You are one with each other, your brothers and sisters and church families, ministries, your work colleagues, acquaintances. Everyone is interconnected to one Supreme Being – God (Source of all) who gives us gifts such as: Grace, mercy, salvation and spiritual renewal, faith, hope, charity and clarity. Believe in your intentions. You will see positive results. Death is transient and temporal. Have no more fear, worry nor anxiety. It is all good. No worries.

Additional Guidance from God and Jesus: Thy shalt pay it forward to others. Serve others when you can. Thy shalt not abuse physically, verbally, emotionally, psychologically, etc. Let neither love not become apathy nor indifference. Thy shalt not use children against any parent or other child. Thy shalt be real (mask off) genuine and true not fake. Thy shalt not betray, afflict nor deceive others. Thy shalt not manipulate, coerce nor inflict any pain. Sing praise, shout for Joy. Happiness abounds. Thy shalt not be passive aggressive. Speak your mind and be more direct. Thy shalt aid and help the weak, down trodden, meek and needy, the afflicted and the poor. Thy shalt teach goodness, the word of God, the Bible and abide in his laws.

Learn, read, decipher, understand and show others the true meaning of the Bible with its prose (poetry), metaphors, stories, analogies, lessons and legends, the truth, salvation and unity. Thy shalt love one another for we are all one with each other, the plants, the trees, flowers, animals, water and humans. The water (Sea) is God, the lakes, rivers, streams (Spirit), a drop of water (Humans). Thy shalt try not to lie often. Thy shalt live in unity and togetherness like a large commune. Thy shalt share, cooperate with others. Thy shalt understand the lonely, aloneness, hermits, distance and suffering. Do not neglect the hermit, the lonely, the orphan, the widows, widowers. Do not force your company upon the despaired and depressed. Let it go and let it flow.

Do you really live in the present moment of time? This instant 2023, or does the past slowly creep up unexpectently. A memory fills your tear ducts and next you are smiling at a love lost. The one that got away. After we worry about the future which has not even commenced. Doubt, worries, fears and sweaty palms. Your heart beat rises with the unknown questions.

There are a few things you should never be without (my personal opinion):

1. Love of people, your country, your work
2. Imagination (Hobbies), prayer words
3. Words, writing, books, all forms of Art
4. Ambition/work/purpose/goals – creativity
5. Servitude and gratitude (Heart) Thank you

6. Humility/Kindness – Try to be nice. I know it is easier said than done. Have some manners.

7. Integrity, Honor, Loyalty (Family/Friends/Colleagues)

8. Be Genuine – A real character (Soul and Spirit)

9. Personable – like people you are one of them

10. Love children you were once one

11. Respect others and be more affectionate. Listen more.

12. Faith/Hope/and Charity - The most important is Love

13. Giving/Generosity (Time and Presence). You cannot have love without giving.

14. Someone to really love soul mate – relationship

15. Kisses/hugs/embraces

When I look at the constellation in the night sky I'm awed by its beauty and majesty. All angels are stars and each star has a name. Satan exists and so does evil. He is a deceiver, liar and counterfeit. Sneaky, cunning an adversary, enemy. He is diabolical is meant to kill to destroy and murder. Wants to take us and separate us away from God. Once he separates our love from God/ Jesus, he will then proceed to use discouragement, disappointment, despair and confusion. One third of all the angels fell from heaven and are assisting the evil one. They work on doubt, insecurity and fear, guilt and shame. He lowers your self-esteem and eliminates your confidence and self worth. Targets the youth through vile lyrics on social media. False doctrine. Evil the devil called Lucifer thrives on the destitute, lonely and desperate and all your vices. Works on your conscious good and bad. Rich or poor no one is safe. The evil one enjoys when you are at your weakest and wants people to kill themselves so he can steal their souls sometimes asking you to sign a contract (give your life/soul away to him forever unless Jesus/God intervenes.). The devil/demons/evil and Lucifer thrives on hopelessness, despair, melancholy and sadness.

Adam and Eve betrayed God 1st sin – Denied God (Temptation) 2nd sin – Vanity (Self centered and Conceit) 3rd sin – Pride (Do it their own way not Gods way). God asked where are you? Why are you hiding? They for the first time felt guilt and shame and were aware of their nakedness. God states – "Surely you will die". Satan contradicts, then tempts and states a lie.

Unity – Church – One God Church. All/everyone in the world will be under one roof. Some will disobey and try to fight the King of Kings/Prince of Peace in the sky who is Jesus returning the Messiah. Many will not be happy. Acceptance of Others – Love thy neighbour. Love your brother. Love your enemies. Love one another. Turn the other cheek. If someone is cold give them heat. If someone is thirsty give them a cold or hot drink. If someone is hungry give them food. If someone has no home at the moment, offer a room in your homes. You will thirst no more – spiritual thirst. Hunger – Spiritual hunger. To know God and live by his good fruits which are offered to us. The most common sin in the world is ingratitude (not appreciating or giving thanks appropriately)... Born Again Christian: Follow Christianity. The Holy Spirit indwells in your body. Live in peace, be kind, and help others. Live in God's family, church family of like minded brothers and sisters united. Ministry is saved. Repent and ask for forgiveness. Be sincere and truly sorrowful for your sins.

God and Jesus give the following gifts: Mercy – (Asking for forgiveness and it is granted). Grace (A gift given freely from God/Jesus/Lord even when we do not deserve it). Salvation (Saving all from sin). Jesus took the burden of sin from the entire world. Love – Always. You are never alone. "Fear not" – He is always with you accepting no matter what. Do not fear is printed and written and repeated three hundred and sixty-five (365) times in the St. James version Bible. Eucharist – is the Body of Christ. Wine – is the Blood of Christ shed for our sins eternally. Forgiveness: Do not count faults. Example: Another fault/another sin/another time

Hatred: Someone has wronged/neglected/hurt/persecuted/bullied/humiliated and belittled you. Took something away and broke part of your heart. Some faults are: Bitterness/resentful/anger/ vehemence/vengeful/revenge/wrath/envy/jealously. Really poor character traits. You want the other person to suffer as much or more than you did. Lesson: I will show you just wait and see. My day will come eventually. You are the one who now suffers more. The other is not concerned, not worked up and does not even think of you. Remember, ten years ago you did this to me? (I forgot get over it, move on get a life). Hatred is a huge word and dangerous sin: Dislike, loath becomes disdain. You might as well dig two (2) graves for revenge. Trees have feelings and emotions. In New Guinea if twelve to fifteen (12-15) tribal men surround one single tree and scream and yell with all their might at the top of their lungs for only a few minutes. About two (2) weeks later the tree falls to its death. Very true and sad indeed.

Heart: Is an organ which you feel emotions through your heart. The heart thinks and has a mind (memories) a feeling organ. So many sayings: My heart is broken, set my heart free, you have a big heart, you are all heart, why are you so heartless, you have a heart after all, she has a heart of steel, heart of gold, heart skips a beat, I can hear your heart, telltale heart, two hearts beating as one, listen to your heart it knows, you wear your heart on your sleeve, aren't you all heart, my heart is full, the heart tells the truth, heart break, cold cold heart, heart full of love, listen to my heart, he/she has a good heart. In love – you get butterflies and the heart rate beats faster. Like walking on air or a cloud. Signs are: nervousness, giddy, talk faster or not at all, stutter.

Why is it that you do not like someone you just met? Nothing they will do or say will change your mind or thinking. Expressions like: "I cannot stand the presence of this person". They rub me the wrong way. They are a bore/bragger/conceited/unloving/selfish. The labels – decide to categorize and judge others. In French there is a saying "I cannot stand the smell of that person". The smell of a person is called pheromones. Do not want to be near or present in the same room. Then the person does something really surprising and kind. You misjudged and misunderstood their intentions. You start to feel ashamed and embarrassed and slightly guilty. You no longer look at the person in the same manner or light. All you saw was darkness around them. Now you can begin to love him/her.

I was reading in the Bible about serving others. Offer yourself help assistant to others, the elderly or friends who need your help. Doing many free jobs in the past. No pay and absolutely no funds for all the help. No compensation just more work and them asking for me to do more. No gratitude thankless work. I learned a valuable lesson. If you help others do not expect or assume anything. Got cheated I got the short end of the stick. Lack of respect, used and disregarded. Yelled at and told what to do. Bossed around and always unsatisfied. Always more, do more, I want more from you. I will walk all over you like a doormat. I felt like easy prey an unwilling target. Is gullible, naive, trusting written on my forehead? Ordered around and obey me. I'm intelligent and could not get out soon enough. My heavenly Father and begotten Son goodnight everyone in heaven. My faith always carries me onwards. God lifts me up and carries me in my weakness. They never forsake us. Never deny our name. We are their lost sheep that strayed away and have been found once again. My hope is resilient and has not failed me yet. God's love and strength, love, grace and mercy make me say thank you. Good night my family.

I have constructed a list of our will versus God and Jesus' will: My will — Want to retain control over your life. You do not like the idea of letting go and let be. Nor letting others lead the way, your direction. No help or ask to take care of us. Do not want to lose our independence. Do not want to be dependent on others or co-dependent. Believe there is another way our way. It is my life and I will take care of it. Waiting — all the doors remain closed. Nothing works. Leave praying and God for a few days or months to go back to our self-serving ways. Our own motives and directions. Lack of patience. You do not have enough faith and belief that God and Jesus will not make the proper choices for your life nor the right decisions, offers, moves, relocation. You do not like or enjoy the answer. The answer is not what you desire, want or need.

God and Jesus' will us the following: There is always a way and everything is possible. He knows you better than yourself. They created your life and have thousands of year's experience. They know the world and the way humans and man thinks. They know we are imperfect with sin. They have all the confidence in us not our choices. Do not interfere with your choices even if they are wrong. Let you make the same mistake dozens of times until you learn your lesson. Do not interfere with your life unless asked. Never forceful. Will suggest loving, be kind hearted. Want a better path and destiny and outcome for your life.

Forgiving and want the best and for you to have abundance and be happy and joyful. Merciful and answer all prayers. Ask for you to serve and help others. Not just you in the world. It's not about you and your Ego. They know we make many mistakes, the same sins repeated. Can point out the right direction and show you the right way. Thy will be done is God and Jesus' will not our own. Sheep are not stupid, not dumb. This is false/untrue. Sheep are meek, mild and gentle and rely on their Sheppard to take care of them and lead the right path.

They know when they are lead to slaughter. They smell the fear, slaughter and death. Sheep are prone to attack by wolves, bears and lions. At their weakest and lost, the good Sheppard searches the valleys, mountains and hills and calls them by name. They have personalities like humans. They understand distinct voices, whistles, commands, directions and love their Sheppard owner. Loyal, kind and unaggressive. Willing followers and are obedient. Sheep only follow their Sheppard and not others. They can distinguish different voices.

Seek Jesus' face. Face to face, in your face. God and Jesus really truly want a genuine relationship with you. They are sincere and wait forever. Prayer + Praise + Worship God is the authority ruler of heaven and earth. The one and only almighty. Is here and yet to come once again. He is The Alpha and Omega, the beginning and the end. Manifest presence of God, Jesus and the Holy Spirit. They give you free will freedom to choose to decide to believe in earnest and to follow him.

1. Start with singing praise with voice, fast songs, lyrics and singing. A choir or solo with musical instruments. Acoustics/drums/cymbals/percussion

2. Lift up your hands open faced to the Lord your God

3. God looks and searches your heart forever near and present. Just call out his name, speak to him and ask for his support.

4. Pray alone or make intercessory prayers for others. They are extremely powerful.

5. Praise and Worship – In a group or church meditate, think, and close your eyes to an all powerful sensation and feeling. Feel Jesus' presence in the room or outside. The Holy Spirit comes in the Church as well as inside your body and at your baptism.

6. Worship his Holy name with slow songs & music. Raise your hands or join and hold others hands or not. Believe with all your heart, strength, mind

and soul. Love one another. In unison that love transcends boundaries. Kind of like radio waves to heaven. Look at this group the angels cry. Let's go visit them. Pure Joy. Let us join them singing. They want to be in the room with you listening and give all the Glory to Jesus. Eyes closed or opened it does not matter. Think good positive and loving kind thoughts. Feel the aura heart vibrations. God is there, everywhere and all knowing.

7. You are at peace and received the gift or grace and God, Jesus' Holy Spirit. Love manifested, created and reciprocated. Smile and have joy and happiness, wonder and awe.

Get into their presence: Heavenly realm. Open the portals of connection with them. Pure acceptance just the way you are made. You want to be and do better and sin less. Seek wisdom and inner peace. Love God, the Bible and other people. You want to stay in this euphoric state spiritual awakening forever. You long for the journey and to be guided and used for a purpose. Enjoy human touch. You want to go to the special feast in heaven and celebrate wearing the white pure raiment (clothing) with your loved ones. Have to forgive your enemies and adversaries for acceptance in the gates of heaven. Celebrate their return to earth, the Prince of Peace – King of Kings. This is life living to the fullest. Thank and have gratitude. You long to see his bright pure white golden light.

Worship – is the manifestation of God and Jesus' presence. Believe and have entire faith of the outcome.

Grace – Intention do not let go and hang on to what God/Jesus has in store for you. Abundance. Keep your dreams intact. God's plan already perceived and acceptance of others. In a sermon there is praying and praise yet in worship the evil show its awful ways. Prayer and praise go together. Pray in complete silence or in a group with others. Sing Praise. When you see a person becoming an animal, crawling, screaming and groaning, panting and scowling you now know that God has victory. The blessed holy water is real and heals. (Holy Water blessed by priests, ministers or others religious believers). My ultimate dream answered would be to receive the gift of anointing by the laying of the hands to help others to walk, to cure skin disorders, bones, tumors, cells, blindness, blood vessels, organs and limbs, nerves. God please grant me the gift of healing. Holy Spirit and Jesus reside in my heart.

Heal others just like Saint Frere Andre in the l'Oratoire St. Joseph in Montreal (Quebec) Canada in the Cote-des-Neiges (Hill or side of much snow) area. His small chapel on the side remains with all the crutches hung on the walls. People, who were paralyzed, had diseases like polio, tuberculosis, paralysis, broken bones etc. There were two (2) million people at his funeral over a two week period. People came from different countries and continents to be present, pay their respects, give thanks and say good bye. He healed so many through the Grace of God and Jesus. Grace equals God, Jesus and the Holy Spirit and your intent. Jesus' yoke – He leads all the oxen to plough the fields. He alone can release your weight too see the light. Let him take over your plight. His yoke is easy to help with all of your burdens.

Righteousness, Sanctification, Holy Redemption (Redeemer for all our sins). Work on the right qualities to please God and honor him. Be humble and obedient. Your character, faults, sins may be corrected one by one. Look deep within yourself you may be the source of what is going wrong in your life. It is not always others, outside factors, paranoia sets in. Not everyone wants bad or evil against you. They want us to mature for his perfection completion.

Sometimes others point out our faults critically and we ignore, confront and get on the defensive. We state that is not true. A stranger may see yourself of your hidden dilemmas. Ex.: Unemotional, detached, distant, aloof, moody, self seeking, selfish, lonely, bitter and mean spirited. Your character grows when we focus on the hearts. Our sadness, disappointments and experiences are etched on our faces.

Take responsibility and ownership for your faults. The nature and cause of most of your issues. Growth is the solution to forgiveness and grief. Once you are open and have a new awareness. Let go of debts, loses, sadness and letting go of loss and the past. When you take up the Good Fruits - Beatitude traits you begin a new connection to God and your relationship deepens. When there is a crisis and Drama in your life look inner to your soul to feel and see the light of God.

Letter to Jesus: I'm embarrassed of my temper and slothful ways of late. Lack of motivation and direction. I need you both God and Jesus in my lift for your will is right and kind. Lately have acted immature and unreasonable. Temper tantrums like a child. I'm ashamed of words spoken and guilt is my plight. God knows who needs growth, peace and quiet reflection. An Angel fly's by me and move some objects. I know you are close and feel a warm embrace. Are you consoling and wrapping me in a gentle embrace of feathers. Angel of secret destinations. Sleep, slumber, lazy. Schedule time clock is off. Life of an insomniac. High energy up for two nights, reading and writing. Please forgive all my sins Jesus. I love you all in heaven. There is nothing better than listening to a Maritime storm on a dark night. What is my calling? What is my vocation? Have you been called? Did you hear his voice? Give me a sign from you and I shall know. Open skies wisps of wings. On most high like fairies. I like my evenings compared to fireflies in a mason jar. Eventually you have to let the light shine. Path, what path? Where? I cannot see the curves. Which way is the right one? Where do we turn? What way can we go?

I am grateful to Mother Nature to bestow us her gentle summer winds. Thank you Arch Angels Michael, Raphael and Gabriel and the other nine arch angels for your protection, guidance and support. I love you God, Jesus, Holy Spirit, Mary, Mary M., the Apostles, angels and Elders. Hi to Mom and Dad and all my relatives and loss of friends. A special hello to my extended family. Say thank you in advance. Inside you are always present. He is all knowing of everything and gives you full freedom of choice. He may message you in a book, letter, email, cellular telephone, friend of stranger even on social media. Talking to you through the wind. You are never alone. Listen for his voice. See his light shine up on you. You can be in a car, walking in the woods, a boat, skidoo, see doo, four wheeler, working for charity, train, cruise, and plane. You may hear his voice like a whisper. See an image come alive. He may send angels his heavenly messengers. There is always another way. God and Jesus are near you in all ways. Everything is possible.

God of Grace, mercy, kindness and love. Jesus of humility, all knowing up above. Mary's seven sorrows no doubt no more. I saw and touched rose petal wrapped rosary beads from France. Mary Magdalene understanding ways and bright smile. Mother Mary you love Jesus your son unconditionally. To all my angel guides, messengers and friends I'm deeply indebted. John the Baptist fierce leader and gentle adversary. We will not be damned nor condemned. All of you understand is God of anger, wrath and revenge of the Old Testament which is totally false and untrue. Yet David knows better he plays his lute and dances in your heart words like honey. We sing now your Psalms. David used to dance around naked was singing carefree.

Believer what do you seek? Oh I lost my faith with a touch of doubt. Only know regrets and cannot forget my past. I have difficulty healing and bitterness prevails. All I think about is getting even, my revenge. Cannot let go and forgive no more. Disease, sins and death is overcome by understanding and applying the divine principles of Christian teaching. Beware of your heart. The wonders above are shining within. The light aura of your heart, soul and spirit energies combine. Togetherness is when your heart is completely full with love; you can rise above the world. Feel true bliss, divinity and joy. Just like an old oak tree from a small acorn to a majestic state swaying still. The roots are ingrained deep. God never lets you fall or fail. It is life experience and your unrealistic expectations, assuming, plotting the map. You think the Lord has created misery and you blame the Lord for all your problems, outcomes, unwarranted sickness, death, accidents and suicides. At all the times you stood weak he stood patient strong waiting close by and sometimes carrying you in his beautiful arms.

He watched and observed from the sidelines your repeated offenses and sins, errors, mistakes. Give up your will to him who means everything and never fear you are never alone. So, you really think Jesus doesn't love you and care? He will always lift up your wings and sing softly. Your favorite song, so come along and walk with Jesus and God. Walk your path(s) proudly beside them. They are on your side and will never let go. Even when you do not believe any longer and lost all faith and hope. Doubt at times in your insecurity. God and Jesus grant you gifts of mercy, grace, salvation and talents. The truth is the light. There is nothing more perfect than Jesus' love. He has an enormous heart and cares so much for the entire world. He knows everything you think, feel, your dreams, wishes, hopes and aspirations. There is nothing like God's strength and endurance. Do not forget he always forgives, is kind and objective.

Even when you were a backslider. He smiled upon me always because people are his glory. There is nothing more perfect than the Holy Spirit to be born again acceptance indwelling in your body. The Holy Spirit is waiting to be called for his guidance, teaching and counselling. Our wonderful counsellor. You are worth life and loved deeply.

You do not have to be right or think you are right all the time. Abstinence, willful, stubborn, pride. No you are not always righteous. Try to become more Christ like in character our saviour is love and forgiveness and charity. Done through actions, words and deeds. Truly repent and believe that Jesus is truly the son of God and Messiah. Triune – (1) God, (1) Jesus the son, (1) Holy Spirit as one. Faith + Hope = Belief (Believing). Drop the materialism it is temporal and you always want more and more impressing people who do not even like you. Leave behind your world goods and baggage. Follow Jesus and take up the Cross. Do not look back. Do not even bury anyone; just go walk your path straight right away. It is time do not delay and make excuses or over think. Learn to listen to change our ways to be a better person. One who is more loving, caring, empathetic, sympathetic, agreeable, and likable. You can hear more in silence. Do not be difficult, temperamental, angry and contrary.

Important words: Praise, thanksgiving, gratitude, blessing, kindness matters, encouragement, genuine thank you, appreciation, well done sincere smile. There is power in a real smile it uplifts others. Soul – light – unconscious level – Identify with your soul. Spirituality – Silence – Alone – Meditate. One in all all in one. God like (God's image), feast, celebration. Believe in intention of your plan and path. Visualize you have attained your desires. Ex: Purchase of first house (Decorated and already moved in your mind everything is done). Think positive thoughts, no negativity. Become aware of your surroundings, people's feelings and vibe(s) energy. Faith – Always have neither doubt nor worries.

Repeat good thought patterns. Believe in God's gifts. God and Jesus reside in you. The Holy Spirit has to be called to enter your body and you need to be ready for a change. Accept the gift of the Holy Spirit to indwell in you today.

Problems with Fundamentalists: Organized religions and forced conversion again one's own will. Secularist with punishments. Racial and bigoted groups. My religion is individual and I do not like yours therefore will not associate with others of different faiths, race and cultures. My way or the highway. There are many facets which shape our divisions such as: Family, children, relationships, culture, language, beliefs, values, customs, integrity, honor, praying, love, peace, mannerisms, heart, protection, world views, current affairs, mantras, communication, caste systems, hereditary, patronage, favoritism, ageism, sexism, nepotism.

Everyone wants to experience true love. Eternal love not temporal. Find a soul mate to share life with. To be on the same level mind/body/soul and spirit. Life is love. There are many forms of love. Relationships – boyfriend and girlfriend, husband and wife (Marriage), siblings, kin, relatives, colleagues, mentors, teachers, professors, love of family and community, church family, homeless, orphanages, widows, love of pets, friends, co-workers, professionals. Everything and everyone has a vibration and energy – matter. Rocks, trees people, angels, saints. God and Jesus want us to have true abundance joy, peace and love. Live life eternally – immortality. Be a child in the kingdom of Heaven (Sheep/Lamb mild and meek in his pasture). We are his children. He is our heavenly father all in all. Saviour and protector. Wear the armour of God in distress, fear and uncertainty. Have no fear or doubt and be courageous. Keep the faith and do not despair. His presence is always there. Call out and ask. "If God is for us who can be against us?" Life is a cycle, a figure eight. Yin and

Yang. An Enigma (mystery). We cannot know our true destiny, patterns and lessons in advance. Everyone wants to seek a higher truth.

Love – can hurt and wound. It is a blessing in disguise anguish divine. Push and pull on emotions and feelings could drive you insane around the bend if you let it. Always pleasing. It is what everyone wants and hopes for. True love takes a lifetime to seek. Sometimes far away, sometimes next door. Love can be either stable or erratic. Calm or a tempestuous storm of confusion. Do not over think and open your heart and mind. Take your time. Do not let it go. Hold on for you will not find another real lover who makes you swoon and takes your breath away. There is no replacement or comparing. When you are ready, take a blind leap of faith. Do not waiver, no stalling. Go for it knowing full well the other heart half is waiting to indulge. Just ask.

His patience and bright smile is warmth. You miss his lips and smell of his shirt. The way he grins and looks at you like you are the only woman in the world. The sound of his laughter and joyful child within. The way he wraps his strong arms around you for comfort. His great ideas and intelligence. You do not choose whom you love it just happens such as divinity is open to anyone who asks for the Lord by name. Can always flirt after many years and desires you still. Just calling to hear your reassuring voice. His spontaneity and energy. Loyalty and kindness. Trust him with my life. The way he listens calm and never rushed. Women are complex this is true yet everyone is an individual. No two are the same ever. We are born to drive men crazy in a good way. We will please you and bring you in our lives and secrets. Oh, not all our secrets where would the mystery remain. I want to be in your world. Nice love notes and sweet words of praise, encouragement. No nagging or alternative reasons.

Shower you with attention, care and be your personal Venus if you would like or a friend, partner and team. Strive to give you your independence and strength to let you shine and take centre stage. Romantic dinners and cafes holding hands and lingering. A woman will do much when in love and has to remember it takes two to make sacrifices for love to flourish and bloom. Both wanting, needing each other. Yes we do love kissing of course. Passion and desire are great and necessary. Attraction is sensed immediately. There is a spark and suddenly you feel very much alive and shy. Whisper sweet nothings in your ear. I must hear your voice.

To me – let him let me be genuine and not pretend. He can give me wings to fly free and the gift in return is I will always fly back. Love is not being stifled. When you look in my eyes and there is passion, understanding and you just know he is the one. Giving of yourself and self sacrificing to make the other happy. It is two (2) beings with one (1) spiritual soul. Not enjoying being apart. Truly missing ones company, soothing voice or advice. The qualities in him I do not possess. It is the differences that make us unique. Some days your personal Venus lover and other days you wish to be alone in solitude to think, reflect, does not mean you appreciate them less. Let them hang with their friend's at times playing cards in their guy basement, garage or special bonding place.

Loyalty, courage, communication and trust are earned slowly. When I look or glance your way and we want to leave together to be intimate just with that special look, smirk, grin or smile. Love is holding my hand in public or in a restaurant, unashamed of looks and does not worry about your image. Showing some PDA (Public display/demonstration of Affection). Pride is weakened. Could you be my strength and I can be your weakness. Less arrogant and more tolerant. Always smiling or singing to yourself. Less mean more kind. New pictures and memories made together. Less irritable and more patient. Love is letting the other grow with you. Helping them succeed in a business or encouraging them opening their own. Doing what is necessary to please them. Listening intently what is unsaid. Submit and admit your weaknesses. Do not be embarrassed to act like a fool, be goofy and show your inner child. Speak your mind and do not start out arguments from events taken place years ago. Remember a year and a half years (1½) ago you did this to me. It is forgotten already move on. Tell him you love him even when he is really not loveable. In the end only kindness matters. Love is grabbing my waist or shoulders in an embrace and feeling your lips and subtle gentle kiss. Surprise me.

Love is being excited just to hear their voice and anticipate their footsteps home at last. Love is showing and encouraging how to do new things. Yes, you can drive standard if you try. Love is believing in someone despite their faults and seeing their warmth and caring smile. Love is defending, protecting and honoring each other. Love is not gossip or hypocrisy, holding grudges forever and withholding love. Love is to be cherished not a bribe. It is not envious nor jealous nor greedy or selfish. Love is bringing food on a rainy day and preparing it to cheer someone up. Bringing chicken soup for a cold. Love is total acceptance of being a human. Being on time or before because you cannot wait to see them. Running into their warm arms, hugging closely. A kiss on the check or forehead. Watching a good movie or riding together on a motorcycle, car or truck, ski-doo or boat. Staying close. Apologize when you hurt your loved one.

Avoid confrontation. Love is taking in the sun and basking in the water together. Wonderful feelings. Love is taking a bath or shower together, shampooing, lathering up and lingering. Love is taking out the knots and pressure points on the back, arms and shoulders, and neck. Candles glowing, a child's laughter. Let us go make some new memories. Love is new adventures and exploring places of the unknown. Love can be mysterious and as complicated as you make it. Or just be genuine and simple. When everything feels right and you want to spend every morning sharing coffee day and night sharing together. When you know you cannot be without them in your life. They are important, beautiful, smart and knowing. You care so much your heart is full and glowing. You are so proud of them you want your friends and family know them too. Love is trying to love and not have the person back off all the time on the defensive with their deep dark issues.

Love leads to the sacrament of marriage. True love is beautiful. When you write your own vows and release your romantic thoughts out loud. Love is despite falling into a routine you enjoy their company the best. Writing a love note and leaving it on the bathroom mirror, fridge, lunch, briefcase, suit etc. Baking them their favorite meal and dessert. Picking up great wine cheese and grapes. Love is spending quality time together. Is having butterflies and shiver every time you meet. They can still make you laugh and still feel excited just looking at them. Love is being quiet, laughing, boisterous, vivacious, silence, talking. Just being in ones presence makes you happy. Love is not deceitful, betrayal, back stabbing, two faced, wrath, revenge vengeance nor lying. The divine heart. I will go where God guides me even though it is not your desire. Longing for autumn once again breezes and rustles of the trees. Love is supposed to be easy free flowing and natural. When love is difficult, breaking your emotions in half.

Wondering, worrying the thought of loss will drive you around a bend in curved road. You cannot pick and choose whom you love. Love everyone, neighbor, friend, fellowman, stranger or an acquaintance. Let your love beam bright at the highest frequency at a dimensional level. Smile not just at your lover, spouse immediate family and relatives. Say thank you, give and appreciate the day. Emotions are rampant, flippant and change frequently. Forever in motion. Your true feelings do not change about a person. How someone makes you feel is ingrained in your soul, spirit and heart. Deep down your instinct and intuition knows. Why do people gravitate is because they want truth, intimacy and closeness. Long to be closer to your smile, scent, skin and lips. Drawing our bodies near. Touch another human being. We are not mechanical robots. Our needs are sometimes insatiable. Your true love never quenches. It continues in another realm.

Yes you can love two (2) people at the same time. Yet your heart chooses the special true love. The one you want to spend time with, think about, and spend solitude and quiet pensive times with. Laugh, giggle and be giddy with. Why try to read minds at all times. Quit asking what are you thinking about right now? Do not form insecurities, doubts or fears. Be confident in your abilities. The more you cling the more your man will run away from attachment. Do not be too needy. Yet we want to form some attachments which are important in our lives. An oxymoron of terms. Being touchy feely is real. I like to run and hug/embrace my lover when he walks through the door. Show him how much I care. Thinking sweet thoughts of kindness. I won't be waiting by the phone. Come find me. We clutch and grasp at hidden meanings.

Breathe new life in leaves of rust and golden yellow rod and juniper. God and Jesus have my heart enraptured. They know the spirit that dwells within you. For they are part of the whole plan, present and future. Our destiny. Jesus holds my hand and uplifts my body out of the white cap tides. God directs and places his reassuring hand upon my forehead and touches my cheek and crown. I am loved and not alone any longer. The angels sing and a voice is heard faintly like the end of a tunnel or echoed from mountain ranges and peaks. For they give us all a fine thread line of silver to travel and explore the world. A connection to other levels and dimensions. The natives and pioneers, the front lines of war. Splendid waterfowls and bird watching. Our relatives past lives. Fear not for now you are floating and flying over cliffs and oceans. Have faith and believe your inner child within. The dream ends and back into my body I fall really hard. I only hope to visit heaven once again. I wish to find the portal or vortex.

I took four (4) photos of a picture of Jesus hanging on a wall at my friend's house. Jesus gave me different images of himself not for keeps just temporary. Jesus: Marble staircase ascending. There is one large eagle, a dove on the left hand side flying and an albino white lion with a light aura. Heavenly light with rays at the end of the stairs. On the right hand side sits a meek lamb. Hearts longing. Beautiful banisters and balusters, misty bright light. The entrance to heaven's gate. Jesus' crown of thorns so real you can touch it. Pressed in hard and penetrating his head. It is harsh to look at. Droplets of blood on his forehead, cheeks and face. His head is strewing drop by drop. Jesus' eyes are closed serenely. He is at peace thinking of the heavenly father, his mission and us. God's grace. The drops so real and huge color or red. His blood is alive. Jesus has long slightly wavy hair to his shoulders. Golden aura encircles his entire head, thick and resonating lighter gold around the aura. Faded image like a dream. Jesus has no blood dripping in this image. He is thinking and reflecting. I see a light burgundy robe, sandals. Thick brown hair tossed behind.

His face is vague cloudy and misty. Almost disappearing, faintly. His eyes are closed and when you stare for a minute his eyes open back up and see right through you. Jesus' head and neck only. Vintage image. He has no pain and is completely peaceful. I touched his face. The red droplets were cupped in my hands I was stroking his cheek. I cried because Jesus was showing his backsliding daughter (me Nora) a glimpse of home. I stared and moved and touched crying out loud. Oh Jesus it is you, really you! Here now a moment never forgotten. He wanted me to believe once again and restore my faith and state fear not I am here. There is hope. You are never alone.

The Bible book is ceaseless, unending, a continuation of the many sequels of life. It defines humans, our weaknesses and sins yet our lessons and growth. Our lack of Glory, God within, mercy, grace. We desire the polar opposite of our lack. Oh, it is not so easy to be gentle, nice, kind, peaceful, good and patient all the time. Our Lord, Adonai, Lord, Jesus, Eloi send us the difficult and irate people to deal with. Perhaps we are already temperamental, difficult, irritating, annoying, and bothersome to others and are totally blinded to our faults until others subtlety points them out like a guide.

Novena – What is the definition a novena? It is a small prayer recited aloud three (3) times per day for nine (9) consecutive straight days. When a miracle, cure, desire, request or what you prayed for occurs and comes true. You then post an advertisement publicly usually a newspaper with the prayer printed so another person could receive another personal gift from God. Praise and Glory be to God. Bless you all in heaven above and on earth below.

There are twelve (12) lost tribes of Israel. The Armor of God is the following: Helmet, breastplate, shield, sword, waist (belt) and boots for the feet

Holy Spirit: Works in you through intercessory prayer. The Holy Spirit is always present in Church. Life is not about you yet helping and serving others through your teaching, direction and dedication. You can receive gifts from the Holy Spirit. Speaking in Tongues from the Holy spirit within you to God and Jesus in their language. They understand all languages for all were created by them. The Holy Spirit wants us to: Adore, pray, worship and praise the Lord and Jesus. Did you ever think about the prophets, apostles, Kings, aids, maidens, sisters and brothers, Queens, disciple's personal characters?

God – Our father in Heaven. Creator of Heaven and earth. Friend. The Alpha and Omega the beginning and the end. Wonderfully made. Abiding, forgiving, merciful. Our leader, truthful, healer. Problem solver, seeker. Heavenly Father, family, powerful, mighty, saves. Changes our perspective and fosters love. Jealous – wants us all to be accepted into heaven. Wise, calm, all knowing, all powerful, all present. Believes in change. Blessedness. Thunderous voice. Slow to anger, giver of many chances. Steers us on the proper stable path to righteousness. Baptism – purifying of sins. Put on the right path. Tall, big, masculine, dark haired, brown eyes and large hands. He has olive green eyes when you see God through others. God and Jesus possess both masculine and feminine qualities of character. Our Eternal father God.

Jesus: His name means Salvation. He is Lord, son of the living Christ. Our saviour, redeemer, our salvation. He is our birthright, baptism. Jesus descended to earth and became a man. His ascension – back to his heavenly father in heaven. After the resurrection. Transfiguration – He was luminous white and glowed. Peter and John were witnesses to his ascension. Jesus is both spiritual and a human/man. No one goes through the gates without his approval. He is on the slim side and tall six feet seven (6ft7"). He wears sandals and different colors of long robes which are sometimes loose or roped at the waist. Only Jesus holds the keys to the Gates of Heaven.

Moses: True believer and needed no proof. All trustful, stubborn, sufferer. Leader, patient, guide, empathetic. Killed one man for racial reasons. Serious, stutterer, doubtful to give speeches. Raised by Pharaoh's daughter who found him floating in a reed basket. Was raised in affluence yet never forgot his chosen people or where he came from.

Twelve (12) lost Tribes: Judah, Benjamin, Levi, Simeon, Ephraim, Asher, Naphtali, Zebulon, Gad, Dan, Reuben, Issachar

David: Sheppard with small stature. Strength in size is in the mind. Ruler, king, leader. Flawed, a sinner, an adulterer, killer. Repented greeted by constant cries. Wrote two thirds (2/3) of Psalms. True believer and never failing love. Musician – played the lute and harp and would dance around naked. Singer. Saw goodness in others and was extremely fair. Always praised God and Jesus. Did not act or believed in being pompous or above his followers. Sympathetic. Prays and is Happy. Feel in lust with his friend's wife and gets her pregnant. Plots to kill her husband because he cannot face his awful sin. Very emotional. His baby son died (he seeded in adultery) and future other son Absalom plotted against him. Great and much loved King. God stated he is a man after his own heart. King Saul become his rival and searched relentlessly and wanted to kill David. David felt no hatred against Saul.

Mary Magdalene – Female first apostle. Learner, sinner, priestess. Generous, kind, loving, sensitive and emotional. Lover of Jesus. Great listener and follower. Guide and truthful. Privileged. In the Bible they portrayed her as possessed by seven (7) evil spirits and as a prostitute turned virtuous. The apostles were very jealous of the attention Mary Magdalene received from Jesus and had troubles accepting her. Her surname Mary of Magdalene often depicts where the person is from. Mary Magdalene was the one who poured Spikenard and Myrrh on Jesus' crown, and feet and wiped her tears with her hair.

I'm honored to receive a gift from Jesus of a real black and white portrait of Mary Magdalene when she was very young with her veils. She looks really beautiful like an Italian or Arabic young lady. I found this really old wooden framed photo in a Church pile of frames and pictures. I thought it was a picture of one of the 5,000* or more saints. When I asked Jesus how did he retrieve this old photograph? As we all know photography was only invented in the last century. He answered everything is possible with God and Jesus on your side.

Abraham: Leader of chosen people the Jews. Smart, a listener, believer of the right way. He was a Mathematician. Agreeable husband and had many children. Was going to sacrifice his only son Isaac. His wife Sarah was barren until very old age. He had Ishmael with Hagar his hand maid servant and another son. His descendents are all the Arabic (Arabians) and Muslims of the world. Abraham has many descendents.

Noah: Was born albino and had three (3) sons and two (2) daughters. Was faithful to God, Jesus and his wife. Creative, mathematician (calculations), Engineer and builder specializing in finished carpentry. He was a listener, believer, dutiful, convincing, hard worker. Noah displayed pure faith and absolutely no doubt in his beliefs. He was quite obsessive, not rich in materialism. Finish and complete a task (was OCD). Full of life. Lover of unity of family. Teacher, sensitive and extremely loving. Good parent and father. Steadfast, abider, lover of creatures and animals. God's creation and nature. Built the Arc in the middle of a dry spell in the desert which lasted many years. Everyone denied and laughed at him. Even his own sons and daughter did not assist him for the first six to nine (6-9) months after he started the Arc. He worked with his wife in unfailing devotion. He is the definition of Hope. The Arc is real, took years to build and is not a fable or tale. The water did rise and eliminated/killed everyone not on the Arc by drowning.

John the Baptist – Cousin of Jesus (was born six months before Jesus). His mother is Elizabeth, Mary's first cousin. Looked very much like Jesus. Thinker, quiet, faithful. Wild at heart, true believer and hopeful. Fanatical, energetic, kind and gentle. Hopeful, big hearted. Lived remote like a hermit. Baptiser to many people. Capable of converting others to believe and he baptized Jesus in water, the sky opened up, God spoke and a dove flew down. Follower and a leader. Lived with nature and lived on insects and honey and wore animal skins. People confused him with others like Jesus and Elijah. Humble and modest. Gave up materialism to follow Jesus. Was a recluse and hermit. People were drawn to him and would seek him out to be baptized.

The world shifts on its axis. Energy spots of the world where deep vibrations of the earth are felt. Integrity + Fidelity = Love. Love shifted to a higher power and dimension. Realms people are now waking up and no longer sleeping. Aware of their awareness. So many beautiful locations on this earth. Special spots where your heart and memories combine. Peace and your soul touch embrace and remain. So few are able to return because of relocations, change and jobs. Families that were so united are now detached, aloof, and alone in their thoughts. No longer yearning for unity; abandoned, forgotten. Change is desired yet most of us come home to our birth place. The people have deep feelings of acceptance. I had so many homes and moved thirty (30) times in my present lifetime and will move one final time to another province. Always felt transfixed on mobility, movement and change. Like an obsession. No rest. The itchy feet and desire to meet new cultures, new languages, new places, new seas and lakes. See other customs. Are they better or greater than mine or just different? I long to see the blond haired dark skinned. All the Peruvian children with their llamas in the Andes Mountains.

How strange to see people living in the cities coming from small towns in search of materialism, money and a so called better way of life. When they had it all living with nature, sunrises and sunsets, trees and ocean and farm fields. Their simple nomadic life of peace, mountains, and higher elevations is what we wish to find and live. As pioneer, ranchers, cowboys, herders, shepherds with our dedicated flocks. Peace to traffic and cement. Highways from Alps and meadows. They were thwarted by bright lights, sex, lust, greed and the big city. The freedom of the clear skies. Colorful woods and distinct hats by locals and good coffee.

I saw depravity in the city where used to desire to live. Saw children living in garbage heaps and dumps. I viewed unhappiness, despair and sadness everyday searching for just one contagious smile. Feeling warmth within. I saw the boundless greed of will by bigger and better. I was not pretty enough, too heavy and a natural girl with viewing cocaine girls in bars in Montreal. I watched their unhealthy deprived bodies with no food. They thought men would only like them skinny. I watched the LSD, angel dust, cocaine, weed, speed, ecstasy, mushrooms, and acid; the pill popping, free love, peace man. Let it be society. The communal people were happy planting their crops and sharing their bread.

Only when jealousy and envy enticed the groups would disagreements, strife and bitterness commence. The fights over who will be the best boss and leader. You choose. The ones who listen, the loners and outcasts. Is that how a cult is born and formed? If you need someone to believe in and lead you the right way choose God and Jesus on your side. They never fail anyone ever. Always got your back and follow you in your demise, complexes and struggles. Listening to great music elevates your mood and spirit. God and Jesus deserve to be glorified, revered and loved. They deserve all of you. For he is Holy, Holy our Lord Almighty. Who is here and yet to come. Your name is Holy, Holy God almighty. Heaven and earth are filled with your glory. Hosanna in the highest. How do you praise the most high? Be your unique gentle self. Have a purpose in life. You are eccentric and a unique being created for life's purpose. When soul and spirit combine in the heart sheds the brightest true colors of a heavenly colorful aura. The energy from your heart remains. A halo or band color around your head from your heart that extends sometimes many feet. Gold, white, purple, light pink, indigo blue, brilliant yellow are some of the most positive wonderful colors of auras.

I always liked and enjoyed the hippies of the 1960's with their long flowing hair, bell bottom pants and psychedelic shirts and Volkswagen vans of colored flower power and peace. Floral dresses, tube tops, shorts, hot pants, boots and hats. Stylish, free with no care in the world or responsibilities. Freedom is a powerful thing. It becomes the envy of others. To live, do what and when you want to do it. To not worry. Speak your mind and opinions. To ignore the status quo and which is normal living. To live on the little land/acreage not wasting water, seeds or labor. Happy with nature, trees and flowers, the woods and forest. The peace and serenity. Not bothered by people or others. To grow your own food like herbs and vegetables and fruit trees and nuts, bake your own bread, catch your own fish and hunt your own meat from lakes and oceans. Kindness to cows, goats, horses, oxen, ducks, chickens, roosters, turkey's, cats, dogs, birds and chicks. The small hobby farm becomes a reality. Who will feed us when there is no clear water, no farmers left to plough the land and grow crops? Respect the sowers and reapers. Let the sowers eat first. Glean when appropriate. When a farmer in PEI shares with me his bounty I am content. He sells me two large bags of vegetables for 15.00 Cdn. $ grown from the red soil Webber farm in O'Leary. I am in awe. Thank you. Thank you for your organic goodness.

What is heaven like? (Answers from God and Jesus to my inquisitive nature). There is only light and the perfect temperature. God is magnified. Gladness and happiness abound.

1. Jesus' real birthday is October 25th in the autumn not December 25th in the winter.

2. The only time Jesus writes in the Bible is in the sand with his index finger. He wrote the qualities and faults of the accused lady of Adultery. "Let he that is without sin cast the first stone".

3. They are forever present. There is no time and space in the realms. They appear anywhere. Also God and Jesus can appear in two places at one time and can also time travel.

4. God is merciful, forgiving, masculine was large hands and strong stature. He is all knowing, all powerful and everywhere all the time.

5. Jesus and God work together like a tag team. Angels do work and earn their wings. They are only jealous of humans for two reasons that they can receive the Eucharist (body of Christ) and of their freedom of choice.

6. Jesus is direct and kind. He likes to tease and calls me his poor little muffin. He wears robes in colors of white, navy blue, burgundy, purple and green, to his ankles with open sandals. Jesus walks everywhere. He will state father Nora is not listening again what shall I do? Must I call my father he will ask me? God is broad shouldered and has a voice like thunder when angry. His voice is really masculine and soothing. Jesus will say to me tough that is the way it is.

7. Mary has two sisters' names also Mary and Mary. They are often called the Three Mary's.

8. There is no hate, strife, worry nor tears in heaven. The temperature is consistent and it is always day time sun shining never night time in heaven. There is no darkness only light.

9. Angels do wear white clothing and have a golden aura.

10. God and Jesus do sing yet prefer to hear others sing. They also prefer others to cook because of how busy they are. They enjoy home cooked

meals and they do eat dessert and drink wine. They can work three (3) days straight without eating.

11. Jesus wants many more of his people (sheep) saved from the fold to welcome them finally to heaven.

12. Ask for God and Jesus' by the name out loud when you are in danger, trouble. Honor and adore our King of Kings and Prince of Peace.

13. At the end of the world and yes it will happen one day Jesus will ride on a large white stallion. He is the Prince of Peace and King of Kings.

14. Armies will try to fight them in the sky. They will be rejected by believers. God and Jesus triumph. Good always prevails of evil.

15. At the Baptism you must understand the following statements: Repent your sins sincerely. Atone and be reverent. Ask for forgiveness. State you are a sinner and get baptized in water. Water washes the sins (blemishes) away to make you whole and purified/clean once again. Believe Jesus is the son of the living God. Believe in the Blessed Mother the Virgin Mary. Pray and have faith, hope and belief. Help to serve others. Read the Bible the true word of God. Listen for his voice. Believe in the birth, death and resurrection of Jesus. He is the living Christ and son of God.

16. They did not spread any viruses ever. They do not want people to ever have to suffer. Evil knocks first on your door step. Do not let them (evil) inside. They corrupt and influence the young by poor music lyrics.

17. God and Jesus are full of love. The Bible book is love. Do not lie. Do not judge least you be judged.

18. Jesus does have five (5) brothers and three 3 sisters and total of nine (9) children Mary conceived. Mary is the virgin with the birth of Jesus as an immaculate conception from the spirit of God.

19. Mother Nature does control the nature and weather. God and Jesus control the thunder and lightning. There is a child who controls the frost.

20. They know you and your parents and the number of hairs on your head.

21. The dent above your lip is God whispering wise mysterious loving words at birth by placing his index finger there making a permanent dent. The baby always cries after hearing God's words.

22. There is no makeup or face paint in heaven. Everyone is in a natural state.

23. Hell and brimstone exists and is real. Evil exists on earth. The evil one has 1/3 of the angels from heavens that followed him and are accomplices and do bad cruel acts of depravity, murder and lies of deceit. Priest, Popes, Bishops and cardinals, ministers who never speak of evil at all should advise Christians of the truth.

24. Purgatory is between Heaven and Hell. All the suicide victims reside there and have a choice to make amends. They can return to another body or the same body and relive their lives once again to learn lessons. They have a 2nd chance at life to repeat.

25. God and Jesus have absolutely no tolerance for people who hurt children or animals in any way.

26. Do not pray selfish prayers such as: I want, I need, Do this, Do that or else. Never command or dare, bribe or be bossy to God and Jesus. They hear all prayers alone, with others and intercessory. Sometimes they wait to change you or for you to change. They are working on your problem or request be patient. They do not work on your time but theirs. They do not argue with what you are asking for and they plan what is best for the outcome. Thy will be done not your own own will. They want you to succeed and have abundance, good things in life. God and Jesus perform

small and large miracles daily. Open your eyes to really see them. They want to spread joy and happiness, bliss and divinity to the entire world population in the billions.

27. At the crucifixion God never forsaken his son Jesus on his cross. He was always beside his son talking to him, listening sometimes in silence. Jesus took on to himself the entire world of sin.

28. Forgive or you shall not be forgiven. No one enters the gates of Heaven without forgiving everyone who has wronged them. Forgive everyone and have no enemies.

29. The present world and life is difficult to live with pleasure as well as heartbreaks. They want more people to love one another and really care. They see everything at every living moment. Be kind. Jesus never said life was fair or going to be easy and it certainly is a challenge.

30. Mary is very upset regarding the number of abortions and pregnant mothers aborting innocent children. Children can hear voices, words of love, worry, denial, rejection and hatred in the womb. Give life or give the child up for adoption. She cries many tears for the unborn children. Another sorrow close to her heart.

31. God and Jesus plan to make their new spiritual home on earth at the end of the world. Jesus holds the keys to the gates of heaven. No on enters the gates but through him.

32. Many good die young it was their time. Everyone's death has a date and time in heavenly realm.

33. Everyone gets along. Great relationships. No arguing. No fighting. No gossip or backstabbing, no judging, no pettiness, no complaining all the time. All are friends. Love is abundant.

34. You have to make peace and forgive everyone on earth in order for God and Jesus to forgive you.

35. Food is cooked on pioneer wood stoves. Simple

36. There are lakes, water, ocean, sea, streams etc. Colors are magnified. There are many more colors than on earth. More spectrum of colors.

37. If you fish in heaven you must place the fish back in the water.

38. Sense – All senses

39. No taking the name of the Lord in vain, nor idols, no swearing

40. Love thy fellowman as God and Jesus love you.

41. Do onto others what you want to be done to yourself (Golden Rule)

42. God and Jesus are present at every birth/death and miscarriage of all people, animals, creatures and mammals.

43. God and Jesus are our leaders and make the major decisions to be respected. Listen to them intently.

44. Heaven is communal. Everyone shares in chores, tasks, jobs. People work as angels, guardians, servants and messengers etc. Angels are messengers sent from heaven to assist people on earth from harm, accidents, natural disasters etc. Everyone has at least one guardian angel. Some people may have three (3) to five (5) angels helping them at all times.

45. No deceiving, manipulation nor lying allowed.

46. Yes, there is a giant huge Book of Names.

47. The stars are all named after millions/billions of angels. (All stars are angels)

48. There is a huge room of blueprints (scrolls) of our entire lives written on earth. Our lives are all predetermined, so is our destiny.

49. At your death and future feast you will see old friends, relatives, parents, siblings, colleagues, mentors, acquaintances if that is your wish/desire to.

50. God and Jesus do not want us to be loners/hermits in heaven

51. There is sharing, smiles and togetherness

52. Judgement Day – Steps – Each step unravels your life in flashes, flash backs of all good and bad faults and deeds like picture animation.

53. God is too brilliant to look at directly with our sins. We have to be cleansed and wear new white raiment.

54. It is beautiful beyond belief and your imagination

55. Jesus is six feet seven (6ft7") and on the slimmer side. He has a beard and long hair light brown to his shoulders. He has either ten (10) colors like a kaleidoscope or his eyes are also bright blue. God is seven feet four (7ft4") with very dark brown hair and brown eyes and no beard. Mary has brown long hair and green eyes, peachy skin and very beautiful. Mary Magdalene is petite small frame with long flowing copper colored hair. She is short and has hazel eyes. Jesus is married to Mary Magdalene in heaven and they have six (6) biological children.

56. Heaven is our real home and final destination Home away from Home

57. There is music and angels. Everyone is obliged to rise and sing at 5:00 a.m. To sing, praise, worship God and Jesus to give them glory.

58. You eat and drink in heaven. God and Jesus are always busy and able to be without food for three (3) days. They enjoy homemade food, baked goods and fruit and yes they do drink wine.

59. There is no disease, no disability, everyone is cured. No picky eaters, no allergies, no health problems. All is well in heaven. Tis very good excellent. People who are disabled walk dance and run in heaven.

60. Babies who died at birth are around seven (7) years of age and very wise. Their wings are dipped in either pink, purples, green or blue. Voices like sweetness.

61. Adults look around thirty years of age.

62. Our bodies will be transformed into perfection. We will have new raiment free from blood (our sins). We will have spirits and soul.

63. Your pets all of them from all of your life will be in heaven. They will greet you at the pearly gates. How cool is that. That made my day.

64. Love – In love you can see the image of God and Jesus in the iris radiating from the eyes and face of your lover. Expressions of tenderness and warmth.

65. Everyone is peaceful and happy. They love and care for others and always assist God and Jesus with messages, errands. Sometimes angels are personal messengers from Heaven to save those in war, disasters and chaos. At other times save you from your own personal vices.

66. Nothing is a coincidence. Everything happens for a reason.

67. No swearing or profanity allowed. No bullying or interrupting others when they speak.

God and Jesus can take any form of any race, nationality, sex and height they desire. They can walk through walls and on water so yes the Bible is true. They can be in two places at one time and travel faster than the speed of light. They can time travel and fly. There are a total of fourteen (14) dimensions/ realms each level divided by a thin veil or drape. They are all powerful and all knowing. The dimensions are like a fourteen (14) level layer cake with icing. Each layer is a new dimension. You can go from ninth (9th) to third (3rd) dimension but you cannot go from third (3rd) to the ninth (9th) dimension. When you are on a lower dimension you are only allowed to raise one dimension at a time when you are totally ready.

Personal Prayer to God and Jesus: Gratitude – Thank you. Holy Spirit for your fullness and grace, mercy and forgiveness. How difficult it is to let go? What do you want of God? Lord to spread the Good news, foster goodness, love thy fellowman. To each a purpose. Be kind and gentle to one another. Please fill us with joy and inspiration to rise each day with a smile and gratitude. Thank the Lord for the sunshine, my health, for food on my table, a safe place to live and a roof over my head. Thank you for my future small home and business and small car. A cheerful giving home to share with others on their voyages and visits. Thank you for the struggles and pain the emotional trauma and sorrow where I learned acceptance, perseverance, strength, determination and wisdom from you of course. Thank you for the rest and crying bouts to learn rest was needed and crying took out all the misery. Sad eyes become content. Thank you for my best friends and family. Thank you for discernment and aging where you do not have to any longer pretend and can "Let go and Let God". Where it does not matter how you dress or how you look or act. Hopefully will age graciously and fully with dignity and piety not scorn. With remembrance, self esteem and true humility. Not perverted with mundane thoughts. Thank you for my beautiful best friend dog Hallie Borderline collie, black Labrador and 1/8 wolf howling at the moon she died on October 27, 2021, from a rare form of leukemia. She is so well missed.

Life has to go on you say when I am all frail and little. No matter, what time does not wait it is a full circle figure eight. Before you know the ones you love are with others because it took too long and was too proud to say how I felt. Too late to take a chance again. Chance missed. Choice made. Pay it forward (To serve somebody) – Little things make God and Jesus smile. Give a flower to a stranger. Take the arm of someone elderly. Do not poke or scare them. Ask permission first and be polite. Is it okay if I help you across the street with your groceries, shovel your driveway or bring you food? Help someone pick up their prescription during a snow storm. Bake and give away cookies, pies or cakes, muffins and fudge.

Cook extra meals and deliver them. At school bring and extra sandwich or apple for a student who has no food at home. Do not make a big event. People have their pride and dislike charity most times. I have extra do you want some? Buy someone a free cup of coffee and make their day. Smile its free. Volunteer – taking phone calls, appointments, hospitals, Salvation Army, serving or making food. Taking out the garbage. If someone is panicking, reassure them. If someone is chocking do the Hemlick maneuver and save them.

If someone is having a heart attack look around quickly and asks for a difibulator and call 911. If someone is drowning, swim backwards and save them. Be courageous. Do not think about wetting your clothes, the temperature of the water or hypothermia. Serve coffee or tea at functions in a cafe or a Tea Room. Be a host or hostess to great and seat others. Make conversation to the lonely. Listen to others problems. Do not interrupt to say you are busy. State I'm sorry or I understand. Sounds like a difficult and trying time for you. How can I help make you feel better? Anything I can do? Walk up extra flights of stairs to bring groceries in an apartment building for mothers with kids. If you have a car, offer a ride to your neighbour to the store and back. Deliver meals on wheels. Volunteer to be a coach, referee at sporting games and events. Clean and hang laundry, towels etc. at a camp ground, inn, Bed and Breakfast, motel or hotel. Offer a hand; suggest you look overwhelmed may I help you in any way?

Are you burdened with problems at the moment? Stress makes people react impulsively instead of thinking. Give up your seat in a bus or metro/subway/ tram/ tub etc for a disabled, pregnant or elderly person, a woman with kids.

Start a Book Club, art gallery, art class, writing class, garden club how to plant, and photography. Help others use basic functions of computer or the Internet. Help someone fill out their taxes or with a budget. Show someone how a tablet, digital camera, videotaping, Y-Tube works. Downloading pictures/JPEG images and PDF file format files. Help someone and show them how social media works: Face book, Instagram, Twitter, Blogs, Snap Chat, and LinkedIn. Show how to open and close accounts. Basic skills. Teach courses.

State it is quite alright to be a follower, introverted and INSF – Intuition, Senses and Feelings (2% of the total population). Angels do exist and people might ask who you are. This never happens. No one has helped me ever. What do you want? How much will it cost me? Is it for free? Really? Services are not supposed to be paid for. Stop charging money for small favors. Just do them for free and you will feel happy and fulfilled. Pick-up someone's dry cleaning. Help clean someone's apartment/house or run errands.

Prayer with and for others. If someone has a loss show how much you care. Do gardening and help with certain chores, picking up the kids from school. Making them lunch or supper. Be there and do not talk too much. Do not compare your life. (I know how you feel only should you have experience the exact same situation). Offer grief counselling and be the counsellor. Car accident – Help with someone's mobility. Ask if they need you to run errands. Insist. Bring snacks and food. Give your time and company. Play card games with others who are lonely. Organize a bake sale, garage sale or offer to organize an Estate Sale. Go for a walk in the park, mall, and beach to a favorite spot they like and enjoy.

Sit on a park bench with someone and just talk. Offer to babysit or take care of teenagers. (Order pizza, watch movies) Let parents have a date night to themselves. If someone works two to three (2-3) jobs to make ends meet and is a single parent make an extra meal or batch of cookies, bread, muffins, cake or meal. Widows and widowers find time hard. They live in the past and are often alone, lonely and depressed. They have no idea how to function and spend their new free time. Before it was us/we and now it is I/myself needs. Help others if their loved one suffers from dementia or Alzheimer's. Volunteer at the burn unit, fire department, children's hospital, sing or rock newborn babies, Boy's and Girl's club(s), girl scouts, YMCA or the Red Cross.

Help raise funds for charities. Running, bowling, selling chocolates, cookies for a cause. Be present at benefits ex. "Cancer patients", loss of a home from a fire, buying a wheel chair. Visit someone you know at the hospital during hospital hours. Ask if it is ok with the patient that you are there. Intensive care is only for immediate family. Hang someone's clothes on the clothes line or in the dryer. Wash someone's dirty clothes, dry and fold them. Cut grass, plant flowers, mulch, plant scrubs, plant a small garden of herbs or vegetables.

Make homemade bread, yogurt, jam, jellies, mustard pickles, and tomato sauce in jars and give them away. Sew, crochet, and knit a gift of mittens, hats, scarves, socks or a baby blanket. Make a wooden sign or address number sign. Offer to take minutes at committee meetings. Organize a food drive and clothes donations. Offer to fix someone's application form. Pick up or deliver a new appliance. If you have a truck, help someone buy new furniture pick-up and deliver. Help at all retail stores. If someone has no room in their present car to fit the item. Assist. Building a tree house, deck, swings, and paint deck chairs for other people and kids. Put together IKEA furniture with someone. Help someone move into a new apartment/home.

Offer to unpack or paint. Offer to paint some of the rooms in your local Church. Offer to clean-up, vacuum, clean a bathroom, dust, wash a floor, empty kitty litter, pick up toys, and empty garbage pails. Help with spring cleaning or major cleaning of an old historical house. Pay for a friend's bus fare or taxi to get safely home. Pay for someone's coin wash or drying or give some detergent, bleach, dryer sheets or fabric softener. Stain someone's deck or help repair or replace one. Help with installation of a door, windows, steps, fire pit, rocks, cinder blocks and patio stones. Make a garden path, bench, bird bath. Help someone make a coffee station, tea corner, sign, decorate their house.

Give suggestions for new colors inside and out depending on their preferences. Bring patio furniture outside and hang flower pots. Do small repairs: Caulking preventing air/wind for winter. Sealing windows, changing furnace, filters and flues. If someone volunteers and you are buying, give funds for gas or free snacks/meals for their help or give a bonus as a thank you. Do someone's dishes/pots/clean the table and counter tops and appliances. Clean someone's oven or inside of a refrigerator. Volunteer as a security guard for children at cross walks from school. Take care of someone's pet dog(s), cat(s), bird(s) etc. Offer to do dog walks for others on their vacation or during emergencies. Drive someone to the airport. See them off on a trip. Offer to use your car for hospital appointments, hair salon or errands, visiting their family/friend(s).

Drive and deliver lunch/supper. Pick someone up at an event/ceremony or drive them to their country house. Wedding/graduation. Someone who does not have a car offer a lift. Be someone's big sister or big brother or hero/idol or mentor today. Drive someone to their mechanic appointment to pick up their car which is being repaired. Welcome people to where you live. Talk about websites, places of interest to visit, amenities, beaches, schools, churches, shopping, banks and restaurants. Make appointments for plumbing, electrician, contractors, dentist or doctor's appointments. If someone gets sick, help them to the bathroom.

Go green. Help people recycle, reuse and save water and different forms of energy. Teach people to cut energy costs in their home and make suggestions. Teach about home equity and residual income, Chip mortgage (reverse mortgage). Suggest proper Life Insurance companies, car, home, vacation homes, yacht, boat, truck, RV, trailer, motorcycle, and bicycle. Suggest combined insurance claims to save money. Teach to lower credit card debt percentage of interest etc. Show how to consolidate debts. Show someone how to budget properly and explain spending habits. Help someone to fill out forms, grants, loans, bursaries, school loans etc.

What does God/Jesus want from us? To become a member of his heavenly family. Have a relationship everyday and friendship also. He wants 100%. God and Jesus desire to know your heart, thoughts, dreams, visions, intentions, desires, ambitions everything. Abiding in his love and mercy, grace and glory. To adore, praise and worship him. To have fellowship with Church members. Be honest. Tell your deep thoughts. Body of Christ is the Church and Eucharist. The wine is the Blood of Christ. The disciples and prophets spread the Good news of God. Having faith and hope, love and charity. To be a cheerful giver. The most important quality is love. To serve God and others: the lonely, the diseased, fellowman.

To be more giving, humble, become like character of God and Jesus. Wise, patient, fearless, tenacious, strength, courage, no doubt, ambition, determination, helpful, kindness, eight (8) Beatitudes (Good Fruit). Be virtuous, modest and wise. Bring forth good fruits on the vine/branches. Bearer of good fruits. Ripen to overflowing abundance. ACTS stands for Adoration, Confessing, Thanks giving and Supplication another way to pray. Jesus and God told me some traits they find displeasing as follows: Conceit, bragging/showing off, hatred, a know it all, too much pride. The seven (7) deadly Cardinal sins are – Pride, Envy, wrath, sloth, greed, gluttony and lust extra ones: Hatred, Vengeance, Envy, and Jealousy.

Baptism: What does it mean to be baptised and born again? Cleansing of all sins. Clear Slate. To become a member of God's family. Forgiveness – Ask to be forgiven. Truly repent and are sorrowful for your sins committed. Born again is a new beginning and the Holy Spirit will indwell in your body. Receive the Holy Spirit. Receive Spiritual gifts. Immerse your body totally underwater. Word of God is love. To be done by a priest/minister someone holy or who has a calling (Saint). Accept God/Jesus as your personal saviour and salvation. Jesus died for our sins. To read the Bible the holy book and Word of God. Heavenly words (parables, mystery, poems, storytelling, legends, truth, history, wisdom, music, songs, life, lessons, generation, tribes, eras, resurrection, and revelation. Life is a series of tests. How we react to stress displays our attitude and character, our gratitude and thankfulness. God and Jesus take our weakest moments and make us surmount them. There is always a way. Nothing is impossible with God on your side. They will carry us.

Marriage is an important topic. Why get married? Love, passion, sensuality, belonging, companionship, friendship, communication, trust, respect, honesty, appreciation, gratitude, thankfulness, romance, other better half. One and only – spiritual and soul. You miss the person when they are not present and want to live, experience every facet of life with them. Becoming a better person. Reciprocal in feelings and emotions. Without love where would we be? Desire, attraction, smell, closeness, togetherness, caring, thoughtfulness, pheromones, in sync, unity and their smile. You cannot imagine or fathom being with someone else.

You are not losing yet gaining true love. Comfort – found the one soul mate with many qualities and some common interests and values. Routine is not boring as long as it's with you I will suffer the mundane routines and the exciting adventures together. Personalities are different. What the other has you lack and desire to be. Differences of sex are obvious. Differences in character are healthy. You do not want to be the exact same how boring. Lover/friend/husband/wife relationships take much work, sacrifice, and trust. Belief in integrity. Honoring the one you love. Defending them. Getting along yet having debates, opinions and talking. Growing, maturing and learning together. He gives you gifts or joy, pleasure happiness, peace completing you as a person.

Need/Want/Have. No owning, no jealousy, no possessiveness, no betrayal. Desire and passion. You cannot wait to kiss him and hear his voice. He makes you smile and want to be hospitable. Meet their friends and family. Company/belonging/secure/confident. A kiss good morning, an embrace goodnight, sharing. Habits – getting to know everything about your loved one. Through good, bad sickness and health. The high joys the low lows. Loss/death/job/moving/relocating/change. You would do anything for them. Their life before yours. Defending courage and bravery. Man becomes less proud when married. Experience reduces to we/our not me/myself and I. The ego. Thank God for meeting and loving this person. Acknowledge your weaknesses. No longer afraid, no longer doubtful. Have a reason to commit. Commitment – Exclusive. Being in love with one person and being totally magnanimous.

Falling in love with the same person always over and over. Daring – taking a leap of faith believing in him. Growing together. Some change, some stay the same. Evolving. No one can replace your true love. Their voice, kiss, laughter, smell, behavior, sense of humor, character, personality, presence, reassurance, reliability, sweetness. Accepting faults bad habits, vices, quirks, opposite tastes. Sacrifice, agreement, tastes, hobbies. Less selfish more serving. Honor and obedience to God/Jesus. Thanking them for the sacred union. Publicly tell the world you are in love. Reading – living through worldly events. Encouragement.

Hugs, embraces, kissing, touching, stroking, massaging, physical touch and feeling. We are human and need other people. We are social beings and need presence of others. People are not meant to be always alone.

Listening to other stories, tales, and discussions. Respecting opinions even if you do not agree. Two people become one. One soul a togetherness and closeness. Your life changes yet for the better. Leave your loved one some space and freedom to roam, drive and see their friends and family. Yes you are included but do not always have to be present. You want to involve the person in your thoughts, life and social events. Children – sometimes people cannot conceive for many reasons. They might have nieces/nephews or a special child and be a God parent. They may be big brother/sister to a kid. Perhaps kids from other relationships become blended families. Partner is love/life and business and share responsibilities.

Help out. Give your share. If someone falls sick or needs a leave of absence be there to help. Learn from each other. See the world and travel together if possible. I never knew. You never told me that. There will always be surprises and some forms of mystery. Someone is always more serious, conservative, economical, strong arm, stoic, punctual, saver versus a spender. Man – the conquest/ conqueror and hunter. A woman is not supposed to take the imitative all the time. She will wait an eternity sometimes for her love to move. Once someone is conquered comes either self involvement, temporary animal sexual satisfaction. Then panic drives next. Notch on a belt.

The true man once conquered begins the real work of beginning to learn and know the person. Steps on a set of stairs, projection, fascination, memories. Go with the flow do not analyze. Some men feel oh there will always be prettier, more attractive in the future. I will be missing out. On what? The one will slip you by before you ask why. Where did she go? Why to another my friend, oh no. Well you did not desire her or seriously consider her as a true lover and wife of your future. You are not a relationship kind of guy remember you want your space, freedom, choice, liberty, no confinement, or questions. Checking in or telling what time will you be home. You detest routine. It is all adventure, action, move and go go go . Do not tie me down. Think will be a bachelor for a lifetime. A long time. What is wrong with him? He has commitment phobia. Is it just the chase that interested him or the beginning of courting, going steady whatever. When you become an item together. What will my friends think? I'm losing my mind. We never thought you would ever settle down ever. What took you so long?

Inner World – 9 Portals on the human body – (2) Eyes, (2) ears (1) mouth (2) nostrils (nasal) (1) vagina (1) rectum the 10th gate in the opening of the third eye Chakra (Third Eye Chakra just above the eyes between your temples on your forehead). The 10th door is your intuition – your mind which influences all thoughts, memories, pictures, opinions, negation, fear, takes hold of soul. You must meditate one and a half to three hours (1.5 to 3) per day to turn off mind totally. Focus concentration above eyes. Not forcing eyes or straining your body falls asleep. The soul moves from the lower cavity from the navel to a higher realm like a balloon when ready only. Peaceful serenity and complete calm is achieved. The word is God's voice (inner). The current is music. Inner is the soul, spirit and heaven. Astral are the dimensions and realms. When the soul is totally set free from the three (3) veils or cloaks or drapes it merges with the spirit. Naked – behold light is brighter. Every day concentrate on the third (3rd) eye and focus. No interruptions and sit in the same position. When your mind wanders off bring it back to no thought. You will be able to see, speak and hear your heavenly father Jesus and God. Ask questions, see his bright light. View the outer worlds. Eventually you will be able to see and hear your true master guiding you to various dimensions one (1) step at a time. Never in a rush. Slowly and thoroughly. Never do this alone without guidance ever.

Master guides you must go through the following steps: Star(s) Blue streaks, white light cluster of stars bursting.

1. Sun
2. Moon
3. Spirit dimension 4th and 5th dimensions

These are all guided by your master.

Like the sea the inner current always presides and is reliable. Always there (melodious). We are a spec a drop in the vast ocean oasis. Coming home and following the familiar. Love – Brotherhood – we are a family and are to love one another. One with God/Jesus/Spirit/Soul. No strife or regulations required when everyone has found their true path and devotes the necessary time daily. There is a repetition of the five (5) holy names and phrases continually (I do not know what these names are called). Inner voice and sounds. We are not our bodies it is a shell containing organs, DNA, blood, nervous system, soul, spirit, mind and brain, collagen, protein, enzymes, nitrogen, oxygen and hydrogen, bones, ligaments and veins.

The mind is Ego – selfishness, pride, lust, blame, judgement, accusations, not sharing, division, owing, bankrupt of feeling and emotions. We have to learn to attain total abandonment of body and self. Saints go to the highest realms. There are no problems, fights, arguments nor disagreements. Nothing bothers you. Floating you see the light a bright light. Celestial. Life and colors. You are able to leave the body by astral projection in the second and third (2nd and 3rd) dimensions realms only the beginning. There is no time, space or dates in the realms. You meet other masters and those who have passed on. Realizing that life is but a trifle. The soul and spirit manifest together. All the pain, struggles, resentment, anger, revenge, victimization, bitterness, disappointment, despairs is now understood. All for a reason your spiritual growth. Evil will avoid you and does not come near and disappears. Good/bad karma.

Everyone's path is never the same and stop comparing your lives and living through others. No bragging you need energy. You are truly blessed. Bless others and share. Have gratitude and thankfulness. Give to others. The time is now we/our world. Not Mine/I. You will desire to be continually in this state (home) your home/my home. It takes some months, years even a life time to attain these levels of awareness. Some open their third (3rd) Eye Chakra almost immediately. It is easy for them. Ex: The very simple person who is high in belief and trust, faith and their intentions. Already knows the outcome will be positive. Spiritual and religious sometimes are born into poverty without things/needs/objects/ materialism with any attachments. No electricity. Does not have technology, or electricity. Eats very little and has a small modest home living with lots of love. Lives from day to day and knows God always provides.

Has no cellular phone/car/radio/TV/DVD/stereo/MP player/computer/tablet no materialism, luxuries, or fine clothes, shoes, accessories, jewelry. Only book is their Bible and a few others. Not highly educated, nor gifted. Unwavering faith and hope of the outcome. Always smiling and positive. Takes suffering and pain as a lesson of learning. No ill feelings toward anyone. No slander, gossip, defamation. Knows kindness, humility, modesty when not to speak. Neither aggressive nor competitive. Not arrogant. Selfless, giving, generous, hospitable, open hearted. Helps others in need and distress. The poorest in the world have the brightest smiles and will offer their last meal or garment, tea, coffee or milk and sugar. The loneliest people hide their veil and pretend to be joyful. The most depressed people you would not even recognize before they have fallen in despair. The happy people accept life with all its tragedies, all hope and faith to pursue and go on steadfast like a mountain goat. Totally open hearted.

The richest people in the world will sometimes donate to charities with a cause for recognition yet would hardly dare give spare change to the needy on the street. Go get a job they say. They abhor sloth. The middle class is slowly vanishing. Even unemployed people need help from the Salvation Army at times for food, clothes for their kids. I am hearing that coffee, chocolate will eventually run out. What a panic that would cause to be without daily java and chocolate. Not getting your caffeine fix would cause anarchy (just kidding). When you feel no way out call on Heaven above you know how to be saved. Ask for your friends by name. Evoke the holy realm. I'm saturated in the cool dark green water of a lake nearby and lay floating above. Just seeking and reaching out to touch your cheek. I see angel clouds with wispy wings. Lying here and floating feeling closer to you. I am dreaming and imagining my future but wait the past is gone and who knows about our future. You said to me it is the here and the now but how do I not worry or cast doubt my inner turmoil surfaces. With a little faith you can believe in what you cannot see. Add a little hope the way it is supposed to be.

Cherish the little things in life. Be grateful. Seventy to ninety percent (70-90%) of communication is non-verbal and body language. It is what you do not say like slamming doors, sighing. I know that silence is not always golden. There is tension, tone and quiet action. Want to talk but do not because you do not want to offend or nag. Glance. Open your mouth and say never mind. Neglect your emotions and to be fulfilled and happy. Yes and no and underlying sarcasm.

Do not forget to ever hug kiss, peck on the cheek and say I appreciate and cherish you. I am lucky we met. Thank you. Quiet and reserved people listen. Talkative mouthy arrogant ones do not know how to listen properly. What I have to say is important. More important than what I am thinking right now? You never give me a chance to speak my mind. O.K. I am now listening all yours. Go ahead now.

(Another Poem by Nora) Books are books and I love to read. For what you learn cannot be self taught. All the lessons you read come true. As if stepping in another dimension of déjà vu. Words floating in my thoughts and mind land softly on my heart and soul sublime entwining my hands in yours delicately. I think of you and smile shyly and the whole world stops and stands still. Dreams and imaginary realms stardust flickering. Stepping stones and fairy tales. Tip toe past yet you do not see me at the garden gates. I linger. I am here nor there nor anywhere. I can be elsewhere two places at once everywhere. It is quite confusing to explain you see. You will have to take my word for it and see my moves visually. Steam rises from hot Chai Coffee or pot of tea. I do believe you can fly and soar above the cliffs and scan the shores like my favorite birds do sweep. It is a secret I'd like to keep. Gliding, gliding on the White Sea caps. True freedom will you will me last?

Suicide the Taboo Topic – The most suicides in the world happen in San Francisco, Britain, Greenland, Canada, USA, Iceland, and Denmark. The most female's suicides happen in Hong Kong and China. The Western world where abundance is supplied such as food, shelter, heat, electricity, technology, cars, computers, toys, boats has more suicides than the Third World countries. Why are so many depressed, despairing to end one's life? Everyone around did not see the signs. Feeling inferior, a failure. Closed off from the world and cannot cope. They see absolutely no positive future. Sometimes childhood memories do haunt people all their lives. Bad/poor abusive upbringing of no love, support, continual sarcasm and no self worth nor esteem. There are signs of giving away personal items, social media comments, letters or sayings.

You will be better off without me, I do not want to live in this world anymore, life is not fair or cruel, I am in people's way and a burden, and I am too weak to live in a cruel world. Life is just too hard to cope any longer. I hate myself and loath others more. Giving away personal pets to others. Drastic changes in moods such as joining a cult, behaviour, attitudes. Moving to an area to be self sufficient and cut off from the rest of the world and existence to live in a middle of a forest with no neighbors. Building underground storage facilities. Joining negative groups who only want to use your weakness. Staying in one room, loner, existing, eating, reading etc. Being a loner or hermit.

Radically changing your personal beliefs and religious beliefs. You have sick and health issues (hypochondriac) all the time. Bathing and personal care to a minimum. No sense of pride and dirty smelly clothes and body odour with dirty hair. Wanting to be someone else or pretending to emulate another's life. Lead someone else's life. Envious and jealous of everyone and everything around you. No hobbies anymore. Destructive behavior and vices: Alcohol, drugs, substance abuse, too much eating (obesity), gambling, shopping, or starving of oneself (anorexia nervosa), binge eating & vomiting later (bulimic). Anger problems. Dislike of authority or criticisms. Disappointment and trying to live up to others expectations. Living through others with no opinions.

Easily influenced as a follower. Critical, negative and dark. Wearing dark colors all the time navy blue, black, dark brown, taupe and grey. Changing from approachable, friendly mean, to distant and aloof. Sexual deviant, low self esteem, emptiness. No self worth or confidence. Fear of life and no motivation.

Cannot move forward to any future. Living in the past only counts. Being controlled by others. Humiliated, embarrassed by peer and sexting. Social media bullying. At school there is no acceptance. A sense of never belonging, the oddball. Fear of abandonment and being left alone all the time. Many are exhibitionists, voyeurs or are constantly on the internet looking at pornographic images to hide those dirty secrets. They want to shock people, are cunning and sneaky.

No togetherness or cooperation, family time. Amalgamated, blended families. Individualism, break-up of family unit. Jealous of romantic relationships and intimacy of others. Feel unloved, not appreciated. Complete devastation. Pain from an accident with constant daily pain and agony. Comparisons often sibling rivalry and competition. Self-hatred, self-loathing, mutilation, cutting. When they are in a deep depression and not seeking counsel or aid getting a proper diagnosis and the correct/right medication for the proper sickness. Thinks they are freaks. Mental illnesses ranging from one or more of the following: Manic, Borderline Personality Disorder, Bi Polar I and II, disorders such as: ADDHD, OCD, Multiple personalities, Anxiety, panic attacks, Manic high highs and low lows, chronic mood swings, changeable, being contrary. Narcissistic, sociopaths, psychopaths, pedophilias and sexual deviants and addictions.

Corruption and living under duress. Wartime or power. Being told how to act, what to say, what to wear, who to talk to, what time you can go out, permission to drive or go out alone in public. Feel repressed. Introvert to extrovert or extrovert to introvert. Peter Pan Syndrome not wanting to mature grow up or move out from your parent's home. Not wanting to be responsible, opening a business, freedom to make choices, relocating or moving. Live in constant dependence on others and fear. Co-dependent personalities on their parents. Cannot advance in the future and remain stagnant. Live in same area and house all your life and prefer routine. Lack of sleep and desperation. Quiet when used to be outgoing. Change of habits and hobbies. Time sleep patterns changing and interrupted. Chronic insomnia no rest or sleep. Lies. Watching violent television and playing games on the computer all day. Too much internet not going outside. Expects other people to do favors for them all the time. Make excuses not to work or finding a job to be continually co-dependent on others makes them comfortable and safe.

Everything is mundane and boring. True apathy. Embarrassed of parents, family, spouse. Do not want to be in the same room for a long duration. Avoidance and one word answers, mumbling. Detests family visits and functions. Substance abuse, problems and many vices. Morning person to night owl. Nocturnal disrupted sleep patterns. Loud offensive music. Ignoring and pretending not to listen. Yet heard every word. Paranoia stop going outside. Sensitive to hot and cold. Feel tired and chronic fatigue all the time total exhaustion and act irritable and moody all the time. Eating patterns and routines are now different. Stop going to church or services all of a sudden. There are many myths about suicide. Most are planned taking weeks, months and years. Some are impetuous and only think about for five (5) minutes to a few hours.

These suicide pacts are terrible. Always the other will entice one to commit suicide before them. Do not get involved in any dare, bullying or be provoked regarding your life. Walk away, say no thank you, I am not interested. The outcome of suicide is complete devastation. You do not know how much you affect your immediate family, friends, relatives, colleagues, mentors, students etc. They will feel guilty for the rest of their lives. Pondering over and over if they could have done something different to help. How they never seen the signs. The eternal question is why?

The burden is great affecting personal relationships, your job and future events. There is a hole, emptiness felt where there was life none is now. You could have been the most important person to someone without knowing it. A mentor someone to look up to. You will never see your talents, watch important family events, see how you grown into maturity, fall in love with someone. Many family members have to live with depression especially if they were the last person to see you before committing a suicide. Or someone from your family finds your dead body will mark them forever in the recesses of their minds, subconscious, sleep, life. Crying is sometimes a daily routine.

You will never see your goals, dreams and aspirations attained and fulfilled. Not experiencing failure a few times to be the best success after all the pain, sacrifice of your time and energy. Not knowing your passion and what drives you forward. To develop the most important relationships of your life. To see how you have learned, improved and gained wisdom. Seeing your talents grow through practice to near perfection. The many friends and new friends who will appreciate and accept you as you are. To thank that special teacher who saw more than others. He/she encouraged you and sees the deeper picture and outcome. You are beautiful and needed, wanted and loved. The world will not be the same without your presence, laughter and smile. God made you special and unique.

Alcoholism (Both men, women, teenagers and some children are chronic alcoholics): I am writing about this topic with much experience living with three (3) kinds of alcoholics and dating more in my youth. The three of them defined as Glad, Sad, and Mad. Depression, melancholy, sentiments, happy, jolly, fun-loving, throwing items, screams, temper tantrums, berating verbally abusive, physical and mental abuse. Emotional, psychological rages and car accidents. Alcoholics have lack of judgement, are innate obstinate. They will grab keys and say, let me drive; I can drive, Give me the keys now and curse. They are stubborn and think are smarter and better than others.

Extremely insecure people deep down. Frightful, swaying, swearing, changing moods and speeds on the road are erratic. They are sneaky and cunning. Do not know when to call it quits or stop. They always want just one more drink. Do not touch my glass or else. They get really upset if you hide or pour liquor down the drain and can become violet with words swearing or slapping, shoving, pushing, hitting someone. Many are ok on beer and wine. It is when they touch moonshine, spirits, Vodka, Rum, Whiskey, Scotch, Rye, Tequila, Gin, Absinthe, Pernod or mixed drinks they become the devil incarnate. Often found in barns, pubs, taverns, hotels, motels, inns, restaurants drinking before going out to dinner. To get a quick buzz on they will have a few drinks before going out. They can be rude, arrogant, touchy, and bossy and live often in the past only. Many drink in the morning at lunch, middle of the afternoon. There is always a reason or excuse to drink. Many drink in their cars before going out I have seen really bad alcoholics who drink while driving which is illegal. Hiding their alcohol in the back seat of the trunk. The compulsion to drink is that great.

Alcoholism is a grave disease and is a depressant. After the high highs of the night before celebrating the next morning brings an awful hangover where the whole family has to walk on eggshells not to wake the person up. Loud noises bother them. They do not feel like eating anything but to start drinking all over again. Some vomit many times (dry heaves) and others are nauseated. Many people kick the habit of drugs and smoking yet cannot seem to stop drinking. Often drinkers start out young either stealing or watering down booze from parents. Some drink with their friends and often peer pressure make them drink even more. Often the person will drink one after another and have no sense of time. No discussions. They are often silent or closet drinkers hiding their stash in a garage, basement, and car or office to hide their habit. Often times end up in hospitals with problems with their liver (cirrhosis) and dehydration or many other health problems caused by too much alcohol.

Some are binge or weekend drinkers. Or there are shot drinkers. Often time drinkers do not want to drink alone and will buy you and your friends a whole gang a few drinks to enjoy their company of getting quickly tipsy, to totally pissed drunk and belligerent. They offer bartenders a drink too. Waiters also get a drink or a toast. The chronic alcoholic will not even offer a drink he wants to drink the last drop to him/herself. At a party they are wasted, alone or in a corner talking to themselves. Many times they will help themselves to Jell-O shots or any free alcohol available before they will start on their own booze. (BYOB)

Many experience blackouts. No memory of their behaviour or how they got home. The next day all apologetic, non-communicative and sheepish or embarrassed often times shy and are recluses hiding in their bedrooms. They often try to bribe to get one more drink or a running tab to pay later. You will notice their change in behaviour immediately when an alcoholic has to pay their bar tab often times arguing the amount as wrong with the bartender. Ranting and raving he/she will claim over charges or the house cheating them. They often sleep on the couch or hog the whole bed snoring. Sometimes you find out one day later they spent the evening at their best friend's house to sleep it off. The characters are: Mean, angry, yelling, screaming, blaming, swearing, name calling, calling down people, belittle, humiliation, put downs of other family members and spouses, friends, relatives, colleagues even their own boss.

Others can be revengeful, and quite vindictive. Always remember a wrong or criticism. Incapable of love, close ties and normal relationships. Immaturity, self-centeredness, self pity. Blaming always others not themselves. You make me drink. It is because of you. God I can use a drink right now. Do you want to go out for a happy hour two (2) drinks for the same price of one? Come on let me buy you a drink. Sometimes they nurse or babysit their drinks hoping others will offer or give them a tab. They often run huge tabs and never keep up or track of how many and are so surprised at the total will often argue with the server, waitress of bartender saying they did not drink that much as if they are cheating them monies. I did not or could not have possibly have drank that much. You are kidding. They also always forgot they offered other people drinks. Drinkers will start early morning or after work and early evening, late at night it does not matter to them when. Some drink at home alone or with other drinkers to become totally drunk. Alcoholics will raise their voices and yell when angry. They often whisper with clenched teeth and a surly mouth in contempt.

They are extremely reckless drivers and cannot see clearly often swerving back and forth from the center line. They drive erratically slow because of guilt or speed up dangerously to pass others. They are too sudden and everything is a blur. Take the wrong exit or miss their exit. Often drives down one way streets by mistake. They are afraid to be stopped by the police.

Some claim to drive better when they are completely drunk. You know this is not true. Most times they never get hurt in car accidents because their body is so malleable and they are not rigid. They injure, hurt and kill or maim others for life in car accidents. Lots of time they cause fatal accidents with head on collisions. Often times run over people who are at a cross walk or even sidewalks. It is not uncommon for alcoholics in the past to lose their license three to thirteen (3-13) times or more during their lifetime and put their family at risk often with erratic driving.

They lie to people they know. It was not that bad. Yeah they took my license away for two (2) years and now I have to have a breatherlizer in the car to start the engine. Many warnings. No one absolutely no one should get into a car with a drinker or drunk driver. If you have to do get in the car with an alcoholic do not speak, aggravate or disagree with them. Say yes and no in curt answers and do not elaborate, say your opinion or talk too much. Do not start a conversation or agitate the driver in any way. Agree with them to avoid confrontation or arguments. Repeat their words and agree with them. They do not make any sense at all and are talking to themselves.

They will talk on and on about their problems or how unjust the world is and life is not treating them fairly or hatred for someone. Do not panic make or eye contact. Get out as soon as possible. Say at the red light I want to go out. They may become paranoid and yell at you if you try to correct their driving skills. Pretend to go get money and disappear and get a cab, call someone. Your life is not worth putting in drunk drivers hands. It is not worth the risk. Go to a police station or have them get off at an exit off the highway or go to a corner late night store, a relative, friend, anything is better than staying in the car.

The silent drunk seethes with thoughts of future actions. They are revengeful. Their personality is passive aggressive. Everything is fine yet not what they mean. They sneer and snarl and spit venom with their words. Nostrils are flared up. Tight or tucked in lips, biting lips and are often agitated. Pretend to be your best friend. Do not tell me how to drive. I have been driving for longer than you been alive twenty-five (25) years and not one accident. I am a great driver. They will start arguing with you as soon as the car door opens. Nice to strangers and acquaintances yet terrible, mean and hateful towards their own family, spouse and kids. Seething with anger to loved ones may become violent. Throwing objects and cursing. Falling down or tripping up the stairs, making noise as they enter the house. They pat you on the back and say you are their best friend and buddy yet they only spoke to the person for five minutes.

Some drinkers become extra sentimental singing ballads or crying at the end of the night they do not want to leave the bar. Life of the party. Attention seekers, loud extroverts. Jealous of others their jobs, clothes, cars, houses, positions, power, influence. Often compares themselves materialistically to others. You will find them at the center of the room talking to complete strangers and keeping everyone entertained. Walks right in a place like they own it. Overly confident, cocky, arrogant and rude. They are possessive and jealous with their girlfriend or wife. Will tell you to shut up and you don't know anything. What are you talking about anyway? They will change 360 degree personalities, nice, shy to rowdy outgoing and obnoxious to quiet and withdrawn. Very moody. You ask to leave their presence. They will say do not embarrass me stay. Flirt and talk to others and lying to you when alone.

They make others laugh with dirty and bigoted jokes, stories, tales and legends. They have a reservoir of information. Quick witted, smart, sometimes a sociopath and borderline personality disorder. Narcissistic. Will argue with bartender(s), hot headed. The next day will go back to pay their full bar tab because they were so rude and walked out without paying. They want to drink again at the same place and like routine and will pay their dues to avoid condemnation. Drink right away upon walking in. No hello. Some have secret stashes, places, small mickeys, bottles hidden around all over the house and barn. Often they drink vodka to mask smell of alcohol and other kinds of spirits and booze. These kinds of alcoholics possess extremely sensitive egos. I'm the one who wears the pants in the family. I'm the man/woman and the boss in our family and make all the decisions because the others are incapable.

The quiet ones often like to drink all alone. Solitary and antisocial hermits. They observe and watch every movement of others. They are noisy and petty. Some friends of the alcoholics like to go over to their friend's house every few days to have free beer, wine or spirits, liquor. They know their friend has a great stash and are too cheap to buy their own alcohol and sponge off these people for years. Many drinkers do not like to drink alone and are very generous to share. Loathe being called out: Think you had enough I am no longer serving you. The drinker will raise their voice and say what do you mean? I will give my business elsewhere if you do not give me a drink right now. Swear and tell someone to get off their chair like it has their name on it. They like to sit in a corner. Alcoholics have great difficulty admitting they have a drinking problem verbally. Many will never admit it to others. They consider themselves weak and social drinkers. What is the matter with a drink once in a while? I do not drink that much just a few. They are often in denial even when drunk.

They have a favorite home away from home close by a bar/tavern or pub where they know people by name. A brasserie or hang out place where they get wasted, forget to eat or check the time. They are selfish, and irresponsible. Often they will eat a large meal before they drink. Some have many jobs losses one after another blaming others for their problems and job/work performance. They are often late. In summer months it's an excuse to drink more because of the warm temperature/weather. Easter, Valentine's Day, Birthday, Anniversary, Mothers or Fathers Day, St. Patrick's. Christmas is occasions spent buying more booze than food. Oftentimes they do not want to go out with their own spouse. Do not want to be bothered or nagged. It is a lonely sad life of self destruction. Why do people drink so much? There are many reasons: Hereditary (DNA/genes), routine/boredom, following, peer pressure, depression, loneliness, settle nerves (shy people become uninhibited and more relaxed), force of habit (meeting at a pub everyday). Everyone else drinks, lack of acceptance, no self esteem, insecurity, alcohol is a chronic addiction extremely difficult to quit/stop drinking. Alcohol does change ones personality.

Ninety percent (90%) of the men I had long relationships with were chronic alcoholics. My father was a social drinker, beer in the very late afternoon and occasional red wine so therefore, do not where this comes from. The only closet alcoholic in both sides of my family was my very shy loner uncle who was so intelligent and loved puzzles, reading and was a professional cartographer. The psychologists state if your father is an alcoholic the daughters have a huge chance of marrying an alcoholic. My father would have a huge family crowd over for Christmas. When he was younger and married he worked after work hours as a part time bartender and never drank with the clients.

So, do I want to save or change these men? Oh how I tried to render them more open hearted and loving. They always choose the bottle over me. Tried to be the perfect optimist, positive, encouraging, and lost the battle with patience. Nothing worked, nothing changed. I was bitter, jaded and completely exhausted in the end. It was a miserable existence. Never went to an Al Anon meeting yet. Was I a nurse in a previous past life?

My worse fault is impatience yet my family and friends think I was a living Saint to live with those crazy people. I tried so hard to care for others. I'm generous, a cheerful giver and truly want to help. Now, in my early retirement years I want nothing better to find a friend, or soul mate. I have nothing against social drinkers who have fun, laugh and enjoy life at its fullest and do not put tabs or count other people's drinks. So I have dated the mad, sad and glad alcoholics. You can say I have personal living experience on this topic and soon get tired of it and it does get pretty old. There are tremendous beautiful men who I would love to date not any longer because of alcoholism. I have grown too mature to search, want, need or desire comfort, security over my sanity and freedom. Oh, how they tried to hide their drinking from me. The secretive drinker likes vodka, hiding bottles in closets, drawers and garages, chewing gum and breath mints. Never drinking in front of me and pretending not to drink in front of their friends. If they had their binges I would never see them the whole weekend. It was always the hard stuff like: Crown Royal, Rum, Vodka, and homemade moonshine, sometimes scotch. The cheap alcoholic will drink beer if he/she is desperate. It is funny how they did not enjoy nor want a beer gut and complained on how long it took too long to get a good buzz. Always using eye drops.

Drugs: Well they change the kinds used almost daily. In my day it was cannabis, weed leaves of the plant (hemp oil now legalized used in hospitals), angel dust, mushrooms, acid and some LSD which are all hallucinogenic drugs. People are dying daily from overdoses of opiates. Today you hear much more about ecstasy the party dance drug where you have no control over your bladder and surroundings becoming touchy feely. Cocaine and heroin is ten (10) times more expensive than cocaine are extremely addictive and expensive drugs with high highs after only one use.

On cocaine you talk sporadically are speedy and tend to always have nose drip. An itch and twitch of the nose. Heroine leaves track marks on the arms, legs, and feet by injections which end up looking like burn marks. Many times you would not even guess someone is on heroine except for the drastic weight loss. You will always see them with extra long shirts/sweaters/blouses their arms covered or turtle necks in winter. They use a long piece of flexible plastic and wrap a knot around their arms to make the vein appear easier, and then inject the vile substance. They lie and say they are sick. Crack is extremely addictive making you edgy and hyper.

Meth destroys your health, teeth and you will age at least thirty (30) years. Uppers and downers have the colors of: red, blue, yellow, orange, pink and white pills. People who have to get up early and work really late can easily get addicted to uppers and downers. Examples of these kinds of jobs would be: shift workers, actors/actresses, security, servers, bartenders, small business owners. There are some drugs which stop or eliminate pain for some time and make your body completely totally numb. Other pills like speed increase your awareness. Appetite and diuretic weight suppressants make your heart beat much faster. Other pills are for insomnia (Small peach or white pills). Percocet or pain relievers for the back and sciatica nerve etc. Morphine used for people for chronic disease to relieve pain is often stolen from hospital pharmacies. Some drugs give you the sense of euphoria and make you laugh and relaxed. Other bad trips are nightmares, paranoia, seeing people, shapes or things attack you. The most common drugs are opiates and pain killers.

The very dangerous date drugs which are slipped into someone's drink by powder or pill or liquid format. The victim(s) becomes groggy, cannot see anything sometimes for a few days. Everything is blurred, and they feel quite disorientated and tired. The effect is immediate so if you only drank two drinks your will feel queasy and sick to your stomach and sometimes nauseated get out of the bar/pub/tavern/inn/hotel and go immediately to the hospital by taxi alone or with your friends.. Many women have been raped and woke up two to three (2-3) days later in a stranger's bedroom apartment or house not remembering a thing and were repeatedly raped not remembering a thing. Always watch the server pouring your drink and never leave your drink unattended even for a second. Keep your drink in your hands. Some drugs in drinks make people pass out faint and fall on the floor.

I have friends who dump the drink, rinse the glass and pour soda into their glasses because they are so afraid of a risk or consequence. Also for others should be on the lookout and watch for those other sneaky idiots pouring the drug or powder in someone's drink approach them and let them know you just saw what they did. Take the drink and dump it on the floor immediately and tell the bartender why. Sometimes the bartender will know and be in denial to associate with these perverts. You just prevented a crime and perhaps saved someone's life. Usually they like darkness, corner tables and much distraction (loud music, confusion, loud drunk people shoving, and crowds). They pretend to be the boyfriend and escort her out in his arms. They look for their victim preferring someone alone or waiting and will offer you a drink or wait until you turn your head just for a few seconds. Sometimes they approach two people and try to hint to the other to leave them alone.

Some addicts use a tablespoon and heat the drug till it bubbles then pump the substance into a syringe/needle through their veins(s). When someone is called a junkie they usually are injecting drug(s) with a syringe or needle(s). They are continually shaking until their next fix. No drug(s) should be mixed with alcohol ever or the result may/can be fatal the result is death. Children/preteens and teens do not ever try, take, sneak or steal your parents (adult) medication(s). You do not know what you are taking and it is extremely dangerous. What drugs does to the victim is terrible yet if affects the entire family and siblings. Some will beg, borrow and steal for their addictions. Lie to you when confronted with additional new lies. This is a form of desperation and despair.

There are drug addicts who rob houses during the daytime now, sell appliances, cars, clothes, food, electronic devices, cameras, computer's and will steal money from anyone they know to feed their habit. All drug addicts have dark circles under their eyes, large pupils or are always skinny or have a great noticeable weight loss and hardly ever eat. Often their personal stories are exaggerations, fibs, set-ups and cons to make you feel sorry for them to give more and more. They will often target the same person many times. Most dislike any kind of intervention. Another much unknown drugs are sniffing various lethal substances in a paper bag to get an instant high. Yet you have to continually do it all the time. There are so many new names and new drugs and different pill kinds and colors it is hard to keep up. Now many are addicted to opiates.

Spousal Abuse: He did not abuse me but was a happy/glad alcoholic. My first real boyfriend who truly loves me for me. He starts not paying any bills or helping and gets high everyday on harmless weed (he states) and you forgive him. He wants that motorcycle so bad and that is his excuse. He sings and is happy, dances and gives you lots of affection. Then he starts a grow up in your basement for months and you do not even know it because you never go down stairs anymore. He takes care of the furnace and wood fire. You get rid of the mother plant and see all these lights and division and the awful smell. You throw his clothes out on New Year's Eve. I was now alone and lonely. He crashed your repaired car while drunk and takes long to pay you back yet he does. I am proud of him and still in love. Very charming, soft spoken and nice. Pays attention to your needs. You love to do things for him. My heart is broken and I begin to distrust men after a year of living together. We met on Valentine's Day and he has a date and breaks up on the following Valentine's Day. Nice. I am just friends because still not damaged.

He is the sad mean barbaric alcoholic. There are many forms of spousal abuse emotional, psychological, mental, and physical. It takes an average of thirty-five (35) beatings before a woman will finally report or press charges against her spouse. The abuse takes over for many years sometimes many decades. What everyone has to learn is that abuse is a form of control, power, jealousy and possessiveness and not love. They want to control everything from what you wear, who you talk to, your hobbies and likes, your family, religion, church friends. Abusers want to alienate you totally from others especially from close friends and family. Listening to phone conversations, stealing your cellular to memorize the speed dial numbers, caller i.d., texts, snoop and read all your personal papers. Often times they review and watch your history on the internet and read all your personal emails on the computer. They scope Face Book daily for your comments and new friends.

Gradually they state I do not like so and so they are not a good influence on you get rid of them. I do not like it when you look or talk to other men stop it now. When you do get visitors they sit sullen and moody until the people feel uncomfortable and leave. They will not give you your phone messages for days. They start timing your errands and asking where did you go and why. Also for the first few years everything is like a dream. Of course their hidden agenda is always a mystery. The once beautiful girl or woman is under constant scrutiny. You dressed beautifully and always had on makeup and nice shoes to match. He complimented you every day. Now he wants you to almost dress in a shroud, cover your shoulders; do not show any cleavage, too much leg. He accuses you of flirting with all men and asks if you slept or dated any of these acquaintances. Pretty soon he is weary of everyone of the opposite sex. Your friends and family slowly do not communicate with you because they dislike your boyfriend, spouse, lover or husband. You are blinded by love or is it just lust or co-dependence?

When you have children that is when you are really stuck it seems. How could I leave the children to no security? Forgiveness, fighting emotional baggage continues for years. He is alright he did not hurt me this time. It is only bruises and cuts they will heal. Sometimes you have to be thrown a brick in your face to finally realize this is a totally wrong way to live. I can protect my children and be safe. Do not need to leave in constant worry, anxiety and walking on eggshells. Often times there are vices: alcohol, drugs, gambling, womanizing, and smoking. Yes they are able to flirt and sleep with others while you wait at home with patience. You are not allowed to ask any questions at all. If he walks in the next day or not at all do not even try to look at him. Oftentimes threats are made with knifes, gun or rifle in the house.

Many times they want to move to a an isolated and secluded spot free of prying eyes like a far away farm, mountain, nature, hut, cottage or even an island and off the grid. Just me a you alone and pretend it is romance and an adventure. They will insist on solar energy etc. to control everything. We do not need internet or a phone you got me and that is enough. I will protect you from any harm. The objective is to close off all communication with the outside world. Or they will threaten I am cutting off internet and the phone you spend too much time talking to others and ignoring me and the children.

If you miss your family and friends and suggest you want to see them a drinking binge of days will begin and all his anger will flash out at you. Humiliating words, swearing, demeaning and made up stories begin. You want to care, change be patient like a nurse. Deep down he is still good. If you shop he checks all the bags and yells at you if you waste anything on yourself. Personal items are frowned upon. Buy only things for the house the basic no luxuries. That means no perfume and toiletries. Sometimes they will be extremely jealous of their own children, pets and threaten that you coddle and spoil them too much. For goodness sake how can he be a man when he is now a mommy's boy? They might spoil their daughters or ignore them totally being the Patriarch of the family, boss and leader. Often times they will compare other women to make you feel insecure about your weight, appearance and self worth. When you suggest to work or get a job the answer is no. If he agrees you will be sure he will be stalking you outside and waiting for your appointment or course to end to pick you up. He is not doing you any favors for he distrusts the world. They will let you go to a course to improve yourself yet will not let you work. Or yes you can work, bring me all the money and cash and I will pay the bills, mortgage and groceries. Suddenly you do not have any clue of how much money is spent or saved. He controls the funds, finances and budget. After twenty years you can by your dream house yet he will never let you experience happiness and joy.

Often times he has a domineering mother or does not have a good relationship with her. Abuse is taught growing up. If his father has lack of respect and swears at his mother he thinks this is normal. He will refuse to cook, clean, keep house that is the woman's job. Or the opposite he will cook, clean and help you like a bargaining tool. Look how good I am taking care of you. You are nothing without me and will never succeed. If he cooks you are only allowed to eat food prepared by him so you never get to go out in public to eat. This is another form of restraint and control. By him/her cleaning the house you feel a bit better about yourself not for long. Your world comes crushing down. You do not speak to anyone about your problems because of fear, embarrassment, shame and guilt. Wrong choice and pattern once again. Why do I choose these kinds of men? Where are the nice, generous, giving men? Is my life going to measure up to nothing? Where is the growth and maturity? Will our kids ever be safe?

If you threaten to leave and begin to show some independence that is when the real threats begin. I will get you, you owe me, and I will find you and do this... to you. All of a sudden there is no way out. He will always find us living on pins and needles. Your children absorb your fear and anxieties also. Do not think the unspoken words are avoided. All the sneers, sarcasm, cynical snaps, swearing words and orders are all learned and impressionable upon them. He grabs your arms and you have bruises the next day. Starts to shove and push you when he is upset. Then the first small slap just to show you who is in charge. You are so shocked and cry all night. He throws a chair or items and bruises your whole arm. You cover the flaws up with makeup, clothing and become more quiet and withdrawn. Where did the confident extrovert go? To a sullen exhausted quiet mouse of a personality.

Next he tells you not to look at him when he talks to you. Look at the ground not me do you hear me? He shakes you often, pinches and starts to use and throw objects. He threatens you with knives, baseball bat or his self defense moves. When you are sweeping the floor he takes the broom and whacks you with it for no reason and laughs. He claims you are not domesticated and never keep the house clean enough like I do. You are a terrible cook. Next day he treats you to coffee and pastry and is soft like a kitten because he wants something from you. Your hair is dull dry and starts to fall out, and roots go grey. The skin on your face is no longer radiant and you have break outs, redness and a pale sallow complexion from the many worries. You decide to cut and color your hair to feel a bit better. Big mistake waste of money. I like you as you are. Why did you cut your hair you should have left it as is. I like it longer, grow it back now. Who are you trying to impress are you going out with someone else or something? Not with the girls I know how that works. I think your dye job looks cheap.

You go out to a restaurant and say hello to the host. He flushes and turns red because the man is young and handsome. He pouts, ignores you and says he is going to the bathroom. Then you find he has left you stranded totally to fend for yourself in the middle of nowhere. He has the car you see. Punishing and branding you as the bad person always is their tactic. You are cheap, a whore, sleep around which are all incredibly untrue. Then you start to believe you are not worthy and resign yourself to listening to verbal abuse daily for hours. It goes on for years with no control. The drinking and drug binges (alcohol and speed) combined are terrifying to say the least. You hide and lock the door hoping he will not find you.

Or now you finally you decide to take matters into your own hands in the middle of winter and just run away and leave. You see car high beams of headlights and hide behind a snow bank, breathe hard nowhere to go. You both live in the country and he only drives. Returning from a family function he drives unsteady and speaks his demeaning words. I want to get out now you state. He laughs in this darkness you will never find your way. Are you nuts? He apologizes and swerves the car along the narrow lake road. There is a huge drop with no guard rails. You become panicked, quiet and do nothing but hold your arms together pray to the angels to get home safely.

Your personal home is no longer your home even though you pay for everything. You have to call the RCMP to have him escorted and leave. Start to sleep in the car in parking lots and you do not want to return home (your home). He threatens you and wants to borrow money a couple of hundreds or more every day until you are entirely broke. Yet his savings are still intact. Yes he controls the finances we know. He will not help with bills, mortgage or telephone, internet, cable, food, wood, heat or electrical bill. Then you find out he has a huge stash of money hidden by accident and lied to you all this time. You are being used to the extreme. He pretends you are wrong. Frugal and cheap they want to grab every cent out of your accounts. Always borrowing and demanding money from you from fifty to five hundred dollars daily (50, 100, 200, and 500 $) daily whatever he can get always expecting it without asking. He thinks you are his personal bank.

I need money for my cigarettes and alcohol and expects though he never pays for himself. Never does he have any intention of paying you back ever. You almost went to court to get back monies owed and he pays you back by second mortgaging his home and blames you for selling his home. It never ends. When he wins at gambling with your money he never gives you any of the winnings. He is the man and of course he won so he assumes your money is his not ours. There are no joint statements or accounts. You will be sure he controls his own finances and never shares. We are not married so therefore you are always going to be the victim.

Drives your new car for six months and then buys it back at a lower price of course. I never got to drive my new car. Here I was taking public transportation while he was driving my car every day to work at a job that was supposed to be mine. Yes, I gave up my new potential job because did not pass just one course. I purchase him a new wardrobe and beautiful huge portrait for his office. People ask me if he is a prince. I laugh because I look so awful and poorly dressed. He wears new clothes while I have none. The portrait was called Beaute sans pardon (Beauty without forgiveness) a medieval gorgeous rendition in a custom cherry ebony frame. He never gave it back to me. He is a sociopath narcissist.

Until one day when you least expect it he chokes your neck and throws you on the wall. You are astonished then petrified. Then you run away to the police barefoot and end the so called one way relationship. Then you move very far away and he follows then turns to you one day in your van with black demonic eyes and states I want to kill you right now then myself pull over right now.

You pray to God, Jesus the Angels in desperation. Get me out of this situation please. I promise will leave him this time. Took the van and drove away while he in a drunken stupor and all baffled. I was one of the lucky ones who escaped. You suspect he is on speed or other hard drugs because he becomes so violent, fierce and screams for hours. All he thinks about is vengeance and retaliation all he has is hatred and anger. He states it is your fault he drinks. He is so disappointed angry and unhappy about his divorce; life and hardly seeing nor living with his child anymore that it destroys him totally. You meet him at the near end of the divorce not the cause of it. He looks in the mirror and talks to himself cursing and spitting at his own image.

The breaking point is when he kicked our beautiful dog. Telling me he knows how to kick without hurting the animal. That did it for me. I took the animal back to live with me after six (6) months when I moved away. Unfortunately a neighbor who just got his license first day hit my dog got impaled by a mail box post and he did not even have the decency to tell me to my face. The dog was out all night dead and alone. I buried her on my friend's property in front of a scotch pine. My nice ex boyfriend was kind enough to help me bury and lift her with my friend. She was one hundred and twenty (120 lbs) a gorgeous black and white Labrador who loved the snow and winter. Her name was Chloe. It was a horrible experience.

He is the revengeful, mean and sad alcoholic. The next boyfriend threw full contents of beer bottle all over you in a fit of rage. He took out the car keys while you are driving at one hundred (100 mph). Makes a scene in a restaurant and screams at you to follow him. Argues with the clerk at a hotel on New Year's Eve. Security gets involved and asks if you are alright. Insulted he begins to yell and scream. On the highway he tells you are going the wrong way. He is so lost. You never make it to the hotel room because you are terrified of his alcoholic abuse. He pouts whines and is a mommy's boy who could do no wrong in her eyes. He is spoiled rotten to the core. You have to call his mother because he stole your car keys and cannot get home.

Starts doing jobs for a hotel and starts to avoid you inviting strangers to his hotel room. You wait patiently to be let down. Embarrasses and humiliates you in front of his new so called friends who are only acquaintances. Tries to sweet talk and bribe his mother to pay for his houses, car, gas and expenses while he sits on his laurels. He builds overpriced, over budgeted beautiful homes and expects mommy to bail him out. You gave your all in this relationship while he flirted with every waitress, server(s) everywhere in front of you. Divorced and unhappy he sees his kids for a few years and blames his ex wife for gaining weight that there was no more attraction and threatens you not to gain weight or get fat.

Tries to manipulate me and wants to second mortgage my personal home at the time so he could build a new one on the large parcel/plot of land. No way. He does not care and awaits his big fat inheritance to squander on himself and hopefully his kids. You saved him at least three hundred thousand (300,000) on his will. He threatens to come over with a baseball bat. Tells you deserve to be beaten up. Nice. You get fed up and tell him to get out of the car. That night he meets a new love for the interim.

Well, he drinks at parties and gets into a fight with the host on your first day making a fool of himself. Also he is drunk before you even go out. He uses you always and takes away your happiness. I'm beginning to speak to myself the same pattern again. Once again I get away safe and sound and refuse to date an alcoholic for the rest of my life. I am alone, single and fearful once again. Does this sound at all familiar to you? The reason is strong intelligent women do make the wrong and bad choices and decisions about their personal relationships. If you give up your strength and do not stand up for yourself eventually spousal abusers demand to take over the weaker sex (they call you their personal property) finances.

They would enjoy controlling all groceries, pharmaceutical items, prescriptions, clothing, car payments, and repairs to a house, credit cards, and bills such as: heating, gas, oil, electric, hot water, cable internet, and cellular phone, mortgage, taxes and all expenses and giving you next to nothing to live on or a minimal weekly allowance. No money for shopping or outings, cafes or restaurants. You have to ask permission to get your own money. He demands you hand over all your salary for your own good. They want to move in on your space and if you think the sail boat, cottage, rental property or your home is off limits think again. They think your property is one hundred percent (100%) theirs even before they met you which is totally illegal.

Often times they are previously scoped/stalked for someone naive, gullible with a huge heart, malleable and influential going to receive a future huge inheritance, real estate property, farms, a widow, someone owning large investments, monies, stocks, bonds, mutual funds, dividends, GIC's, parcels of land/acreage/ hectares, small/medium or large business, antiques, jewelry, art, coins, rare items, race horses, mines, oil, inventory. They inform themselves on all tax and capital gain laws. The irony in some cases is if they smoke and drink they refuse to have their spouse do the same. There are many derogatory names and actions such as: the wife, woman, she, her, that one over there, Sheila, bird, nuts, crazy, seeing someone, snapping the fingers for attention etc. Often times the woman is not even introduced and stands there like a mime waiting for permission to speak. Worst of all they drive you crazy and say you are insane and everything is all in your mind.

I received a few sacred memorial medals. Instead of Mary's hands and arms above her head hands outstretched with both palms facing upwards and rays of light and she clutching the middle a globe (which represents the world/earth). The medal is depicted cast palms downward with rays pointing downwards and no globe. There are twelve (12) crowns which I think depicts the twelve (12) Apostles. So the original mold would have to be redone with corrections. One foot is planted on earth the other is in water. Mary always has a shroud (Navy Blue) and white dress. Sometimes she or Jesus holds the Eucharist (Bread of Life). She holds a rosary of amber and blue beads in one hand and a cross/necklace around her neck. She is depicted with ivory porcelain skin with rosy cheeks. Beautiful green or blue eyes. Perfect composure. Immaculate Mary. Mary is mother of all mothers.

Sacred heart with seven sorrows. Behind the medal is a large M and below (2) separate hearts Jesus with thorns, Mary with arrows piercing her heart crossed. She is barefooted with one foot planted on earth and the other in water (sea or ocean). So the original mold prints silver oval medals is probably in Italy would have to be recast correctly. The colors blue and white are for the sea and foam. I would suggest that the original mold/cast to the medal be changed to please Mother Mary. She pointed out these flaws.

Saints: Oh saints thy saints, ours to behold martyred and misunderstood. Hermits, isolation on a foreign isle homes far off in total obscurity. Banished to oblivion. Giver and maker of good deeds. Private cells and years of complete silence. Visions of prophesy and no socializing reading hearts and thoughts. Some predicting future events (Prophecy). Infantile admission to monasteries, convents and sees. Life of piety, goodness, humility and modesty and many times poverty. Forever attaining the truth and justice.

They had difficult lives of the narrow arduous paths. Life forlorn. Tortured, hung, drawn and quartered, boiled in oil or water, cutting of tongues, limbs and fingers. Thrown over a cliff in a sack to drown, slow suffering and chained, often imprisoned. Extreme mortifications and severe penances, spiritual aridity. Diabolical assaults and levitation. Life of extreme austerities. Ecstasies and visitors and mystical experiences. Running away from pre-arranged marriages and tortured youth. A choice or a calling. Working with the plagues, leprosy, poor, orphans, children, boys and girls, widows and widowers, the oppressed and lonely. Often opening hospitals, churches, personal homes, monasteries, estates and castles. Giving away all riches to charity, the poor and needy. Often die in poverty as an elder. Holy helpers, ransoming members of your flock. Devotions to Blessed Virgin Mary, the Eucharist, Trinity and the Sacraments.

Miracles of healing upon their tombs (graves). Tormented, obstinate and perplexing characters. Life of pious strict obedience and austerities. Self imposed pain and sorrow. Taking up the cross literally. Some feel the whole passion of Christ and receive the Stigmata. Others are dripping with blood from either their hands, feet or eyes. Unfortunately sometimes abandoned and forgotten by most. All that remains now are the legends. Inherited gifts from heaven most high. They opened thousands of schools, churches, buildings, hospices and convents. They were often descendants of Sheppard's, merchants, farmers, royalty, nobility, and affluence, poor, rich. Lack and abundance. Love and charity, giving on their minds always. Power and leader struggles. Sees, titles and positions such as Abbess, Bishop, Deacon, Tertiary etc. The many conversions and cruel endings. Rubbing shoulders with politics and being peace keepers, referees and arbitrators. Avoiding paganism, idols, and cruel rulers who run to hunt and haunt you. They would provide shelter to priests, Catholics and Christians. At their death bells would toll on their own and people would be hearing the saint's voice. The more than 5,000 registered, appointed and approved saints of the world were confessors of love to Jesus, God and Mary. They would not ever recant their beliefs ever even in death or torture.

Pride, courage and bravery were often their positive traits. Pious, kind, meek, modest and humble. They despised hurting others. They created enemies often by others stories and legends, slander, defamation and gossip. Prefabricated stories of envy, jealousy plots to their demise. Accusations made up stories some fabricated. No witnesses. Often accused of guilt until proven innocent. Give up to the Queen, King everything against your entire beliefs and will. Why are you not celebrating on the feast day of your enmity? No boasting, vanity, pompous nor arrogant. Kind and generous giving clothing, food, caring for others. Always serving and self-sacrificing. A loving hand and smile of encouragement. Patron/Patroness of countries seamen, sailors or ailments.

Joy/Truth/Love: God and Jesus can work through your imagination. Bring you to the right thoughts, words and feelings at any given moment for the purpose at hand using one or several ways. All people are special and all moments are Golden. If you acknowledge my message that you have received them directly. You are then responsible for interpreting them. Some people are willing to actually listen, to the heart and are will to remain open to communication even when it seems strange, fearful and wrong. Listen to your feelings. God has no form or shape. He can take any form or shape which you can understand in the 3rd Dimension. He is the great unseen.

Today I believe men and women to be: More romantic and appreciate your man/woman. Do not fear to be authentic yourself. Let go of your huge Ego(s) which is selfish and self serving. Laugh more, stay charming. Grin, wink, and smile more. Learn to flirt well again. You do not have to be always on, macho and rugged. Listen more and pay attention to their words. Hold hands. Walk hand in hand it is comforting and nice. Stop spending more time on your phone than with your spouse. Give your opinion more and give taste for decorating too. Learn to cook and clean too. Be more loving, caring and show your emotions & feelings. Do not fear a women if she is more successful. Be a team and encourage. Do not hate feminist women.

A man can be a leader or a follower. More love of others and kids. Do not worry what you do. It is what is in your heart, thoughts mind, soul and spirit that count. You don't have to be competitive. It is absolutely ok to lose. Stop worrying about performance being the best all the time. Brag and boast less. Stop bullshitting and lying so much. Communicate by talking on the phone. Stop texting so much! Do not cut off people mid-sentence. Keep your integrity and word of honor. Stop being flippant and a flake. Do what you say. Stay real and reliable. Be what you mean. Take action and stop talking crap at would of, could of and should was hype. I cannot do this now. Have less worries and regrets.

Women have too many expectations of life of men. No more lists. Social media web dating sites are lies, deception and problems. Not reliable and they are just social masks and not being authentic and true. Do not want to hurt others, avoid reality. It is an escapism and leads just to depression. Plastic surgery, vanity, narcissistic, and self loathing body images in magazines, selfies and air-brushing. Self-mutilation – society wants and needs are not your own. There are so many more tattoos, piercings. Some are too conceited overly confident, cocky, arrogant and grandiose too.

Much outer body image is not love. No soul/spirit/bible return to your roots pioneer and simplicity. Women have too much criteria wants/haves/in their minds, thoughts, heads. Lists of chores, post it notes, Time Management. Too much ambition and little communication. Texting is crap. Women forgot to be romantic, soft and feminine. Men are confused about their roles. Women want to work, have a family, be a great lover and have a great relationship. They are on anti-depressant drugs to cope with reality. A superwoman does not exist. Too many meetings, committees, commitments, make a very boring uninteresting person. Alcohol – too many cocktails.

Aggression, tempers, fighting, arguing, blaming non-caring. I am better than your comparisons. Not calm very hyper too much type "A" personalities. Some love themselves too much. Difficulty sharing/giving/charity/self sacrifice. Very selfish at times. Big egos and me, myself and I. Playing victims and co-dependency. Judging, checking people out and gossiping. Very petty. How they act and what is said and the sense of style of others and fashion. Comparing others. Fighting over custody of children and divorce. Kids are used as pawns. Do not want to care for elderly parents nor spouse when ill. Lost family dynamic. Abortion is cruel. Too many categories and need social identity. Women often want careers before family. Sacrifice time and love for money. Success position and relocation. High expectations. Value themselves too highly. Overly perfectionists. Bothered and bitter about small events, nitpick habits and like Drama.

I am neither a leader nor follower rather a loner who is not always alone. Those who have not known failure, disappointment, sorrow or loneliness are lying. Eyes of sorrow are the most memorable. Be my window of the soul. Solitude could be beautiful. Faint angel music, softly ringing in another dimension. Love conquers all. Believing is seeing. The greatest form of love is listening when you are a speaker/talker.

No one enjoys being always alone. How are you supposed to get to know yourself with no freedom? I think we have fleeting moments of happiness and mere bliss. Joyous moments are not anticipated nor expected. Sheer joy is a child's laughter. I miss your advice, stories and voice. Do you miss me yet? I miss her elegance, beauty and refinement. Share your sowing. Give away what you reap. Keep a small portion only. Give a smile today even if it is a grin or smirk, curled up lip, top teeth showing, wide agape mouth, crooked lips, pucker the pout. A smile is free yet to the recipient ecstasy. My lover is my desire and best friend, where minds meet. We cannot live without human touch or sociability. We are beings not robots. Feelings are not microchips. I would rather have a meaningful conversation than keep up with technology. Love without reserve; do not withhold your true essence. I will still love the unlovable. You are the change within. Not all is what is appears. Do not believe the media hype, shock value, doom and gloom all the time. It elicits no morality. Tu me manque. Ti amo. Social media is not always social. Do not text me. I want your voice. What lays deep is your soul's awareness. To be self aware is to elevate your emotions. I am rarely bored just indifferent or complacent. I feel communes are a great idea. Until the situation arises when there are too many leaders clashing. A leader always has followers.

I'm going to write and talk about Evil. Yes, it does exist and is present on earth at this very moment. Evil is the opposite of Good and heaven. No one wants to discuss or talk about the bad real evil. In order to rid ourselves and set our sins free you need to understand what enables you, pushes, influences, inspires. What drives you? Well since the most beautiful angel (he was called the morning star) fell from heaven and brought a total of 1/3 of the entire angels with him. Why did he do this? He taunted God and did not obey our creator, his creator. Lucifer that is his name (evil) thought he was bigger, better his ego and greed overpowered him. His sins were greater than his belief and trust. We have to rebuke and bind evil. Ask their names and ask them to leave the body alone in Jesus' name. Continuously read passages of the Bible and pray.

Lucifer doubted God and Jesus. He actually thought he could take over heaven and influence others. Now God always has a plan and he waits. This means he does not act hastily. He is candid and kind, patient and all knowing. Gentle and forever forgiving. He knows all our mistakes, thoughts and actions before we do. O.K. yes there is a real genuine place called Hell. It is full of fire, brimstone, an awful, lonely, despairing place. Purgatory is where you get a second chance. Now those who commit suicide or give up on their lives because of despair are asleep for awhile. Then God and Jesus intervene. They are given a chance to repent. Now life any form of life is not for us to take, giving up, assisted or mercy killing, suicide, murder, etc. Life is God's gift to us and we are to live. God never said life is going to be an easy ride or simple. He said it is beautiful and challenging. It is so easy to choose the easy path, use others, manipulate, and be selfish. The black book is the opposite of the Bible in every way.

The devil is here to kill murder and destroy others who believe in God and Jesus. Likes nothing better to cause unforgiveness, envy, petty gossip, slander, defamation, hatred, strife, bickering, fighting, disagreements, jealousy, confusion, ostracizing, and abandonment, forgetting a person, depression and finally suicide. Lucifer loves to separate others from the love of God and Jesus. He will try to entice, tempt or bribe you with fame and riches monies/gold/gems/jewels/investments/real estate/cars/ boats/toys or other desires/wants/needs in exchange for your soul. Note that it is consumerism, materialism and nothing spiritual knowledge in return. There is always a price. If it sounds too good to be true that is because it is.

Often times he asks for you to sign an agreement or contract thinking you are legally binded to evil forever. God and Jesus can break these contracts. He thrives on desperation, despair and disappointment. This fuels his ego. Lucifer loves to control people with addictions. If you take a picture of a chronic lonely junkie addict when he/she is at their lowest moment in life near death, often times evil will appear in the picture smiling. Lucifer trembles at the mention of God, Jesus and Mary's names. The devil knows them all by name. Also he enjoys when you do not touch or read the Bible often. Evil will make you late for an important meeting or appointment, cause drama, ruin relationships and cause infidelity/adultery with lies and deception in couples breaking the family unit and children. Lucifer taunts and wants people to die by his own hand or by his other leagues.

Life is difficult. You have to work, have high morals, a job, be part of a community and family, have sense of work integrity, dignity, and honesty, be good, be kind, care for others, have sympathy, empathy, and be selfless. Give your love to others every one and serve others. Volunteer, give to charities, plan for the futures, retirement, get an education and have your children educated. Be a pillar of society, respected, honorable. Now not everyone is perfect but God and Jesus. We fall hard. We are afraid, have doubt, lack confidence, motivation etc. Fear drives us. We begin to doubt our thoughts and become negative. Constantly feel guilt and shame for no reason.

Thinking that our mistakes or past will haunt us forever. Forgive yourself, love yourself, and love your enemies. Do not wish badly on anyone. We plot for nothing, worry all the time. Our fear of failure and have insecurities of not being good or smart enough. Not being successful and falling by the wayside. Forgetting our strengths and only seeing weakness and meekness. We struggle, are contrary, fight, are bickering and arguing constantly like kids. Fighting leads to dislike and apathy eventually.

Prayer to Virgin Mary: Mother Mary please protect me immediately. I need your help right away. Now please this is urgent. I'm scared what can I do? Could you please comfort and protect me and ward off all evil? Mary can manifest herself – present weapons of destruction (Bullets, guns, knives etc. Stop wars). Of course she has assistance from the Arch Angels (12) of them. Leagues, dominions, principalities, seraphim's, cherubim's. She is our advocate, redeematrix and Queen mother. She represents Government, Nationalities, conflict, war, families – unit all a whole, children, babies (unborn), politics, against all evil forces. At the crucifixion John was to take Mary as his mother for the world's suffering.

Father Joseph (Step father to Jesus) – He married Mary and had eight other children besides Jesus. He worked very hard as a professional carpenter to provide for his family. Joseph taught Jesus as a little boy he would sit with Joseph on a bench and watch everything with his pet puppy. A fast learner Jesus was soon apprentice and professional like his step father. Now many do not know that Joseph is the Patron Saint of Workers and Builders. Also, there is a huge beautiful place and building commemorated and dedicated to Joseph's name in Montreal (Quebec) Canada in Cote-des-Neiges called l'Oratoire St. Joseph where you can get true blessed holy water. It has a huge church atrium and dome with many massive steps where people pray on each step for their sins or requests to God.

Joseph believed the angel when she told him fear not that God and Mary's is a spiritual union. The Immaculate Conception. He could have left Mary pregnant yet he loved her very much. Joseph travelled for a census with her and of course was there for the birth of the holy Jesus. The love Joseph had for Mary and Jesus is undeniable. All we know from the Bible is that Joseph died probably when Jesus was a young adult. He took over from his father to provide for the family and that is why his great miracles, parables and speeches only started from his age of thirty to thirty three approximately. Say one Hail Mary and repeat three times per day "St. Joseph pray for us" and you will be taken care of.

How was Jesus when he was young? He was able to produce tall grass and grain to hide in an instant. Jesus would play with mud, shape them into birds and they became real doves or sparrows. He learned carpentry from his Step Father Joseph. Provided food, home, shelter for a family of five (5) brothers and (3) sisters. Joseph died when Jesus was very young. His brother James the lesser is one of the Apostles. The rest of his brothers were jealous and did not believe Jesus was the son of God. He was a great communicator, scholar of laws, Judaism, Torah, etc. Jesus is the Messiah. Jesus played with Mary Magdalene and Lazarus when he was a young child. Jesus watched and learned as a child how to become a great carpenter. He absorbed everything and was a natural with languages, communication, parables, meaning of life. Calm serene and wise before his years. Patient. He could put people in their place by shame, humility, respect and more learning.

I have written a list of characteristics of the twelve (12) apostles. All the apostles were Jewish. Luke a prophet and disciple was a gentile and converted to Judaism. Phillip and Mark were also prophets and disciples.

John – is a fisherman born in Bethsaida. He stood at the cross with Mary weeping taking all they had worked for was done. His love so enduring from heaven came sweeping when Jesus whispered the words, "Woman, behold thy son". John grew gentle to all men a brother. He prays little children to love one another. John was the greatest disciple of all. With years of sailing through rough waters he made a strong follower. One on whom Christ could count on and call. His depth of faith and good understanding helped when he wrote of Christ and the times they shared. Outdoor life was so demanding; ritual and spiritual words were told on how much God cared.

James the Elder (The Greater) - He was a martyr for Christ and his words fill no pages. His silence speaks out down through the ages. James as the silent disciple who walked close to the Savior with Peter and John. Though he never spoke out, others who talked found him a disciple to depend on. He was lean and tanned, strong, straight. The son of Zebedee whose mother became a disciple too. James the Elder slept on through the prayer of Gethsemane. Was rudely rejected for being a Jew. Christ called James and John "The Sons of Thunder" because of their tempers. He rebuked them when they sought to be first. It was James who saw Christ's deed of wonder and heard him plead on the cross, "I thirst". All Jesus was given was bile and vinegar for his thirst.

James, the Lesser (Younger) – He was the biological brother of Jesus. Although little is known of him, Christ saw in him favor and righteousness. One of the mysteries yet to be solved. We know his mother was deeply involved. She was Mary who came to the tomb because they had spices and wanted to anoint Jesus. It was Christ who chose to appoint him one of the twelve Apostles and gave him work to do. "Provide no script for your journey, no shoes. Heal the sick, cleanse the leper. He said go into whatsoever town you choose. Cast out devils and freely give raise the dead".

Peter – He was blessed with great physical strength. Strong hands and big stature to haul all the nets from the sea. At the Lord's command, he left his wife and children and became a fisher of men for eternity. Still he said the wrong things at times. He did the wrong things and often came up short when put to the test. Christ saw much more than his strength. He saw how strong Peter's faith which brings in the potter's hands, the mark of the best. How human were his faults and he knew that God of all grace will strengthen you in your weakness. Peter, that impetuous fisherman is the favorite of many people because his life was real and a constant struggle to win the adversaries. His name was changed from Simon to Peter (Petra the rock) upon which he would build great churches in the name of Jesus. Jesus being our cornerstone. He was crucified upside down.

Paul was a strong ruler of Jewish faith, doctrine, books, and laws. He ousted many gentiles and had taken part in their torture. He had a rude awaking on the road to Damascus, lost his voice completely for three days and fell to the ground and could not look up at the bright glowing light. He was a very hard working, relentless believer who travelled all over the world to spread the God news and open Churches. He made many friends, disciples and a following. Paul had an arduous life being ship wrecked, imprisoned, flogged, lost at sea, tortured, poor, hardly any clothing or anything to eat at times. He prayed daily and fought the good fight (life). Paul endured hardship with great faith.

Matthew – He was a business man and saved cash and done the accounting. The least likely candidate one could choose to be a disciple, or apostle. Matthew had bad opinions surmounting, Jesus said to Matthew, the sinner, Come. He arose without any thought or questions. It was a sign that no one was excluded from this new order that Christ's new coming had brought. Matthew was a publican. He left us the gospel that bears his good name. Jesus had eaten with Matthew's disreputable friends while the Pharisees exclaimed in disgust. He said "I come to call men from their sins. God is faithful, forgiving and he is just.

Thaddeus (Judas, not Iscariot) – He was fine and true. The name means

"Dear one" or "from the heart". Those who walked daily so near to him knew he was humble and loving right from the start. Judas not Iscariot, thus John wrote, being careful to show which one he meant. So much is told of Judas you will note. But of the other only one event. At the Last Supper Christ's teaching was heart. To Judas who questioned, came words of praise. If a man loves me, he will keep my word. I and my Father will love him always. A name can mean much or nothing at all. It is how lives are lived that others recall.

Judas Iscariot – Now Judas was headed for destruction. Bound and determined to have his own way. One of the twelve who had heard Christ's instruction. Money was the trap that led him astray. True, he was the tool authorities used. The promise of money was all he asked. He stood before Christ. It was time to choose. One of the twelve chose that devilish task. That one of the twelve could have betrayed Christ the Lord has been recorded in God's Holy Word. Repenting, he tried his best to appeal. Stating: I betrayed an innocent man. He took his own life. They bought potter's field. Ancient prophets had told of the plan. He hung himself from a tree and the plot is barren to this present day.

Simon: He was political with one goal to free Judea from the Roman rule at the time. Jesus chose Simon for a different role. Simon loved and honored Jesus. He was a Zealot, was a servant of God with great enthusiasm that could inspire others. He walked daily the paths Christ strolled and was zealous to set the world on fire. A patriot yes with a different plan. He gave his all for the cause of God and man. From the Mount of Olives to Jerusalem was only one Sabbath day away. Here Simon came to an upper room and with others began to fast and pray.

Thomas – was the twin so the legend is told. Thomas was one who doubted that Christ lives again (The Resurrection). I would see for myself he said so boldly. I would see the nail prints that caused him pain. Christ, knowing his heart, appeared once more and came to the place where the apostles had strolled. They had hidden away behind a closed door. He heard Thomas say. "My Lord and my God". Christ said, be not faithless, but believing. Christ said Thomas who doubted now believed instead. Later they fished in the Tiberius Sea. All night with not catch at all. When the morning arose Christ called to them. Children have you meat? Cast your nets to the right? Then their nets overflowed with abundance of fish.

Andrew: - The first of twelve, it was Andrew who came to see the Messiah and eager to learn to walk the straight road in the Savior's name. Convinced by the prophet John his concern was for another, for Simon his brother. They grew up together near Galilee. He had heard of the Promised One from their mother. For them the promise was reality. Later it was Andrew who found a young lad with loaves and fishes, and the hungry were fed. Always very helpful and giving he made others glad. Christ said, I will make you fishers of men". Andrew was first, a man set apart. A true disciple will have love in his heart.

Phillip: (A prophet and disciple) – Jesus found Philip a practical man. He called out to him saying, Come, follow me. At once Philip followed without a plan. Walking beside him and happy to be. Next he shared Christ with a friend of old Nathaniel-Bartholomew by name. Come and see him of whom the prophets told. Nathaniel-Bartholomew came and followed. Still seeing that things were practically done, Philip came along to the Upper Room. He knew not that Christ and the Father were one till the day Christ arose from the tomb. Then this practical man found the faith to employ. He preached to them Christ and brought the world great joy. Mark, Luke and Phillip are all prophets.

Never lose your will or the most blessed instrument played the mind. The mind keeps time, pulses, struggles. Every flowing words, thoughts, phrases or stories and knowledge bursting to be remembered, renewed and cherished. The mind dull with no growth is like fungi, waiting to be mastered, and rekindled. A mind is a terrible thing to waste. All our memories, growth and every growth spurt, words, languages and cues. A confused mind gives perplexing thoughts. All information stored in our mind would make microchips and Intel envious. The vastness, storage of tender moments. Our lives and defense.

Your mind can be bitter or creative you choose your thoughts. Your thoughts become a whole new you. The mind is a sponge, feed it, fuel it, and nourish it with care. There will never be a complete mind at rest for even at sleep and slumber it is still active with dreams. You can experience out-of-body experiences, travelling, people, faces, emotions and déjà vu. Learn experience, read and enjoy life. The mind is music to the soul and creativity's friend. There is end in friend, be in believe and if in life. I cannot help the person I am yet can change to what I want to become. All is possible. Faith believes without seeing. Believing is done with your whole heart. Truth is great yet we run away and close our ears to directness and honesty. Hope is everything on our last limb and breath. What you wish for will come true. The broken heart mends. It bends, it breaks, and it cracks and pulls. It hurts. A heart loves and nothing is without purpose. Our path(s) and our future, our meaning and purpose is not planned by us but given as a gift from above. You can only control your destiny so much.

Courage is having no fear at a given moment. To think to save another. Courage is selfless, assists and is reactive. Words do hurt and are a weapon. Do not talk about money all the time. Speak about your dreams or aspirations. If you do not have any more dreams you can make other new ones come true. Say you are wrong when you are wrong. Take the blame and do not be a coward. Apologize, be brave, and be courageous, a giver. Say I love you more often.

Give to charity. Kiss like there is no tomorrow. Be kind, try if you cannot bite your tongue. Sometimes people do need a good tongue lashing. Do something nice for someone else besides yourself and do not charge money.

The Holy Spirit: Helps define parables and the Bible. To think more clearly. Releases confusion. Settles us down to concentrate, read, learn and ask more questions. Wants you to be joyful and happy. Helps with forgiveness, and mending your heart. Works on our traits and faults to better ourselves and our conscience. It only takes one day to change so take a chance. A gift bestowed from God and Jesus. Guides you, teaches, inspires. Gives you a sense of peace, love, calmness and warmth surrounds your body. Makes your heart feel warm inside. The Holy Spirit is forever present in Churches.

The Holy Spirit/ghost is always present. You want to be more generous and help others any way you can. Help with Church fellowship and acceptance. The Holy Spirit comes in praying and intercessory praying for others. Is present during Baptism. Aids you to be humble and modest. Helps with beatitudes which are the good fruits to become more like the character of God and Jesus. Wants you be more like the image of God. Molds, shapes and kneads you like clay and goes far beyond our faults. The Holy Spirit encourages us to do good and spread the word and good news. The Holy Spirit is part of the holy Trinity. Be of service to others. Be more loving and kind. Love thy neighbors as God loves you. Wants you to see you smile often and to become a better person. Repeat what you ask for and never give up on the outcome or intention. Gives us new found peace. Be charitable and a cheerful giver. Help the lowly, needy, sick, lonely, orphans, widows and elders. Dwell on the present not the past. Does not criticize, does not dictate and is not authoritative. It is up to you to make changes. The Holy Spirit is always there to help along the way of your journey. Stay on the straight and narrow path; the hard route not the easy one.

I would like to speak to you about a special anointing from the Holy Spirit, Jesus and God. What is it like to be anointed? Anointing could be done on the crown of your head or an touch/imprint in the palm or your hand which produces anointing healing oil. Or intercessory anointing of a group of clergy praying to help and heal the sick. How come there are only a select few who receive these tremendous special gifts in the world? The gifts of healing, prophecy, speaking and interpretation of tongues, knowledge and wisdom, spreading the Good news/Word of God, performing miracles, rebuking/binding/casting out demons/Satan/Lucifer/Demons/Evil. You have to have so much desire and hunger inside, beg, plead, demand, ask for God's special grace. How would it feel to receive the genuine whole Holy Spirit? Would it be like a burning, on fire, to be touched, to be truly blessed? Some people scream, yell, wail, moan, roll, shake, tremble, fall to the ground, are silent, loud, roar like a lion or meek as a lamb in true peace and silence resting on the ground on their backs looking at the celestial sky. Some speak in tongues the language only God/Jesus and spirit understands. You are not to speak in tongues for fun or try to impress your friends with the spiritual language. Also not to boast nor brag about your gifts least they be taken away as fast as you receive them.

Some people are in this heavenly spiritual awakening for hours/days/weeks or months. It is extremely exhausting and makes one very weak in a good way. The blessed ones feel completely alive, at ease/peace, purified, loving, engaging, compassionate, sympathetic, empathetic, joyful, experience true divinity like they can take on the world. There are thousands of ministers, priests, nuns, saints, monks, martyrs, writers, deacons, cardinals, bishops, missionary workers who have received the extremely rare special gifts from

God/Jesus/Holy Spirit above. They can touch you to become part of the special love force and do the work like the Apostles did: healing/anointing/casting out demons, prophesy, speak in tongues, miracles, touching others, intercessory group prayers, single prayers and then touching a person to impart a gift(s). Let Jesus mold you like clay and be his instrument. Let him use us all for the whole good of the world.

An example of healing (intercessory) anointing by clergy was done to my friend Cheryl Gallant. She was anointed by about six (6) clergy at the Nazarene Church. They surrounded close to her and laid both their hands on her head, shoulders and back while she prayed. Cheryl has been ill from birth and has Spina Bifida (curvature of the spine). She is in a wheel chair yet was on crutches until twenty years old. Cheryl has had one hundred and fifteen major surgeries under anesthetic. Also she is presently living with the longest shunt (from Dr. Shunt created for his daughter to drain spinal fluid). Finally she has flat lined at least five (5) times.

That means declared dead her heart completely stopped clinically. It all simply means she holds three (3) world records and should be placed in the Guinness Book of world records. Her character: Definitely not shy and quite talkative, caring, compassionate, sympathetic, empathetic and loving. What else? Hmm she had had cancer in her bowels, and her stomach was cut open and took an entire year to heal, blood in her urine, unresolved kidney problems. She has a stoma and is on heavy pain killer medication presently. Cheryl has a hole in her pallet and cannot eat certain foods. She had septicemia (blood poisoning) at the age of five years old and lived in the hospital alone without her parents. She was returned home at five (5) years old and small and skinny as a rake at seventeen (17) pounds. This is when she learned to know her brothers and sister.

Hospital bills added to an excess of 100,000 by the time she reached five years old. Both sets of grandparents spent all their monetary and life savings funds to help save her. Leonard her father had to put a second mortgage their home many times. Her mother Jean was a registered nurse who worked in surgeries and eventually ran the nursing department. Cheryl witnessed much abuse and death of other children in wards who were murdered before her eyes. She was struck by lightning sitting in a car. Cheryl was tormented, pursued by the devil/evil and I decided (with of course Jesus', God and the Holy Spirit's assistance/help) to rebuke and cast out the demon to leave her body to leave her alone. I used a special holy water which was lost the next day. I never done this in my life and asked the Lord for courage, bravery with an unbending faith, belief and intent. Praying for hope and a miracle.

Cheryl had a child at twenty (20) years old and the welfare system wanted to take her child away until her parents intervened. Her daughter is a chef in a hotel. Cheryl lost four babies, the boy twin David, Garth, Chelsea, and finally Kendall. She told me just because you do not have the use of your legs and can no longer walk does not mean you cannot love. Man, that was a lesson in humility in itself. At twenty years old her fiancé who has a grave mental illness put her in a wheel chair before she used crutches. In a fit of rage he blamed Cheryl for the death of their son (one of the twins) David who died at birth. She is courageous, intelligent (CPA Accountant), has a quick wit, sensitive and adores all children. People tend to look down upon her disability and think she is deaf, dumb or mentally challenged. I get a kick at watching people's reactions. They just stare blatantly at her feet (which are swollen) and are continuously rude and see only the wheel chair not her. What I see is the whole person and not fear or ignorance of her chair any longer.

Cheryl saved a little girl from sexual abuse who was kidnapped. Also she took care of nine children babysitting during a fire and saved everyone. She even jumped from the balcony with a baby cradled in her arms and landed safely into the snow bank. It took twelve long years for Cheryl to receive a new proper wheel chair that worked. Her case worker gave her the worst terrible runaround possible, was rude, lazy and always lied. I had to get the Mayor of Summerside (PEI) Canada at the time to intervene on her behalf. Purchase orders delayed for months or never sent for parts, battery and always breaking down on the old used wheel chair. This wheel chair is her mobility, her legs. I never had to deal directly with her case worker because if I did would have jumped over the counter for an attack to defend my friend lol. I was the one who wrote all the numerous emails and contacted the Mayor. Also called the pharmacies responsible for the repairs and followed-up for my friend. Without her wheel chair she is completely immobile and house bound. It took an extremely excruciating exasperating twelve years (12) for Cheryl to finally receive her brand new wheelchair.

She was on wish lists from the Shriners Hospital/and Children's Wish Foundation with a near death experience and met Freddie Mercury at a live concert in person. He was her favorite singer at the time from the group called Queen. Cheryl is now fifty-six (56) years old. She is the longest survivor and on the committee which gives advice to parents who have new born children with Spina Bifida. What is rare is Cheryl is born with two lungs and others are born with only one lung. The cause of this disability is simply a lack of two different vitamins between both parents. Lacking vitamin C in the Father and vitamin E in the mother. Also the lack of Iron in one or the other or both parents.

She has about eighty (80) active severe allergies some are: all latex, bananas, mushrooms, whole wheat bread, coffee, bees, hornets and wasps etc... Cheryl

Gallant gets up early is very active and ultra sensitive. She loves a good religious movie that touches her spirit and soul. Her new addiction is Diamond Point (3 dimensional glitter images done with a special pen). Also quite creative by drawing geometric shapes in pencil like a pro. I would say she is an extreme extrovert. She is now engaged to be married and is very much in love. She enjoys adult coloring books. Cheryl can quite protective off her loved ones and is a real soldier defender for many causes and justice. One of her favorite past time is babysitting other people's children. Her second home is Tim Horton's coffee shop. I could not be any more proud or happier for her. She is an example and the Glory of God. I can go on and on about this topic. If my friend is not a living miracle I do not know who is. Thanks to our Lord and Saviour. Blessed be.

The gifts God and Jesus and the Holy Spirit bestowed unto me are: Generosity, understanding, giving, sharing, love of animals, sympathy, empathy, ultra sensitivity, trusting, the word of God and hearing their audible voices, eloquent speaker, communicator, spreading the word (Good News) writing, knowledge, some wisdom (could always use more), mercy, faith, belief, hope, charity, intent, praising, worshipping, research, praying, intercessory prayer, compassion, Creativity: art (drawing & painting), making jewelry, some singing, performing different voices.

I'm lacking in the following gifts: remove all the drama, being less angry and bitter and temperamental, show more gratitude & thankfulness, less complaining & judging, withhold grudges (revenge/vengeance), more sense of community, more presence in Church with church family, to be less rude and arrogant, forgiveness of others, patience, humbleness, modesty, less pride, less Ego, to be less selfish, togetherness, more grace, prophecy, healing hands, receiving and giving others anointing for healing & a gift, manifestations, deliverance, miracles, binding, rebuking and removing the Devil or demons (from people who are possessed, captured, influenced), even though I'm not a minister nor nun I can/could learn to perform exorcisms, (casting out pure evil), work on envy & jealousy, work on removing depression & despair, work on removing lethargy/sloth (stagnation with no motivation), missionary work, and building more churches. By the Grace of God I do ask for more gifts according to his will not mine. My desire is for the gift of impartation from others who already have the gift and are freely giving their gift to others by the laying of hands – anointing to heal others.

I'm not high maintenance yet I try to be always clean and neat. My itchy, sensitive skin attracts insects from summer humid sweat. So fear of malaria is ever present. While visiting three different Latin American countries I drank water and food which made me ill for six months and was on heavy medication. I'm not afraid of garbage, dirt, filth, squalor, and living without luxury. It is not comfortable living without an internet connection because I write and do research. So some people call me difficult.

In Cuba I had gastro problems and this old lady who was missing a few fingers and looked like a live witch gave me a shot of I think vodka, pepper and other ingredients and cured my stomach problems right away. I thought at the time if I do not drink this she will harm me. It was a scary experience.

Fallen Angels: When fallen angels procreated with the humans the Neptilim race happened. Giants. with huge heads and bodies which were mostly destroyed by scientists at the beginning of the 19th century because they were scared and did not want the world public to panic. God forbade fallen angels to have relations with people on earth so this was the outcome and result.

When one door closes many others will open. It is easy to be discouraged and impatient. We want everything here and now. An automatic easily gratified society we live in. Demanding here right now. That is not how the heavenly realm works. Not instant gratification. This will lead to despair and misery when we do not get what is requested soon enough. Expectations cause anxiety. Everything is a test of patience and waiting. Pray every day without ceasing. Think of God and Jesus everyday even in your routines. In the simple things and chores. Serve one God for he counts our tears and holds them in a vile. God is on his time not yours. God is working on it and is not finished. God is making you wait for something even better. Intuition is the spirit talking to us.

Listen for God's audible voice or whisper. Listen for the hum and music from angels. Just listen and wait. Do your ears ring? How can we hear if we are always talking? It is important when speaking to someone to have direct eye contact. Look at the person and do not cower down. People that do not want others to make eye contact or look at them have serious problems. There is a difference between a look, glance, glare, stare and stalking someone. You are not above me or others only God is and so is the sky. Do not crush someone else's day or glory. There is no class system in heaven. You are not better than I, nor worse. Your sins are not better than hers. Stop comparing, there is only one you. God created everyone different why would you want to remain the same? God gives many gifts and talents to people. Use them wisely to teach, counsel, help.

There are lies of omission; well you did not ask me. God and Jesus want our lives to be of servitude. Serving others not being served by others. Truly humble yourselves. Do not do anything for show or boasting, watch me now, look how much I give of my time, money, energy. I am a good person see. No, just give freely without an agenda. Let Jesus and God be your judge. Why should we judge others? Jesus said that it my job not yours. Your sins will be accounted for. If you judge others everything will be revealed on judgement day. What makes you think your sins are better than others? They are not.

God and Jesus have forgiven murderers, killers, evil doers, Satanists for they have truly repented with remorse and believe Jesus is the son of God. Ask for salvation and deliverance from your sins. Ask for forgiveness. They rely on the grace and forgiveness from God. They are scared, afraid and with doubt in their previous hateful lives where there was no way out for humans, soul and spirit. You are freed of temptations of lies of deceit. Do good instead of bad. Good always prevails. We actually think we are better than others. I look down at times. Their mannerisms, ignorance, way of dress, vulgarity, rudeness and class systems, education, clothing and outside appearance. Do you look at the deep felt heart like Jesus and God do? Do you see the spirit auras and chakra energy fields? Are you on the same wave length or dimension? You have eyes to see? Do you really read expressions?

You have ears to hear and listen. Do you brush others away and think you are more important? Do you scream, yell in anger and distress because you fear self doubt and are insecure and lack confidence and love? Do you touch and feel the person's constant fight with depression, suicide, manic, ADDHD, hypomania or other mental mind illnesses?

There are one hundred and fifty million at least (150,000,000) people or more in India who are among the caste system called the untouchables. They do the vilest low work that no one else wants to do. Their parents and perhaps ancestors have a contract unpaid with interest which carries to the next generation and the relative/person inherits the debt with taxes. It seems the interest and payments are never fulfilled for their entire freedom and interest continues to the next new generation. This does not seem fair at all. They work hard all their lives paying interest forever on a debt which is unending.

Jesus cried, and sweat blood spilled over his cheeks in the Garden of Gethsemane. He was apprehensive and anxious for he knew his fate and future.

To take on the worlds sins. Thy will be done – God's will not his. Jesus prayed to be freed of such an agonizing fate. Must he take on all mankind's sins to save them to atone for men's sins and mistakes? Was the burden placed on his shoulders only? He was the pure sacrifice. The lamb, meek, loving and kind. A lamb will not fight when lead to slaughter. His expression is meek as a lamb, cuddly. He had inner strength and was a deep thinker and pondered. The wind, air, electricity, God and Jesus are all invincible. Blessed are those who believe without ever seeing. My soul I long to keep. Internal spirit do not weep for I will change my ways. Patience give me some time. I make the same mistakes daily over again. Pleading why do I fall again when I know right from wrong? Do not want to fall in an abyss of darkness and brimstone. Never willing to hear the millions of awful moans, groans, screams and torment. The other side is so easy and right justified and free. God and Jesus let me fly and sail with wings like a bird flight free flowing. I lift my wings in unison with the wind, the speed of light that is my plight. All I ask is for a warm house like pioneer days. A wood stove and fresh well water.

Nora Gravel created daily Prayer (written poem): God with us Jesus in us. Above, below, throughout our soul. He protects is just and we love him because he is mild and meek. Strong like the wind. Humble and modest. Neither boasting nor blame. Light brighter than the sun. A candle flickering. He puts our sins to shame. No guilt ridden or strife. No more crying or war. God and Jesus give you wide wings to thrust and soar high above as if a dove. Finding you were lost then found. In God's love we are secure. In Jesus we trust. I am their star.

Second poem (Written by author Nora Gravel): Lord above us always. More than the crimson sunsets and your parents you hold dear. Above your soul mate who brought you so near to God. Your family and annoying siblings. More than the kaleidoscope rainbow of seven colors and all the world's many wonders. It is time to discover a better truth. Jesus above all else. Closer to the shores of the glistening strait. Warm waters and red clay soil supple ripples under my feet. Not just Innu shucks built by the Inuit with rocks so high to state we were here; look like they were placed and balancing forever as statues eventually some disappear. More than opal caves of precious stones of turquoise, jade, soap stone and pink crystal.

More than the seals, orcas, polar bears, narwhals and my favorite puffin birds. Better than Vikings and their runes, legends and fables of yore. The Celts and Druids with crosses of gold. The solid rock of Newfoundland and fields of PEI. The many quaint towns of Nova Scotia and New Brunswick. Lovely as the colors of houses on the Isle of St. Pierre de Miquelon. PEI's fields of mustard, purples chief potatoes and green hills and valleys. Sky bluer than blue can ever be imagined and cotton candy pink clouds. The lobster boats and dories sit mighty flowing lightly in Cape-Egmont cove. Sheer laughter, joy and all your memories wrapped up in one thought. Jesus above us all. Piper plovers, starlings, finches, chickadees, blue jays and wild barn cats. My precious dog friend Hallie who is more human than most. A friendly multi colored calico with light green eyes.

Greater than golden Junipers, Spruce and the mighty Elm trees. The cosmos, marigolds, tulips, oriental and blue Icelandic poppies so fair. Country flowers with herbs everywhere. Higher than cliffs and refreshing clean crisp salt air. Seagulls, swallows and piper plovers, beware of their nests in the sand. No tramping around the Piper Plover bird's nests around National Parks and beaches. The rich rocks so vivid and smooth. All the lonely light houses no longer run and held by keepers. Old farmhouses with walls that can speak. The kindred young wind bashful and strong. August apples and raspberries and plump juicy strawberries, Cortland and Honey Crisp apples in U-pick patch. Seafood and homemade cheeses. Do not forget the goat soap in Brackly Beach.

The eleven (11) pet goats which live five minutes from my home. So cute. One is dressed in a dress with a pearl necklace and visits hospitals to cheer up patients. Friends who are near to those overseas whom think of you and smile about your younger years. Greater than the babe you hold close to your chest and the triplets on the way. The majestic mountains of Innsbruck, Laurentians, Eastern Townships, Bavaria and French medieval towns, Tuscan country side and the Baltic Sea. More than the best Italian meal you ever have eaten sublime.

The gentle cassis wine, sumptuous desserts refined. Huge brilliant sun and its beauty and glory of the glowing full moon and astral stars. The many galaxies still unseen. Seeing the most glorious spectacular unforgettable days of sunshine. The brightness vitality and light. Feeling of the cool night's breezes after swimming all day long. Your life, vigor, bliss and joy. Smiling at the entire world of art at dusk. God above all of us. Forever and ever, eternally. Amen

God my father, Jesus Christ the son of the living God. God my creator, master, king and friend. Jesus the redeemer and saviour till the end and hereafter. Forever and ever promised. Our salvation we are saved from blemished sins that remain constricted in our hearts. Yes, guilt that tears us apart. Jesus saved us, yes. The least we can do is save ourselves and walk towards him. Believe and accept Jesus and he set us free from total misery. Jesus not only died and atoned for all our sins; it is the way he died. Alone and praying. Mary, Mary Magdalene, Elizabeth and John bending by his cross in total disbelief.

The soldiers mock of bile and vinegar. Stabbing his side and out rushed blood, water and wine. His one hundred and fourteen (114) scourging (floggings). The Body of Christ, the Blood of Christ. We are all washed away our sins through baptism. Believe, repent, have faith and hope. God and Jesus want to know you more and have a true relationship with them. They know all the hairs on your head. Know all your worries and cares. Erase doubt and all of your fears and it will make you hopeful. Keep the faith, keep on. Jesus, God and the Holy Spirit will make you whole once again. Be still and know I am God. You knocked, you searched and you will find. We are quick to blame them for our inequities.

Why? Woe is me. Why me and what did I do to deserve this treatment? Why not? For the glory and power in God. Someone put a curse on me. Am I hexed? All bad luck and a dark cloud is following me. Cloud and doom. Guess I cannot be lucky. I need a break now. Give me another chance will you? Others get what they want without ever trying. They live a better life and are happier and seem ecstatic. What happens behind closed doors? What happens here stays here. Too afraid to disagree and stare in silence. When you finish blaming others for your problems, complaining then you begin to live not just exist. I listened to many people whom are really downcast and quick to blame others. God and Jesus even for everything that goes wrong in their lives.

I asked God and Jesus to tell me something I do not know. Well they totally baffled and surprised me. So, I am told that I have five (5) additional brothers and sister for a total of ten (10) children in our family instead of five children/siblings whom are presently alive. My mother had triplets, fraternal twins, identical twins and finally another set of identical twins one after another. My older brother was one of the triplets and two died at birth. My older sister had a fraternal twin brother who died at birth. I had an identical twin sister who died of spinia bifida at birth. My younger brother had an identical twin brother who also died at birth.

Their names are in order as follows: Aaron, Zachary, Isaiah, Nathalie and Jean-Mathieu. Well I am so happy to be a twin and knowing having an extended family in heaven. The only problem is my immediate family would never believe it. Why did my parents keep this huge dark secret(s) for so long? Apparently they were so sad and found this a private matter between themselves. It would have been nice to have known sooner. I forgot to ask God if the triplets were identical. Apparently that is really rare.

I'm taking this opportunity to tell the first true story about my younger brother Jean-Marc who is also known to his friends as J.M., Jimmy, and Jammy. I call him Mark. I know you will believe in angels after you read this true story. My brother was with three (3) friends driving in a medium sized car on a highway in Quebec. What happened is they were riding on one spare tire. Of course you cannot go as fast on a spare. Well you know Quebec drivers are not that patient and drive at fast speed, quickly and are reactionary. An eighteen (18) wheeler truck rear ended them at full speed.

What happened after was somewhat disastrous. One person ended with a broken hip another had lacerations. The driver was lucky he received not a scratch. My brother Jean-Marc was the unlucky one. Well, in his words he told me his nylon jacket caught on fire and he was trying to shield his face and got his arms and one ear burned third degree. There was not much time to get out of the car. He was the first to awaken; the others were in a daze. Apparently some good Samaritans stopped and said they had experience in first aid. My brother panicked and rolled down his window to get out. From here he was in full shock and walked a few steps and fell on the ground. The two men immediately came to his rescue. Now he did not know it at the time but he broke his neck (2) vertebrae's that control the arms and shoulder movements. These were completely crushed. Jean-Marc was transferred to another hospital from the highway in Quebec to the south shore hospital called Charles Lemoyne in Greenfield Park, Quebec. His injuries were too intensive. A neck specialist was required immediately to examine him.

When I received a call at work from one of my sister's I continued working on my computer. I do not even remember who called me. It is really shocking news and I was in total shock. My boss had to force me to go to the hospital. Was not looking forward to this. What was I expecting to see?

Was he ok? How bad could it be? When they finally wheeled him in he spoke to me saying I don't feel too bad Nora. Then he said do I look ok and I lied. Guess the pain killers were working. His entire head was wrapped in gauze like a mummy. I did not even recognize my own brother only his voice. We were all pretending to put on brave faces. Next he was examined with pins in his legs and arms to see if he had any feeling. The doctors were so surprised. Said you are really lucky you can feel that? JM screamed and said yes, that really hurts. Suddenly he lost the feelings of his arms, hands and shoulders immediately. Just like that. They rushed him into surgery. The surgeon at the time was only thirty (32) years old and an expert in neck injuries. He was trying a new way of operating by going in the front of the neck instead of the back.

Well, my brother could not move at all because he was in traction. That is where they literally drill screws in your forehead with supporting thick wire to stabilize the neck with a kind of silver band. His hair grew really long because he was in the hospital for many months. I remember spraying dry shampoo and we took turns brushing his teeth and using the suction to get out phlegm because he would have chocked. He listened attentively to his doctor and aides. He was really afraid of being disabled in a wheel chair. Told me straight out I do not think can handle not being active. Well the first operation was a success. They shaved his pelvic bone into two disks/vertebrae's (4th and 5th). Jean-Marc is really a handsome man to others. I never took this view for he is my brother. He was really proud as a peacock. So he asked me look Nora my teeth are hanging by a thread and they were. His perfect straight teeth were almost all lost. For months they shifted and he ended up with slightly crooked teeth. Who cares I said to him at least you have your teeth strong back into your gums. Let's not be so vain. He laughed and what a smile he has.

Also a burn specialist was flown in from Switzerland took really good care of the burns on his ear, face and arms. He had to wear what looked like stretched thick nylon compression bands for 23 hours a day. They scraped the burns putting on treatments. Burnt skin smells foul. They scraped off his skin because it curled up. His ear looked like dumbo the elephant so huge. It was literally five to six (5-6) inches all swollen and I thought well he is going to lose his ear for sure. His arms were really burnt badly too. So he had so many friends visiting I lost count. Some of them could not take it seeing him so weak like this. My poor brother was dating a girl and didn't she break up with him at his weakest moment. He asked me should I send flowers to her? I was like what?

You are thinking of someone else when you are suffering yourself. Too much. She never visited him and broke his heart at the time. I thought that was so shallow. Maybe she was just young and scared. One of his friends did not even want to enter his room to see him she was petrified and started shaking. I can't see him no way. He thought this was comical and said come on in. She refused. About a few months later they let Jean-Marc out of the hospital to go home for Thanksgiving supper. Now, it was the only Thanksgiving that I missed. Maybe it was better. I would have screamed for my brother that day and would have caused more drama and making him nervous. He pulled in his chair to enjoy a huge meal for once and then, snap his neck cracked and broke a second time. Well this was on a Friday night and he had to wait in agony until Monday because they could not reach his doctor on the weekend. He was in so much pain. They rushed him into a second surgery once again. We were all praying all the time. Silent and intercessory prayers, pleading begging bargaining with God to save him. Tears were running down everyone's faces in our immediate family. His doctor managed to put in a four to six inch (4-6) steel plate into his neck for support. We all joked that he would be stopped at all the airports; the device they use will always ring.

Now if you do not believe in miracles I hope you do now. Jean-Marc went into extensive physiotherapy to walk again. Shame on me I never thought he would walk properly again. We were all doubtful. He proved us wrong once again. The fact he is not disabled nor in a wheel chair and can walk and run with no problems is a true blessing. These are a few miracles that happened before our eyes. Now the weight lost was incredible. He was skinny for many years after that. I think he lost forty (40) to fifty (50) pounds. There were so many traumas and he began to be paranoid of the neighbors thinking they were watching what he was doing all day. He slept until 2:00 p.m. for years and did not want to work. Finally, he got the courage to go out and face the world again. I think about fifteen years later he saw his Doctor who operated on him twice on a date and he did not recognize my brother. That must be the greatest feeling being a surgeon. He gained weight back, was really healthy. Well, my brother visited other patients who had neck injuries and could not take it any longer. One of the girls was only twenty-four (24) yrs old and she was driving a Ferrero convertible car a two (2) seater and got hit by a bread truck. She was paralyzed from neck down and her spinal cord was severed. There was no chance of an operation or recuperation for her. I think that is when he realized just how fortunate he was thanks to God, Jesus and the team group of angels.

He told me when he went to thank the two men who stopped to help on the ground at the scene of the accident there were gone, vanished. They managed to pull out three of his friends from the car and fifteen (15) seconds later the car exploded just like in the movies. The eighteen (18) wheeler trucker dragged them for one and half (1.5) miles. Now I was told the driver either feel asleep at the wheel or was drunk. We never found out. He did not even realize he hit them until they were crushed underneath his truck, dragged and completely stopped. The driver wrote my brother a long apology letter. My younger brother did not want to go to court to relive this tragedy. JM had trauma and nightmares every night at midnight for years. He would yell out no no, get me out of here please. I do not want my face to burn.

So I talked to God and Jesus finally about all this. They said there was a large group of angels assisting my brother that day. What is a group six or eight? He said between 100 to 1,000 angels were there. I was saying no way. He said there was some lifting and moving the crushed car, others, helping the victims, others making sure the truck did not explode. Others making sure no one else would get into an accident on the highway. God and Jesus told me there were so many angels at the accident scene, at the hospital and recuperation and that my brother was very fortunate that day to survive.

It was neither his time nor destiny to die. My brother could have died instantly yet he was so brave. I still do not understand how he can be running and walking with no limp. He had no facial scars, his ear healed completely with no scaring. The only scar is from the neck operations about two inches only and both his arms. His recuperation did not come overnight. My brother was always exhausted or fatigued. His burns on his arms took many years to heal. He still has his scar on his neck and was told he could have plastic surgery which he avoided. After they grafted skin from other parts of his body for his arms and made two (2) discs from his pelvic bone I think he was done with being prodded. I am surprised at his resiliency and positive outlook. During his time in the hospital he did not cry at all during all the times I saw him. He was stoic, rigid and serious. One time he begged me to get his a smoke meat sandwich instead of that plain hospital food. Well, my father was in his hospital room when he devoured his sandwich. Next thing he knew his upset stomach would not digest the meat and he got sick. The tricky part is have you ever got sick in traction? So, I promised never to do that mistake again even though I felt so sorry he could not eat roasted chicken, pizza, lasagna etc. his favorites.

My brother Jean-Marc is a huge Wayne Gretzy fan and there was an awful flood in the house. His shoeboxes with all his perfect wrapped hockey cards were wet, damp and completely destroyed. He was devastated. His favorite was a perfect shape rookie card. I know you are not supposed to cling to anything materialistic yet he really was careful collecting, talking to friends. He even went to places with others to sell their cards. My older brother lost his calling and should have been a sports announcer. They drove me nuts with points, spreads, scores, teams, all star players and averages. Memorizing plays they knew everything. Well, I would find Gilles and my neighbor Michael Beauregard pretending to speak into a microphone hours for many years. Go figure Michael Beauregard became a sports announcer on CFRA radio in Ottawa deserved his career. See what I mean by missing your calling? It was not just hockey but basketball, baseball, football also. They were sports junkies' lol.

The irony is my mother was terrified of car accidents. She would say my biggest fear is seeing one of my children in a car accident. Well, I think she must have been one of the guardian angels ministering to my brother that day. She died just two years prior the accident took place. My mother was really nervous in a car and would scream at my father if he passed any car or large truck and held onto his arm for sheer life. My little brother was one of her favorites and it was just not his destiny or time to die that day. Today, Jean-Marc is fifty-one year old doing well and works on highways the irony go figure. He loves the outdoor life and dislikes working indoors.

My discussions with God and Jesus about angels go as follows. God says all angels earn their wings in heaven. God speaks individually to each person as he/she enters heaven as he sits on his throne. For example: If you spoil your children emotionally and do not let them take a chance or grow and smother them he then shows and directs you lovingly. An angel can choose any body form before being born. They enter a body and remain in it for the rest of the person's life. That means there are literally angels alive and walking all over the earth already. God and Jesus talk to everyone about their qualities and faults. My parents were told they spoiled us too much emotionally. They are now guardian angels who earned wings and get told their duties from above. It can be any natural disaster, accidents, depression, suicide, murder, saving people from fire etc.

Timing is everything. Yes they can time travel. The expression just in time is relevant. Yet Jesus tells me there is no time and space in heaven. Angels appear to us like a large round light orb, light about six (6) to seven (7) inches travelling really quickly the color of white, light yellow or golden. Many children see angels as tall and transparent. Children are more open than adults. When a child says they see a pink or purple angel(s) it is the aura or halo around the head or body that they visualize. Many parents will say they have active imaginations and disregard their thoughts. Not everyone in heaven becomes an angel. In the sky at night time I was witnessed many times what I call angel lights of amber, white, golden, red, blue and green. They flash constantly and it is like a faithful friend flashing like snowflakes visiting. When I have a problem or feel emotional distressed or crying and look out up at the sky through my window a light appears one at a time. They look like a band of multiple lights large enough. An angel can be male or female. They all sing at 5:30 a.m. exactly early every morning before the sun rises to praise and worship for the glory of God and Jesus. Children and adults choose the color of their wing tips. Yes, some just have huge plain white feathers.

Angels: They fly faster than the speed of light. There are twelve (12) arch angels, twenty-four (24) elders. It is a fact that angels fly faster than the speed of light. Yes they can so get used to it. As soon as God and Jesus give their messages, directions, commands they sprint off right away. Angels minister/assist/help always because there is so much work and assistance needed on earth. Angels are messengers, aides and guardians of humans. They await their assignments with great trepidation, anticipation and love to help people. An example of a human angel: At a corner of a busy traffic section they will pull back on your shoulder to avoid you getting hit by a car. Many angels have jobs helping people on earth. They can walk through walls or doors. Young children who die at birth are about seven year old angels with melodious voices. I would describe their voices as pure, innocent, sweet and wise and the prettiest tone ever. Adults are about thirty (30) years of age in heaven. Everyone has auras and have duties like cooking, cleaning, ironing, taking care of children. It is communal living with total peace, quiet and serenity. They have a different tone, vibration or frequency which is really high when angels speak and sing. They live on a higher plane/dimension. Please God and Jesus I loathe ironing. Hope I do not get stuck with that job in heaven one day.

There are about sixteen (16) Arch Angels named as follows: Michael, Gabriel, Raphael, Ariel, Jophiel, Raziel, Chamuel, Uriel, Zadkiel/Sachiel, Raguel, Metatron, Jeremiel, Azrael, Sandalphon, Haniel, Cassiel

Heaven is a perfect paradise. There is no darkness just light and warmth. Jesus told me wait until you see the different colors and flowers we have in heaven. There is more of a vast spectrum and everything is more vivid and bright. Since I am an artist (paint & draw) and love all colors and flowers I was really happy to learn this fact. Even the more boring colors like grey and brown can be made beautiful mixed with others. You can paint with soot/ash/peat from fires and have spectacular white and blacks. Just mix with water and do not forget your sealer at the end of your projects. I also paint with coffee grinds at times.

Scientists will be pleased to learn that there are a total of fourteen (14) dimensions in heaven. Not everyone in heaven is an Angel. Angels are God and Jesus' messengers who protect humans from harm. They guide us to safety and can protect your personal home from robberies, theft and fire. Angels often veil their faces before God because his bright light is too much. They feel humbled in his presence. Angels work and do God's duties and do not want to be praised or worshipped instead of God or Jesus. The only things angels envy about humans are our free will, freedom of choice and the fact we can receive the Eucharist. Angels are spirit beings who represent the heavenly realm. They do watch and observe us and smile.

Other names of groups of angels are: Thrones, Powers, Rulers, Authority, Dominions, Principalities, Leagues, Holy Ones, Mighty Ones, Fire and Wind, Seraphim's, Cherubs, Cherubim's, Hosts, Chariots, Holy Watchers, Living Creatures, Elders, Guides, Angel's of the Lord, Messengers, God's Servants, Order and Harmony. Satan's angels are called leagues, fallen ones, demons and Satan's Hosts. One fact is they are represented by the elements wind (air) and fire. Fire needs air to start and we cannot see wind. Angels often appear just after a strong wild wind or they appear like flames of fire, their eyes blazing, sword shining and the warriors/defenders wear the garments of heaven (sword, helmet, breastplate, boots, belt and shield). The arch angels do not have to wear a helmet. Often times they appear visually to the enemy guarding a building, site, house, business or an army of protectors etc.

I often times reflect on the elements earth and water which is meant for humans. The earth meaning sowing, planting and reaping, flowers, birds, valleys, mountains. What is stable and tangible? We feel the soil in our hands. The water ebb and flow of life, white caps warning dangerous temperatures ahead. The water our natural element needed to survive and for our gardens to grow. We are the drop in the vast ocean. We can float and feel at peace swimming in the water. Also catch fish to feed the world. An owl which hoots in the daytime warns of a severe storm to follow the same day or next.

My personal true second story. I visited some small towns about twenty-five (25) years ago in Guatemala. It was tropical and incredibly humid. So much my cotton tops were soaked with sweat. The locals laughed at this saying nothing yet staring. OK I told them would like to see you in a -35 degree day in a Canadian winter if you can take it and chuckled. It took me two years to speak Spanish relatively well. Today I lost the language completely. Not practicing Spanish over the years. They could not even imagine my remark because never saw snow in their entire existence. I was on a day trip with a boyfriend, his mother and niece we headed for the border of Mexico and Guatemala.

I never knew racism and bigotry between Latin American countries until that fateful day. The Mexican border patrol man let me go and pass in because I was Canadian but held everyone back even though we all had the correct proper papers, passports and visas. I had to head out to Chiapas (St. Cristobel de las Casas) and was going to meet a month later at their relative's house. After a few days at the relative's house/courtyard I noticed they were extremely inhospitable, felt in the way and took up a hotel room. This is a long story.

So I travelled with my boyfriend at the time on an old amber and black school bus which was yellow and black. The ones from Canada that are no longer in service or required. In walked I would say about at least fifty (50) people three to a seat/bench, chickens, fruit baskets, boxes, groceries, mothers and children mostly, some day workers/laborers and I the only blond (pelo rubio), sturdy (they called me gorda I know means chubby/overweight ha) and grey eyes in the entire country. The locals would stare at me so much I would laugh. What is it? It is like being an alien. So with the chickens squawking, the kids singing and the adults raising their voices it was a routine trip. Well, they drive like maniacs passing a bus when a car is coming right at them. So half the time I would gasp or scream out look out. Omg. There is much beauty in Guatemala, mountains, hillsides, lakes and waterfalls. Beautiful greenery and countryside. This is where Tim Horton fair trade coffee comes from and is grown. Yes way.

So at a pit stop on a mountain in a valley with the bus I bought a nice real jade and hematite necklace etc. as a souvenir. The local people picked fresh coffee beans, roasted them and crushed them in a marble bowl with a mortar and pestle. The Guatemalans people are beautiful, friendly and really nice. They boiled water with a kettle on a fire. We drank with brown sugar and milk from a goat. That was the best incredible coffee in my life. I asked a question about how they find the tourists. They laughed and responded we speak way too much and like to giggle. Fair enough. I tried in vain to pay for my coffee. Just put some bills and change down on a bench near the fire. They refused and kept on saying uno regalo para ti. A Gift for you.

When we were all on our merry time I noticed there were no guard rails on the routes, highways, roads at all and the incline drop was really high. All of a sudden the bus front tire blew out and the driver tried to take control. Then I remember praying a fast one. Please guardian angels protect us from any accidents. I am not going to die today neither is anyone on this bus. It is not my time yet. Thank you so much for saving us. That was weird to pray in advance of an event.

Miraculously and yes it was a miracle two huge sand pits or domes appeared letting the bus slam into them to a complete halt. People were yelling, screaming it is the end the end I say. Signs of the cross and Dios mio was shouted. The sounds and wails of the children will never be forgotten. I was near the end of the bus and looking at the rear door thinking if we go down this cliff I'm going to open this door. It never happened thank you God. We were all saved not a scratch on anyone.

Even the bus driver looked at me and knew me as the back seat driver because I spoke in English. He laughed really loud and shrugs his shoulders. I do not know why these sand domes appeared they were not there yesterday. Also people heard me pray mouthing with whispers in English. I got off the bus to have a group of people surround me saying Angelitos. What is that? No no I am far from an angel believe me. You angel, you save us from crash. Thank you. God blesses you. This felt so strange. I insist God and Jesus and his angels did the saving and work not me. You golden girl from heaven. This was too much even I denied it vigilantly. They nicknamed me Barbie. This is comical because I'm curvy and have hips/thighs/calves and butt while Barbie is a skinny plastic doll with no shape.

Well after my father died I put on a VHS tape one day and it was Kevin Costner's movie, "Dragonfly". Our accident happened in exactly the same place, curve and area reinacted in the movie sequence it was errie. Guess what happened in the scene? His wife goes over the cliff and dies in the exact place/area/location in the same looking school bus we were all in. The movie is about dealing with grief. I just lost my father and it was really appropriate. Wow. Was there a message to get this movie or what? So our experience was really a happy ending like a fairy tale. Kevin Costner movies are so inspiring and he is a great actor. I highly recommend this movie as it grasps at all senses. Love you Kevin as my brother of course.

I do have another third and final interesting very sad true story to tell. My uncle Paul Tardy who is the brother of my mother Raymonde Tardy was conned and scammed is the lowest way possible. My uncle won the lottery 6/49 when he turned sixty (60). He never told anyone until a year later to my older surviving aunt. Paul was a private person who loved riding his bicycle, swimming, nature, flowers, trees and grapes. He was a faithful Catholic Christian who read the Bible to my mother over the last three months of her life. The last week he recited many passages out loud to Raymonde my mother. Paul's sister (my mother) turned to him and said I want to die on a Sunday. Low and behold my mother died the day after the final prayer at approximately 9:00 a.m. on a Sunday.

My Aunt Nora Tardy also died on a Sunday. My father died twenty years later also during the month of March. I have decided to call this the ides of March. Paul decided to sponsor people from a small Caribbean country in the 1990's I believe. I do not have the exact dates and names. He must have sponsored at least ten to twelve (10-12) people because they were all present at my Grandmothers Mary Jane O'Brien's funeral. They surrounded my uncle in a circle with crossed arms not wanting any of the immediate family or relatives to speak to him directly. I found this really unusual and weird behavior. My grandmother lived to ninety nine (99) being of strong tough northern Irish descent.

I believe my grandmother must have had at least seven (7) or eight (8) older sisters who were like clones. Very dark brown hair almost black with light blue or green eyes, pale white ivory skin, very tall with long arms and strong shoulders. She was only three in the picture I saw with golden white hair, stocky build, strong legs and shoulders and very short. So you could imagine the contrast already. She had no brothers. The whole family immigrated to Canada in approximately 1905 from Northern Belfast, Ireland. My grandmother had eight children and brought them up well.

They were very poor yet proud with only two bedrooms in a small house with 10 people and the Weston horse and buggy used to leave bread to my grandmother. My Aunt Nora and Uncle Paul would meet every Sunday over coffee for hours and chat about what they would do when they would win. I found them so funny. They were so sure to win that they spoke as if they won the lottery already. This went on for twenty years. Yes it did. When my aunt Nora died of breast cancer after a very long nine (9) year battle, Uncle Paul won six months after her death. I asked him what were his special numbers and he answered the birthdays of my brothers and sisters and even the extra number was a birthday from his immediate family.

Well I thought that was really nice and wished them luck over the years. Six months before he won my uncle Paul had two brain aneurysms and almost died. The blood vessel unclipped and it was really dangerous. He also got blood poisoning. Paul changed nothing in his habits and even went on collecting empty plastic bottles to clean and beautify the surroundings in the park. My uncle could eat five (5) pounds of bananas a week. Paul Tardy was a carpenter, athletic and always suntanned. He told me he saved all his life before winning the lottery.

I would describe my uncle Paul as about five foot five, muscular, athletic, broad shouldered, light green eyes, dark brown hair which turned mostly grey, and a large moustache. He wore dentures and was very tanned all year round. He spoke in a low voice sporadically in French. Paul was never overweight and kept up a vigil to stay in shape. (Walking, bicycle riding, swimming, working, landscaping). His stomach was flat. He was very independent, kind, witty, low key and loved to laugh. He was very proud of his outward appearance yet cared for people. He had the qualities of empathy and sympathy for others. In his late twenties he devoted his life to taking care of our grandmother Mary Jane O'Brien for almost the rest of her life. She was placed in a nursing home very late in life and hated living there. She continually cried, complained and wanted to go back to her original home to live out the rest days in peace on her large favorite famous wooden rocking chair.

One day Paul took me on the side of his pool for a talk and said Nora I want you to be the Executor of my will and showed me a copy of his original will yet I never found out his lawyer's name. I was very concerned and yet flattered and asked him why me? He answered I never married and worked hard and my life was not easy one. He also said I was a very fair person and not a greedy one. I did not ask him what he meant. Never did see that same original Will once again. Paul's original Will was destroyed during the demolishment of his small family house in January or February 2019. A new will was falsified by fraud and made my uncle sign under duress. My uncle was engaged twice and never married. He hired a chef/guard right away after he won the lottery and was paranoid of people trying to get to his money/funds.

The sponsors and so called adopted son bulldozed my Grandmother's Mary

Jane O'Brien's house down and sold the lot just two months after my uncle died in November 2018. The whole immediate family nor relatives were never told what he died of, where, when and what disease or sickness he had. Also we assumed he was cremated due to no autopsy. I am positive there was foul play. We still do not know where he is buried and what he died of and the date. Why would someone do this? They followed him, surrounded him all the time. All these years they refused family communication. It was almost sect like and he was definitely brain washed, influenced and coerced.

All of a sudden I learned that my uncle was forced under duress to sign a Power of Attorney and sign over papers (a new Will) for an adopted son. Now this is where it gets interesting. My uncle never wanted children of his own nor adopted and he repeated that all his life. He was a loner and called children little monsters lol. Also he was very frugal and careful with money coming from a very poor family. Paul Tardy bought a house in Arizona sold it, and then a condo in Mexico sold it then returned to the small family home where he grew up for years. He bought one car and it lasted twenty years.

Now instead of going through years of future litigation and putting many people through pain, humiliation and embarrassment or shame in prison, I have decided to let this book speak for itself. Someone will come forward who has a conscious perhaps even apologizing and tell me the truth of what happened/transpired and make a donation. The Power of Attorney and new Will can be traced and copies of the documents can be sent to me in Prince Edward Island (Canada) by courier.

I plan on purchasing an eighty to one hundred and twenty (80-120) year older small home in the Maritimes (Newfoundland) near the ocean, a small used car and a used Italian Vespa scooter with proceeds from a donation, contribution etc. As long as my bills, taxes are paid and I eat and have the basics for now I am good. With any additional funds/monies I plan on contributing and help pay back the Caribbean government for a complete investigation with the proceeds/monies returned from the false adopted son and sponsors.

In the near future the consulate will get a copy of this book and they can retrace all the steps of the sponsors' names in full, home addresses, telephone and cellular numbers. They can also find out all bank information, wire transfers, investments, stocks, mutual funds, annuities, dividends, GICS, bonds, treasury bills, insurance, new purchases of homes, commercial property or businesses, land/lots, cottages, cars, sailboats or yachts, etc. The government can investigate if the sponsors put property or funds in another person's name such as a family member, spouse, friend or relative. Also numbered corporations or registered companies can be searched and retrieved.

Real Estate Properties (Houses/land/lots, commercial properties, condos, duplex, triplex, cottages, vacation rentals) may/can be seized, resold and the proceeds of the sales to be paid back what is owed. Also the information of the original name(s) on the Agreement of Purchase and Sale from the Real Estate Company of the large corner lot property on Barthelemy Street in Longueuil (Quebec) sold approximately in January or February in 2019. Finally they can track down all the names involved by paperwork of the Power of Attorney, new Will and Adoption papers of the so called fake adopted son.

The total the thieves had stolen with interest and investments is approximately between 12,000,000 to 15,000,000 million (Cdn $) including interest. Not a small feat right? What an awful embarrassment, disgrace and shame to those who have done this crime and government since my Uncle Paul Tardy sponsored at least ten to twelve (10-12) people from a small Caribbean Island to help them prosper not take advantage of him. This is the absolute short version of the whole story by facts only. Well, I will be waiting patiently. Patience is not my best quality or virtue. I fear require a lot of work regarding good fruits and Beatitudes. I will be awaiting answers, follow-up and solving this case. What is expected is return in monies (Cdn $) of a large portion/donation from the government after I'm reimbursed in full. I will be delighted and happy to compensate the entire investigation and also to make a huge donation to the Government in return as compensation for their efforts. I am also a cheerful giver. Of course I do not expect the whole amount after three years. What I do expect is fairness. I am available to help/ assist in any way required to solve this case and missing links.

Excuses – When you know in your heart of hearts that you are telling the truth God and Jesus know also. Maybe they have another plan, venture, challenge, direction, relocation, adventure, job, they want you to grasp and take a risk. There are signs and gifts also talents. How and when we use them is important. Do not sit idle for years. Change and take a chance or risk. Think out of the confinement of your box. Do not worry what others think or say.

Do what you love without explanation. Sacrifice some time to learn. Be curious not noisy. Speak and communicate the Good News. Do not gossip. Read and learn more lessons every day. Listen to others and grasp information, storytelling, tales, lyrics, songs, ballads, poems, verses, sonnets, fiction, history, biographies, sci-fi, science, architecture, art, manuscripts, collecting or whatever your interests and passions may be varied. Pray and talk to God and Jesus about anything.

What the following definitions or words are like: Atonement, Sanctification, Righteousness, Redemption, Sacraments, the Body and Blood of Christ and taking up one's cross literally mean? What is the difference between worship, praising, and for the Glory of God?

Atonement: To be truly repentant for ones sins. To atone for ones sin is to acknowledge regret, have shame, guilt and not desiring to sin again. To self a process to improve ourselves not in an egoist way. Living daily with spiritual qualities such as giving, loving, togetherness, and sharing spiritual direction. We will all receive a pure new heart. To become renewed and changed. Total transformation and to self improve.

Sanctification: We are all sanctified through the body and blood of Jesus Christ.

Redemption: Wiping the slate clean of sin. We are free from sin because of the love of Jesus to the entire universe. Originating from our ancestors, protegeny, and previous generations Adam and Eve at the beginning of time. Jesus is sometimes called the second Adam.

Born Again: Means - You absolutely implicitly accept and receive the perfect gift the Holy Spirit to indwell in your body, spirit and soul with all your belief. For the spirit perfects teaches and counsels your life for the better. What better gift? Also he never forces merely gives suggestions to better your present life situation. You will feel elated, young, inspired, happy, content, and blissful and experience true divinity. Find yourself smiling more. He will open your heart to new dormant talents and show you the way to practice and have passion for your work. To fully experience Joy. "Let go, and let God". Of course you always have the freedom of choice and you will the Holy Spirit and he just tries to guide along your path and calling. The Holy Spirit will never tell you what to do and when. Of course God and Jesus want you to have a life of abundance. The Holy Spirit never interferes with the choices you make in life. In our stubbornness we all try to go our own way. It never works out eventually we crumble and fail and fall.

There are Seven Sacraments: Baptism, Eucharist, Reconciliation, Confirmation, Marriage, Holy Orders, Anointing of the Sick.

Taking up the Cross of Jesus: Jesus led the way and example on how to live with meaning and serving with total humility. For Jesus the son of the living Christ is the true unblemished lamb. Perfect and untarnished. Free from faults and sins. Jesus did the grandest greatest sacrifice on earth. He gave up his life to us to free us from sin. Jesus resurrected three days later as promised. He ascended into heaven (ascension), came back and will come back once again. Jesus is the true Messiah. What more could he give greater than his life - absolutely nothing. Jesus became man although he was also spiritual. So he is spiritual and man. Jesus (Calvary and the stations of the Cross) - literally took up his cross and walked to his own death dragging his beaten bloody body with sinews showing and huge wooden heavy cross to the mount of death Golgotha until someone else finally aided him near the end of his route. We were literally ransomed and bought back from God and Jesus.

For we belong to them and no one else. Our hearts, minds, strengths and souls reside in their power. God and Jesus are the all knowing, all powerful, all believing, here there everywhere. "I am what I am". Alpha and Omega. Beginning and the end." For there is only eternity living in peace when we give up our lives to Jesus Christ and will ourselves to his will and way not ours. To surrender submit, abide and humble ourselves totally body and soul. Believe in the son of God who is and yet to come. For everyone's true strength, power comes directly from heaven from God and Jesus. We would be dust, a drop of water, a grain of sand, nothing without them. We are presently clay to be molded and tended properly. They want us to really live, breathe and be content with your life. Not merely exist. For God gave you the gift of life not to be taken away. "Abide in me as I abide in you".

The Body and Blood of Christ: The body of Christ is the Eucharist. A symbolism during the Last Supper (Jesus with all twelve Apostles) of the body of Christ that God, Jesus and Holy Spirit will reside in our body in our whole being. Therefore, the expression the body is your temple is real. The Blood of Christ is symbolism of how he had shed tears of blood on the Cross in order to free us completely of sin. How Jesus received one hundred and fourteen (114) scourgings rendering his body limp, still, weak and lifeless for he was forced to walk with a heavy wooden laden cross. Also it represents the Crown of thorns placed on his head in mockery. Jesus shed tears of blood in the garden of Gethsemane and also when the Crown of Thorns was placed on his head. Blood is also all the animal sacrifices and offerings made by people in the past. Herod demanded that his guards kill all the children two years and under all over the country. He wanted to kill baby Jesus the living Christ.

The imagery or metaphor is Jesus will always indwell in his apostles and he sent the gift of the Holy Spirit to live in their hearts. Jesus and the Holy Spirit will indwell in us also once we are born again. (Receive the gift of the Holy Spirit)

There was a room attended once a year from the High Priests called the room of Holy of Holies. This room was so sacred that no one could enter it but high priest/ministers/bishop/cardinal/pope only once per year. The Eucharist (the body of Christ) and the special wine (the Blood of Christ) were prepared for the congregation. When Jesus died on the Cross God had the large handmade embroidered drapes in gold and other colors rent from top to bottom. Meaning access to God and his heavenly realm and son could be at any time. Just call upon them by their names. You must ask for help from them verbally. Remember the story in the Bible about the gentleman who accidently touched the Ark of the Covenant he had died right away.

The prized animals: Ram, Bull, Sheep, Ewe, Goat (males or females) free of total blemish which means a perfect specimen of offering in God's eye. An animal sacrifice offering to our Lord most high for he is Holy. You receive tenfold. Sow and reap. Give, take, sharing and receiving. Making one's living with Good Fruits in the image and the perfect character of the Lord. The Blood of Christ also means the story of spreading the Blood of a lamb on the entrance of all homes to protect them from having their eldest child from being killed. The ones with the front entrance doors washed in blood of the sheep homes were spared damage, and death of their children. So the houses were literally skipped of oppression.

Please note and understand an animal sacrifice was considered a great privilege and honor in those times. An animal was highly valued for food, meat, milk, eggs, cheese, wool, clothing and survival. Currency was not highly available. Many were working poor farmers in feudal system working and tendering leased plots of land. So many did not even own a small portion of their own land working generation after generation forever for the owner with minimal profits or just breaking even. The animals required care, attention, love, seed, hay, food, shelter and fresh water for the animals. Stagnant water for lambs because running water makes them bloat and die. Many times they were behind a year if their crops were not successful for only one year. Some were able to pick their plots of land and many were stuck with hard land with plenty of stones and hardly any pastures and greenery required to feed the animals in spring, summer and the autumn. Crops like vegetables and grain had great difficulty succeeding on these plots. There was waste of seed, resources, time and labor.

There was always the fear of starvation, robbery, drought, locusts, mice, rats or nonstop rain and flooding and natural disasters. The owner would even take their crops and leave them almost starving and treat the workers as serfs. It is a sorry frustrating way to live not getting ahead in business and ever owning a piece of land. The rich back then were only selected few from royalty, ancestry, hierarchy, willed estates and titles in patriarchal societies. This is why there are many parables in the Bible with analogies regarding planting, sowing and reaping. The people could relate to this. The expression I can never get ahead reflects this era. There was no fairness and only division. So their way of living was currently how presently the caste system works in some parts of India. There was a huge pestilence problem (rodents – mice, moles and rats which were able to eat almost all the grain, corn etc.) leaving nothing for the winter months.

Worship: Praying with deep reverence and adoration. Satan detests true worship. He slithers, crawls and begs you to stop. Any singing, devotion in a group puts salt on his wounds. The devil knows God, Jesus, Mary and his angels by their personal names. Reading the Bible, learning its passages and have true devotion are signs of worshipping. Your church family, community and personal family pray together and will stay together. Living united. Raising ones hands in supplication up to the Lord. Singing and clapping from the soul. Holding hands and blessing others are all signs of worship. Feeling your emotions and total adoration. People who are demonized or possessed by the devil or demons crawl on all fours in a church and will speak out loud in another authoritive voice begging for everyone to stop their worship and prayers immediately because it bothers them. God, Jesus, Holy Spirit and some angels are always in a Church setting silently observing.

Praising: Praise the Lord and his son Jesus. Speak praises for they are Holy and good. So holy, holy, holy God Almighty. He is most deserving of our love. Some are in deep prayer and meditate on God's word. We make God happy and satisfied at times. He watches his flock/fold reverently like a father. Remember the Holy Spirit is always in a house of prayer when people unite in true love, Repentance and devotion (Church). Your church members and/or Minister/Priest anoint others in a prayer group with holy water and oil on their crown or forehead. Praying solitary, in groups or with a rosary is faith, belief and praising our Lord. God and Jesus hear all our prayers and answer on their own good time not ours. Intercessory prayer for others is a great quality of character and personality. To put others needs in front of your own. There is no better friend who lies down his life for a friend. God is good, God is great. Prayer groups once a week can and do change the world one prayer at a time, one person at a time. Small deeds do not go unnoticed. Angels praise God and Jesus every single day by rising at 5:30 a.m. to sing before dawn for the glory of God. Yes, everyone in heaven must get up at this time. Too bad you insomniacs like me.

Glory of God: For God's Glory happiness and contentment and complete satisfaction. To humble ourselves and become more modest in God's presence. To bend, bow and pray and supplicate. In the end of the world (earth), everyone will be on bended knee. Some will not be pleased trying to fight off Jesus in the sky. Abide in him as he abides in us. Surrendering our will to his will we will feel the Holy Spirit counsel and teach us to produce the good fruits character (image of God and Jesus). It is nobler to be humble and modest.

Finally, I asked God and Jesus what they thought of religion. They answered they do not agree with religion because it divides people. They did not say not to be religious nor demand that people stop believing. They love when people pray, worship and praise God and Jesus for their glory. Also they look down from heaven when people celebrate Christmas with love, a great supper gathering with your loved ones present celebrating the birth of the begotten son Jesus. He is indeed the son of the living Christ.

God told me to invite the single, orphaned, foster children, lonely or widows also. Do not forget them for everyone wants to feel a sense of belonging and love on Christmas day. It is a difficult time for many because they live with memories from the past. We have to live in the moment of now that is all we have. They enjoy the lights and the warmth in people's hearts. What they explained is bitter disagreements within a Church. Everyone is welcome in my Church they state. People should be concerned about being and not just doing. There is absolutely no reason to rush around your life and stress yourself out for nothing.

When one group insists their religion is better than others. Not to force of coerce your beliefs. If someone wants your help to understand your religion then it is alright to spread the word of God to them. Martial law, conformists and fundamentalists are all problems faced in our society today. Also, you do not have to have a church in gold, marble nor the most seats, icons and state of the art sound etc. Religion is not for show. In many countries people gather in a small humble church, barn, house or small building because they feel sometimes ostracized and judged for their beliefs. They are extremely saddened about priests or ministers taking advantage of young children (little ones). "Revenge is mine" is stated quite clearly. Also "judge not least you be judged".

Prayers - Our Father (The Lord's Prayer):

Our Father who art in Heaven. Hallowed be thy name. Thy kingdom come. Thy will be done. On earth as it is in heaven. Give us this day our daily bread and forgive us our trespasses as we forgive those who trespass against us. Lead us not into temptation and deliver us from all evil. Amen. As it was in the beginning, and now ever shall be world without end.

Apostles Creed:

I believe in God Father almighty creator of heaven and earth. I believe in his only begotten son Jesus who was conceived by the power of the Holy Spirit and born of the Virgin Mary. He suffered under Pontius Pilate was crucified died and buried. He descended to the dead. After three days he rose again and ascended to heaven and he is seated at the right hand of the heavenly Father. He will come again to judge the living and the dead. I believe in the Holy Spirit, the Holy Catholic Church, the communion of Saints, the forgiveness of sins, the resurrection of the body and life everlasting. Amen

Hail Mary:

Hail Mary full of grace the Lord is with thee. Blessed are you amongst woman and blessed is the fruit of thy womb Jesus. Holy Mary mother of God pray for us sinners now and at the hour of our death. Amen.

Psalm 23:

The Lord is my Sheppard I shall not want. He maketh me to lie down in green pastures and leadeth me beside the still waters. He restoreth my soul. He leadeth me to the paths of righteousness for his name's sake. Even though I walk through the valley of shadow of death I fear no evil. His rod and his staff they comfort me. He prepareth a table before me with my own enemies. He anointed my head with oil. My cup runneth over. Surely only goodness and mercy shall follow me the rest of the days of my life and I shall dwell in the house of the Lord forever. Amen

Hail Holy Queen

Hail Holy Queen Mother of mercy. Our life, our sweetness and our hope. To thee do we cry poor banished children of Eve. To thee do we send up our sighs, mourning and weeping in this vale of tears. Turn then most precious advocate thy eyes of mercy towards us, and after that our exile. Show unto us thy fruit of thy womb Jesus. Oh Clement, oh loving, oh sweet Virgin Mary, pray for us mother of God so that we may be made worthy of the promises of Christ. Amen.

Glory Be:
Glory Be to the Father, to the Son, and the Holy Spirit. Amen. Blessed is he who comes in the name of the Lord Hosanna in the highest

*Nicene Creed:
I believe in one God, the Father almighty, maker of heaven and earth, of all things visible and invisible. I believe in one Lord Jesus Christ, the Only Begotten Son of God, born of the Father before all ages. God from God, Light from Light, true God from true God, begotten, not made consubstantial with the Father, through him all things were made. For us men and for our salvation he came down from heaven, and by the Holy Spirit was incarnate of the Virgin Mary, and became man.

For our sake he was crucified under Pontius Pilate, he suffered death and was buried, and rose again on the third day in accordance with the Scriptures. He ascended into heaven and is sealed at the right hand of the Father. He will come again in glory to judge the living and the dead and his kingdom will have to end. I believe in the Holy Spirit, the Lord, the giver of life, who proceeds from the Father and the Son; who with the Father and the Son is adored and glorified, who has spoken through the prophets. I believe in one, holy catholic and apostolic Church. I confess one baptism for the forgiveness of sins and I look toward to the resurrection of the dead and the life of the world to come. Amen.

*Prayers to St. Joseph – Head of the Holy Family, Protector of the Church, Patron Saint of Canada

Prayer to St. Joseph: O St. Joseph, whose protection is so great, so strong, so prompt before the throne of God. I place in thee all my interests and desires. O St. Joseph do assist me by thy powerful intercession and obtain for me from the Divine Son all spiritual blessings, through Jesus Christ, Our Lord, so that having engaged here below thy heavenly power, I may offer my thanksgiving and homage to the most loving of Fathers O St. Joseph. I never weary contemplating thee and Jesus asleep in thy arms. I dare not approach while He reposes near thy heart. Press Him in my name and kiss His fine head for me and ask him to return the kiss when I draw my dying breath St. Joseph. Patron of departing souls prays for us. Amen.

*Prayer to St. Joseph for Our Family

Great Saint Joseph, you were chosen by God to be the Head of the Holy Family. Kindly look down upon us and bestow your fatherly protection upon our home. Model of the most lively faith, obtain for all the members of our family the grace to believe firmly what God has revealed and bear witness to our faith in all that we do. May we ever remain bound together for the salvation of souls. In order to fulfill our role in the great family of the Church and be reunited after this life in the happiness of Heaven. Amen.

*Prayer to St. Joseph for Canada:

Hail St. Joseph, Patron of Canada, protector and guardian of our beloved homeland. Keep under your sovereign patronage in this hour of crisis, the unity, the faith and integrity of your children, the Canada people from sea to sea. Amen.

*Morning Offering: O Jesus, through the immaculate Heart of Mary, I offer You my prayers, works, joys and sufferings on this day for all the intentions of your Sacred heart, in union with the Holy Sacrifice of the Mass throughout the world in reparation for my sins, for the intentions of all my relatives and friends, and in particular for the intentions of the Holy Father. Amen.

*Prayer before Meals: Bless us, O Lord and these gifts which we are about to receive from Your bounty through Christ our Lord. Amen.

*Prayer after Meals: We give You thanks for all Your benefits O Almighty God, who lives and reigns forever, and may the souls of the faithful departed through the mercy of God, rest in peace. Amen.

*Act of Faith: O my God, I firmly believe that you are one God in three divine persons, Father, Son and Holy Spirit. I believe that your divine Son became man and died for our sins, and that he will come to judge the living and the dead. I believe these and all the truths which the Holy Catholic Church teaches because in revealing them you can neither deceive nor be deceived.

*Act of Hope: O my God, relying on Thy almighty power and infinite mercy and promises, I hope to obtain pardon of my sins, the help of Thy grace and life everlasting through the merits of Jesus Christ, my Lord and Redeemer.

*Act of Charity: O my God, I love Thee above all things, with all my heart and soul, because Thou art all-good and worthy of all my love. I love my neighbor as myself for love of Thee. I forgive all who have injured me, and ask pardon of all whom I have injured.

*Angel of God: Angel of God, my guardian dear, to whom His love entrusts me here, ever this day, be at my side to light and guard, to rule and guide. Amen

*Memo rare: Remember, O most gracious Virgin Mary that never was. It known that anyone who fled to thy protection, implored thy help, or sought thine intercession was left unaided. Inspired by this confidence, I fly unto thee, O Virgin of virgins, my mother to thee do I come, before thee I stand, sinful and sorrowful. O Mother of the Word incarnate, despise not my petitions but in thy mercy hear and answer me. Amen.

*Daily Prayer for Priests:

O Almighty Eternal God, look upon the face of Thy Christ, and for the love of him who is the Eternal High Priest, have pity on Thy priests. Remember, O most compassionate God, that they are but weak and frail human beings. Stir up in them the grace of their vocation which is in the by the imposition of the bishop's hands. Keep them close to Thee, lest the Enemy prevail again them, so that they may never do anything in the slightest degree unworthy of their sublime vocation.

O Jesus, I pray Thee for Thy faithful and fervent priests; for Thy unfaithful and tepid priests, for Thy priests laboring at home or abroad in distant mission fields; for Thy tempted priests; for Thy young priests, for Thy aged priests, for Thy sick priests, for Thy dying priests; for the souls of Thy priests in Purgatory.

But above all I commend to Thee the priests dearest to me; the priest who baptized me; the priests who absolved me from my sins; the priests at whose Masses I assisted, and who gave me Thy Body and Blood in Holy Communion; the priests who taught and instructed me, or helped and encouraged me; all the priests to whom I am indebted in any other way particularly (Name) O Jesus, keep them all close to Thy Heart, and bless them abundantly in time and in eternity. Amen.

*How to Pray the Rosary: (1 to 59 beads)

First decade – We offer Thee, O Lord Jesus this first decade in honor of Thy Incarnation and we ask of Thee, through this mystery and through the intercession of the most Holy Mother, a profound humility. One Our Father, Ten Hail Mary's, Glory be to the Father, the son and the Holy Spirit. Amen and Blessed Be.

Grace of the mystery of the Incarnation, come down into my soul and make it truly humble.

Second Decade: We offer Thee, O Lord Jesus this second decade in honor of the Visitation of Thy Holy Mother to her cousin Saint Elizabeth, and we ask of Thee through this mystery and through Mary's intercession, a perfect charity towards our neighbor. One Our Father, Ten Hail Mary's, Glory be to the Father, the son and the Holy Spirit.

Grace of the mystery of the Visitation come down into my soul and make it really charitable.

Third decade: We offer Thee, O Child Jesus this third decade in honor of Thy Blessed Nativity, and we ask of Thee, through this mystery and through the intercession of Thy Blessed Mother, detachment from things of the world, love of poverty and love for the poor. One Our Father, Ten Hail Mary's, Glory be to the Father, the son and the Holy Spirit.

Grace of the mystery of the Nativity come down into my soul and make me truly poor in spirit.

Fourth decade: We offer Thee, O Lord Jesus, this fourth decade in honor of Thy Presentation in the Temple by the hand of Mary, and we ask of Thee, through this mystery and through the intercession of Thy Blessed Mother, The gift of wisdom and purity of heart and body. One Our Father, Ten Hail Mary's, Glory Be to the Father, the son and the Holy Spirit.

Grace of the Mystery of the Purification come down into my soul and make it really wise and really pure.

Fifth Decade: We offer Thee, O Lord Jesus, this fifth decade in honor of Thy Finding in the Temple among the learned men by our Lady after she had lost Thee, and we ask Thee, through this mystery and through the intercession of Thy Blessed Mother, to convert us and help us amend our lives and also to convert all sinners, heretics, schismatic's and idolaters. One Our Father, Ten Hail Mary's, Glory be to the Father, the son and the Holy Spirit.

The Sorrowful Mysteries (60-100 beads)

Sixth Decade: We offer Thee, O Lord Jesus, this sixth decade in honor of Thy Mortal Agony in the Garden of Olives, and we ask Thee, through this mystery and through the intercession of Thy Blessed Mother, perfect sorrow for our sins and the virtue of perfect obedience to Thy Holy Will. One Our Father, Ten Hail Mary's, Glory Be to the Father, the son and the Holy Spirit.

Grace of Our Lord's Agony, come down into my soul and make me truly contrite and perfectly obedient to thy will.

Seventh Decade: We offer Thee, O Lord Jesus, this seventh decade in honor of thy Bloody Scourging and we ask of Thee, through this mystery and through the intercession of Thy Blessed Mother, the grace to mortify our senses perfectly. One Our Father, Ten Hail Mary's, Glory Be to the Father, the son, the Holy Spirit. Amen.

Grace of our Lord's Scourging, come down into my soul and make me truly mortified.

Eighth Decade: We offer Thee, O Lord Jesus, this eighth decade in honor of Thy Cruel Crowning with thorns, and we ask of Thee, through this mystery and through the intercession of Thy Blessed Mother, a great contempt of the world. One our Father, Ten Hail Mary's, Glory Be to the Father, the son, and the Holy Spirit.

Grace of the mystery of Our Lord's crowning with Thorns, come into my soul and make me despise the world.

Ninth Decade: We offer Thee, O Lord Jesus, this ninth decade in honor of Thy Carrying Thy Cross and we ask of Thee, through this mystery and through the intercession of Thy Blessed Mother, to give us great patience in carrying our cross in Thy footsteps everyday of our life. One Our Father, Ten Hail Mary's, Glory Be to the Father, the son and the Holy Spirit.

Grace of the mystery of carrying of the Cross comes down into my soul and makes me truly patient.

Tenth Decade: We off Thee, O Lord Jesus, this tenth decade in honor of Thy Crucifixion on Mount Calvary, and we ask of Thee, through this mystery and through the intercession of Thy Blessed Virgin Mother, a great horror of Sin, a love of the Cross and the grace of a holy death for us and for those who are now in their last agony. Pray One Our Father, Ten Hail Mary's, and Glory Be to the Father, the son and to the Holy Spirit Amen. The Glorious Mysteries: (100-150 beads)

Eleventh Decade: We offer Thee, O Lord Jesus this eleventh decade in honor of Thy Triumphant Resurrection and we ask of thee, through this mystery and through the intercession of Thy Blessed Mother, a lively faith. One Our Father, Ten Hail Mary's, Glory Be to the Father, the son and the Holy Spirit.

Grace of the Resurrection come down into my soul and make me really faithful.

Twelfth Decade: We offer Thee, O Lord Jesus, this twelfth decade in honor of thy Glorious Ascension and we ask of Thee, through this mystery and through the intercession of Thy Blessed Mother a firm hope and a great longing for Heaven. One Our Father, Ten Hail Mary's, Glory Be to the Father, the son and the Holy Spirit.

Grace of the mystery of the Ascension of our Lord, come down into my soul and make me ready for heaven.

Thirteenth Decade: We offer Thee, O Holy Spirit, this thirteenth decade in honor of the Mystery of Pentecost, and we ask of Thee, through this mystery and through the intercession of Mary Thy most faithful Spouse, Thy holy wisdom so that we may know, really love and practice Thy truth, and take all others share in it. One Our Father, Ten Hail Mary's, Glory Be to the Father, to the son and the Holy Spirit.

Grace of Pentecost come down into my soul and makes me really wise in the eyes of Almighty God.

Fourteenth Decade: We offer Thee, O Lord Jesus this fourteenth decade in honor of the Immaculate Conception and the Assumption of thy holy and Blessed Mother, body and soul, into Heaven, and we ask of Thee, through these two mysteries and through her intercession the gift of true devotion to her to help us live and die holily. One Our Father, Ten Hail Mary's, Glory Be to the Father, to the Son, and to the Holy Spirit.

Grace of the Immaculate Conception and the Assumption of Mary, come down into my soul and make me truly devoted to her.

Fifteenth Decade: (Last) We offer thee, O Lord Jesus this fifteenth and last decade in honor of the glorious crowning of the Blessed Mother in Heaven and we ask of Thee, through this mystery and through her intercession, the grace of perseverance and increase of virtue until the very moment of death and after that the eternal crown that is prepared for us. We ask the same grace for all the just and for all our benefactors.

One Our Father, Ten Hail Mary's, Glory Be to the Father, to the son and the Holy Spirit.

We beseech Thee, dear Lord Jesus, by the fifteen mysteries of Thy life, death and passion, by Thy glory and by the merits of Thy Blessed Mother, to convert sinners and help the dying, to deliver the Holy Souls from purgatory and to give us all Thy grace so that we may live well and die well – and please give us the Light of Thy glory later on so that we may see Thee face to face and love Thee for all eternity Amen. So be it. Blessed be and peace to all. Amen.

*Prayer for Strength and Healing: Through the intercession of St. Peregrine

Loving and gracious God, in faith and trust we (I) place ourselves (myself) before you. Fill us (me) with your healing love. In St. Peregrine, you have given the world an outstanding example of courage, faith and hope in the midst of pain and affliction, and you showed your greatness and compassion by the miracle of his cure. Now we (I) ask you, through the intercession of St. Peregrine, to help N. (me), your servant, to endure his/her (my) illness with courage and, if it be your will, to restore him/her (me) to health. Through Christ our Lord. Amen.

*The Use of St. Peregrine Oil: St. Peregrine oil is blessed by a Servite priest in honor of St. Peregrine Laziosi, the 13th century friar of the Servite Order (Servants of Mary) who is a patron Saint of people with cancer and related illnesses. It is a sacramental of the Church and prayer should always accompany its use, whether that given on the reverse side of this card or another intercessory prayer, even in one's own words.

While the sacrament of anointing of the sick is reserved for those who are seriously ill and is not regularly repeated, blessed oil as a sacramental may be used frequently for the benefit of those who need it, whether their condition is life threatening or not.

The oil may be applied daily by oneself or another to the afflicted place (s) on the body or near to it. If a priest, deacon, or deputed lay minister performs the annointing, the celebration of the order for the Blessing of the Sick is appropriate, with the annointing immediately following the prayer of blessing, and avoiding any confusion with the sacrament of annointing of the sick. Sacramental's are primarily for the benefit of Catholics, but they may also be given to other Christians who requests.

*Prayer for the Unborn: Jesus, Mary and Joseph, I love you very much. I beg you to spare the life of (baby's name) the unborn baby that I have spiritually adopted who is in danger of abortion. (Say this prayer every day for nine months to save a baby's life! Prayer of Archbishop Fulton J. Sheen

*Spiritual Adoption: To help stop the anti-life push in the world at that time the late Archbishop Fulton JU. Sheen encouraged the spiritual adoption of an unborn baby. This is done by praying that one particular but unknown child's life will be spared from abortion and allowed to continue to live. To help accomplish this, it was recommended that an individual say the daily prayer for a period of nine (9) months.

*St. Joseph, you who protected the child Jesus and his mother from the murderous hand of Herod, assist us especially in this undertaking.

*St. Michael Defend us. Prayer to Saint Michael the Archangel. Saint Michael the Archangel, defend us in battle; be our defense against the wickedness and snares of the devil. May God rebuke him, we humbly pray. And do thou, O prince of the heavenly host, by the power of God cast into hell Satan and all the evil spirits who prowl about the world seeking the ruin of souls. Amen.

*Almighty God, we thank You for having called Your servant, Angus Bernard MacEachem, to become a missionary to all cultures in Eastern Canada and to be the first Bishop of Charlottetown. May his outstanding love for the people, his tireless missionary journeys throughout the Maritime region, and his singular dedication to offering the sacraments of the Church continue to inspire all the faithful to imitate the love and mercy of Jesus Christ, our Lord and Saviour. May his concern for Catholic Education, which led to the first institution of higher learning on Prince Edward Island, foster in Your people the gifts of faith and reason that they may develop a fuller knowledge and appreciation of Your abundant goodness.

Confident in Your steadfast love and mercy, grant us, we beseech You, the favours we now ask through the intercession of Bishop Angus Bernard MacEachem. Amen

*Novena to the Divine Mercy (Excerpts taken from the Diary of St. Faustina Kowalska, titled Divine Mercy in my Soul (C) 1987

Congregation of Marians of the Immaculate Conception, Stockbridge MA 01263

"Say unceasingly the chaplet that I have taught you. Whoever will recite it will receive great mercy at the hour of death. Priests will recommend it to sinners as their last hope of salvation. Even if there were a sinner most hardened, if he were to recite this chaplet only once, he would receive grace from My infinite mercy. I desire that the whole world know My infinite mercy. I desire to grant unimaginable graces to those should who trust in My Mercy. (Jesus I trust in you)

*As revealed to St. Faustina Kowalska, Novena to be recited before the feast of Divine Mercy starting on Good Friday. Jesus: "I desire that during these nine (9) days you bring souls to the fount of My mercy, that they may draw there from strength and refreshment and whatever graces they need in the hardships of life and, especially, at the hour of death. On each day you will bring to My Heart a different group of souls, and you will immerse them in the ocean of My mercy, and I will bring all these souls into the house of My father. I will deny nothing to any soul whom you will bring to the fount of My mercy."

*The Chaplet of Divine Mercy (to be recited on ordinary Rosary beads)

Begin the Chaplet with OUR FATHER.....HAIL MARY.....THE APOSTLES' CREED.

Then on the Our Father beads you will say the following words:

"Eternal Father, I offer You the Body and Blood, Soul and Divinity of Your dearly beloved Son, Our Lord Jesus Christ, in atonement for our sins and those of the whole word:

On the Hail Mary beads you will say the following words:

"For the sake of His sorrowful Passion, have mercy on us and on the world."

In conclusion, you will recite these words three (3) times:

"Holy God, Holy Mighty One, Holy Immortal One, have mercy on us and on the whole world."

First Day: For All Mankind Especially Sinners

"Today bring to Me all mankind, especially all sinners, and immerse them in the ocean of My mercy. In this way you will consol Me in the bitter grief into which the loss of souls plunges Me"

Most merciful Jesus, whose very nature it is to have compassion on us and to forgive us, do not look upon our sins but upon the trust which we place in You infinite goodness. Receive us all in the place in You infinite goodness. Receive us all in the abode of Your Most Compassionate Heart, and never let us escape from it. We beg this of You by Your love which united You to the Father and the Holy Spirit.

Eternal Father, turn your merciful gaze upon all mankind and especially upon poor sinners, all enfolded in the Most Compassionate heart of Jesus. For the sake of His sorrowful Passion, show us Your Mercy, that we may praise the omnipotence of Your mercy forever and ever. Amen. The Chaplet of Divine Mercy

Second Day: For Priests and Religious

"Today bring to Me the souls of priests and religious and immerse them in My unfathomable mercy. It was they who gave Me the strength to endure My bitter Passion. Through them, as through channels. My mercy flows out upon mankind."

Most Merciful Jesus, from whom comes all that is good, increase Your grace in men and women consecrated to You service, that we may perform worthy works of mercy, and that all who see us may glorify the Father of Mercy who is in heaven.

Eternal Father, turn Your merciful gaze upon the company of chosen ones in Your vineyard – upon the souls of priests and religious; and endow them with the strength of Your blessing. For the love of the Heart of Your Son in which they are enfolded, impart to them Your power and light, that they may be able to guide others in the way of salvation, and with one voice sing praise to your boundless mercy for ages without end. Amen.

Third Day: For Devout and Faithful Souls

"Today bring to Me all devout and faithful souls, and immerse them in the ocean of My mercy. These souls brought Me consolation on the Way of the Cross. They were that drop of consolation in the midst of an ocean of bitterness."

Most merciful Jesus, from the treasury of your mercy, You impart Your graces in great abundance to each and all. Receive us into the abode of Your Most Compassionate Heart and never let us escape from It. We beg this grace of You by that most wondrous love for the heavenly Father with which Your heart burns so fiercely.

Eternal Father, turn Your merciful gaze upon faithful souls, as upon the inheritance of Your Son. For the sake of His sorrowful Passions, grant them Your blessing and surround them with your constant protection. Thus may they never fail in love or lose the treasure of the holy faith, but rather, with all the hosts of Angels and Saints, may they glorify your boundless mercy for endless ages. Amen

The Chaplet of Divine Mercy

Fourth Day: For Unbelievers and Those Who Don't Yet Know God

"Today bring to Me those who do not believe in God and those who do not yet know Me. I was thinking also of them during My bitter Passion, and their future zeal comforted My heart. Immerse them in the ocean of My mercy.

Most Compassionate Jesus, You are the Light of the whole word. Receive into the abode of Your Most Compassionate Heart the souls of those who do not believe in God and of those who as yet do not know You. Let the rays of Your grace enlighten them that they, too together with us, may extol Your wonderful mercy; and do not let them escape from the abode which is Your Most Compassionate heart.

Eternal Father, turn Your merciful gaze upon the souls of those who do not believe in You, and of those who as yet do not know You, but who are enclosed in the Most Compassionate Heart of Jesus. Draw them to the light of the Gospel. These souls do not know what great happiness It is to love You. Grant that they, too, may extol the generosity of your mercy for endless ages. Amen.

The Chaplet of Divine Mercy

Fifth Day: For the Souls of Separated Brethren

"Today bring to Me the Souls of those who have separated themselves from My Church, and immerse them in the ocean of My mercy. During My bitter Passion they tore at My Body and Heart, that is, My Church. As they return to unity with the Church My wounds heal and in this way they alleviate My Passion."

Most Merciful Jesus, Goodness Itself, You do not refuse light to those who seek it of You. Receive into the abode of Your Most Compassionate Heart the souls of those who have separated themselves from Your Church. Draw them by Your light into the unity of the Church, and do not let them escape from the abode of Your Most Compassionate Heart; but bring it about that they, too come to glorify the generosity of Your mercy.

External Father, turn Your merciful gaze upon the souls of those who have separated themselves from Your Son's Church, who have squandered Your blessings and misused Your graces by obstinately persisting in their errors. Do not look upon their errors, but upon the love of Your own Son and upon his bitter Passion, which he underwent for their sake since they too are enclosed in His Most Compassionate Heart. Bring it about that they also may glorify Your great mercy for endless ages. Amen. The Chaplet of Divine Mercy

Sixth Day: For Meek and Humble Souls and the Souls of Children

"Today bring to Me the meek and humble souls and the souls of little children, and immerse them in My mercy. These souls most closely resemble My Heart. They strengthened Me during My bitter agony. I saw them as earthly Angels, who will keep vigil at My altars. I pour out upon them whole torrents of grace. Only the humble soul is capable of receiving My grace, I favour humble souls with My confident."

Most Merciful Jesus, You yourself have said "Learn from Me for I am meek and humble of heart: Receive into the abode of Your Most Compassionate Heart all meek and humble should and the souls of little children. These souls send all heaven into ecstasy and they are the heavenly Father's favorites. They are a sweet-smelling bouquet before the throne of God. God himself takes delight in their fragrance. These should have a permanent abode in Your Most Compassionate heart O Jesus, and they unceasingly sing but a hymn of love and mercy.

Eternal Father, turn Your merciful gaze upon meek souls, upon humble souls, and upon little children who are enfolded in the abode which is the Most Compassionate Heart of Jesus. These should bear the closest resemblance to Your Son. Their fragrance rises from the earth and reaches Your very throne. Father of mercy and of all goodness, I beg You by the love You bear these should and by the delight You take in them; bless the whole world, that all souls together may sing out the praises of Your mercy for endless ages. Amen.

Seventh Day: For Souls Who Especially Venerate and Glorify My Mercy

"Today bring to Me the souls who especially venerate and glorify My mercy and immerse them in My mercy. These souls sorrowed most over My Passion and entered most deeply into My Spirit. They are living images of My Compassionate Heart. These souls will shine with a special brightness in the next life. Not one of them will go into the fire of hell. I shall particularly defend each one of them at the hour of death."

Most Merciful Jesus, whose Heart is Love Itself, receive into the abode of Your Most Compassionate Heart the souls of those who particularly extol and venerate the greatness of Your mercy. These should are mighty with the very power of God Himself. In the midst of all afflictions and adversities they go forward confident of Your mercy; and united to You O Jesus they carry all mankind of their shoulders. These souls will not be judged severely, but Your mercy will embrace them as they depart from this life.

Eternal Father, turn Your merciful gaze upon the souls who glorify and venerate Your greatest attribute that of Your fathomless mercy, and who are enclosed in the Most Compassionate Heart of Jesus. These souls are a living Gospel; their hands are full of deeds of mercy, and their hearts, overflowing with joy, sing a canticle of mercy to You, O Most High! I beg You O God:

Show them your mercy according to the hope and trust they have placed in You. Let there be accomplished in them the promise of Jesus, who said to them that during their life, but especially at the house of death, the souls who still venerate his fathomless mercy of His, he, himself, will defend as His glory. Amen. The Chaplet of Divine Mercy.

Eighth Day: For Souls in Purgatory

"Today bring to Me the souls who are in the prise of purgatory and immerse them in the abyss of My mercy. Let the torrents of My Blood cool down their scorching flames. All these souls are greatly loved by Me. They are making retribution to My justice. It is in your power to bring them relief. Draw all the indulgences from the treasury of My Church and offer them on their behalf. Oh, if you only knew the torments they suffer, you would continually offer for them the alms of the spirit and pay off their debt to My justice."

Most Merciful Jesus, You Yourself have said that You desire mercy; so I bring into the abode of Your Most Compassionate heart the souls in Purgatory, souls who are very dear to you; and yet, who must make retribution to Your justice. May the streams of Blood and Water which pushed forth from Your Heart put out the flames of Purgatory, that there, too, the power of Your mercy may be celebrated.

Eternal Father, turn Your merciful gaze upon the souls suffering in Purgatory, who are enfolded in the Most Compassionate Heart of Jesus, I beg You, by the sorrowful Passion of Jesus Your Son, and by all the bitterness with which His most sacred Soul was flooded: Manifest your mercy to the souls who are under Your just scrutiny. Look upon them in no other way but only through the Wounds of Jesus, Your dearly beloved Son; for we firmly believe that there is no limit in your goodness and compassion. Amen. The Chaplet of Divine Mercy

Ninth Day: For Lukewarm Souls

"Today bring to Me souls who have become lukewarm and immerse them in the abyss of My mercy. These souls around My Heart most painfully. My soul suffered the most dreadful loathing in the Garden of Olives because of lukewarm souls. They were the reason I cried out: "Father take this cup away from Me, if It be Your Will." For them, the last hope of salvation is to run to My mercy."

Most compassionate Jesus, You are Compassion Itself. I bring lukewarm souls into the abode of Your Most Compassionate Heart. In this fire of Your pure love let these tepid souls, who like corpses, filled You with such deep loathing be once again set aflame. O Most Compassionate Jesus exercise the omnipotence of Your mercy and draw them into the very ardor of Your love; and bestow upon them the gift of holy love, for nothing is beyond your power.

Eternal Father, turn Your merciful gaze upon lukewarm souls, who are nonetheless enfolded in the Most Compassionate Heart of Jesus. Father of Mercy, I beg You by the bitter Passion of Your Son and by His three-hour agony on the Cross: Let them, too, glorify the abyss of Your mercy. Amen. The Chaplet of Divine Mercy.

*Gifts of the Holy Spirit: Wisdom, Knowledge, Understanding, Piety, Counsel, Fortitude, Fear of the Lord

*Fruits of the Holy Spirit: Joy, Charity, Peace, Patience, Kindness, Goodness, Long-suffering, humility, fidelity, modesty, continence, chastity

*The Beatitudes: Love/Joy/Gentleness/Goodness/Meekness/Faith/Peace/Long Time Suffering

*The Seven Sacraments: (A Sacrament is an outward sign instituted by Christ to give grace) Baptism, Eucharist, Reconciliation, Confirmation, Marriage, Holy Orders, Anointing of the Sick.

*In God there are Three Divine Persons: 1) God the Father 2) God the Son 3) God the Holy Spirit (Ghost)

*The Cardinal Virtues: Prudence, Fortitude, Temperance, Justice

*Seven Capital Sins (Cardinal Sins) – Pride, Covetousness (Greed), Lust, Anger, Gluttony, Envy and Sloth

*Seven contrary virtues are: Humility, Kindness, Patience, Diligence, Generosity, Abstinence and Chastity

*Theological Virtues: Faith, Hope and Charity

*Last Things: Death, Judgment, Heaven, Hell

*Spiritual Works of Mercy: Counsel the doubtful, instruct the ignorant, admonish the sinner, Comfort the sorrowful, Forgive injuries, Bear wrongs patiently, Pray for the living and dead

*Corporal Works of Mercy or Seven Acts of Christian charity are: Feed the hungry, Give drink to the thirsty, Clothe the naked, Shelter the homeless (stranger), Visit the sick, Visit and minister to the imprisoned, and Bury the dead

Prophet(s): What is a real or true prophet? A person spreading the good word, news and good fruits like character of God and Jesus. Someone who has faith, hope, charity and love and is a dedicated Bible reader who sacrifices his/her life for the greater good. Some possess the gift of healing. Some may visualize the future. Possess wisdom, knowledge and awareness of our fellowmen. They can live a much longer life. Have been known to pray and change the weather patterns such as: rain, drought, storms. Definitely understand there is both good and evil in the world.

Some prophets became saints. Possess resilience, a strong disposition and are ultra sensitive.

Compliments of: Salvation Army Prayers (Sowers of Seed pray for us." Personal Bible verses of Comfort, Assurance and Salvation). Given directly to me red and black small booklet). Continue reading your Bible. Its truths are true today and forever. For extra copies write to: (See References). Read daily quoted Bible verses.

"Man shall not live by bread alone, but by every word that proceedeth out of the mouth of God. (Matthew 4:4), Holy: From a child thou hast known the holy scriptures, which are able to make thee wise unto salvation through faith which is in Christ Jesus (2 Timothy 3:15), Memorize: blessed are they that hear the word of God and keep it (Luke 11:28), Thy word have I hid in mine heart, that I might not sin against thee (Psalm 119:11), Every word of God is pure: he is a shield unto them that put their trust in him (Proverbs 30:5), Thy word is truth (John 17:17), Study to shew thyself approved unto God (2 Timothy 2:15), If ye continue in my word, then are ye my disciples indeed (John 8:31), Every house is builded by some man; but he that it is appointed unto men once to die, but after this the judgment (Hebrews 9:27), A man's life consisteth not in the abundance of the things which he possesseth (Luke 12:15), For what shall it profit a man, if he shall gain the whole world, and lose his own soul? (Mark 8:36), For the wages of sin is death; but the gift of God is eternal life through Jesus

Christ our Lord (Romans 6:23), God hath given to us eternal life, and this life in his Son. (John 5:11).

These are written that ye might believe that Jesus is the Christ, the Son of God and that believing ye might have life through his name (John 20:31), And this is life eternal (John 17:3), He that believeth on the Son hath everlasting life: and he that believeth not the Son shall not see life; but the wrath of God abideth on him, God is angry with the wicked (Psalm 7:11), Come now, and I will give you rest. (Matthew 11:28), ... and him that cometh to me I will in no wise cast out. (John 6:37), Verily, verily, I say unto you, He that heareth my word, and believeth on him that sent me, hath everlasting life, and shall not come into condemnation; but is passed from death unto life. (John 5:24),

Jesus answered and said unto him, Verily, verily, I say unto thee, Except a man be born again, he cannot see the kingdom of God. (John 3:3), Ye must be born again. (John 3:7), Jesus said unto her, I am the resurrection, and the life: he that believeth in me, though he were dead, yet shall he live: and whosoever liveth and believeth in me shall never die. (John 11:25, 26), For God so loved the word, that he gave His only begotten Son, that whosoever believeth in Him should not perish, but have everlasting life. (John 3:16). For God sent not his Son into the world to condemn the world: but that the world through him might be saved. (John 3:17), but he that believeth not shall be damned. (Mark 16:16).

Nevertheless the foundation of God standeth sure, having this seal, the Lord knoweth them that are his. And, let everyone that nameth the name of Christ depart from iniquity. (2 Timothy 2:19), For we must all appear before the judgment seat of Christ; that everyone may receive the things done in his body, according to that he hath done whether it be good or bad. (2 Corinthians 5:10), So then every one of us shall give account of himself to God. (Romans 14:12),

God is not mocked: for whatsoever man soweth he also reap. (Galatians 6:7), But God Commendeth his love toward us, in that, while we were yet sinners, Christ died for us. (Romans 5:8). Who his own self bare our sins in his own body on the tree... (1 Peter 2:24), ... If we walk in the light, as he is in the light, we have fellowship one with another, and the blood of Jesus Christ his Son cleanseth us from all sin. (1 John 1:7).

...Christ died for our sins... (Corinthians 15:3), Neither is there salvation in any other: for there is none other name under heaven given among men, whereby we must be saved. (Acts 4:12), How shall we escape, if we neglect so great salvation? (Hebrews 2:3) ... behold, now is the accepted time; behold, now is the day of salvation. (2 Corinthians 6:2), FOR ALL HAVE SINNED, and come short of the glory of God. (Romans 3:23), ... what must I do to be saved? (Acts 16:30), ... Believe on the Lord Jesus Christ, and thou shalt be saved, and thy house. (Acts 16:31) JESUS SAID: BEHOLD I STAND AT THE DOOR AND KNOCK: IF ANY MAN HEAR MY VOICE, AND OPEN THE DOOR, I WILL COME IN TO HIM. (Revelations 3:20)

"God be merciful to me a sinner! I believe Christ died for me and that His Precious blood will cleanse me from all my sin. By faith I now receive the Lord Jesus Christ into my heart as my Lord and my Savior; trusting Him for the salvation of my soul. Help me Lord to do thy will each day. In Jesus; name I pray, Amen.

BELIEVER'S NAME: These things have I written to you that believe on the name of the Son of God; that ye may know that ye have eternal life, and that ye may believe on the name of the Son of God. (1 John 5:13).

Therefore being justified by faith, we have peace with God through our Lord Jesus Christ. (Romans 5:1), My peace I give unto you. Let not your heart be troubled, neither let it be afraid (John 14:27), And the peace of God, which passeth all understanding shall keep your hearts and minds through Christ Jesus. (Philippians 4:7), Casting all your care upon him; for he careth for you. (1 Peter 5:7),.

...Thou shalt love the Lord thy God with all thy heart, and with all thy soul, and with all thy mind. (Matthew 22:37) (Matthew 22:37), ... Eye hath not seen nor ear heard, neither have entered into the heart of man, the things which God hath prepared for them that love Him (Corinthians 2:9)

* The Stations of the Cross is a school of faith, the faith which by its very nature "works through love". (Galatians 5:6). Let us pray.

Brief pause in silence

Jesus, innocent victim of sin, receive us as companions on Your Paschal path, which from death leads to life, and teach us to live the time that we spend on earth rooted in faith in You, who have loved us and given Yourself up for us. You are the Christ, the one Lord, who live and reign forever and ever. Amen.

This verse is said after each station is announced:

We adore You, O Christ, and we bless You. Because by your holy cross You have redeemed the world.

1. Jesus is condemned to death
2. Jesus takes up His cross
3. Jesus falls for the first time
4. Jesus meets His Mother
5. Jesus is helped by Simon the Cyrene to carry his cross
6. Veronica wipes the face of Jesus
7. Jesus falls for the second time
8. Jesus meets the women of Jerusalem
9. Jesus falls for the third time
10. Jesus is stripped of His garments
11. Jesus is nailed to the cross
12. Jesus dies on the cross
13. Jesus is taken down from the cross
14. Jesus is laid in the tomb

Let us pray. Brief pause in silence.

*Jesus Lord rich in mercy, You were made man so as to become our brother and by your death conquer death. You descended into Hades so as to free mankind, to make us live again with You, we are risen and called to sit with You in the heavenly places. Good Shepherd who leads us to restful waters, take us in Your hand when we cross the valley of darkness, so that we may stay with You and contemplate forever your glory. Amen.

Why will we all wear white raiment at the end of the world? Good question. White signifies innocence and purity. It also means salvation, and absolution of sins. White has all the colors combined of the spectrum so yes white is a color. We will be free of our blood stained sins in the end. There are many shades of white just ask someone who is an interior decorator/designer or painter. Religious rites are usually performed with some part of white clothing such as a: shirt, pants, blouse, dress, skirt, headpiece, handkerchief, scarf etc.

A ritual for examples is being present in a church and lighting a candle or candles for your loved ones. Praying and remembering memories of your past life and the beloved person who died.

There are some people who live in houses with everything in white such as: paint on walls, furniture, floors, cabinetry, throw rugs, carpets, pillows, accessories and even dress in white. The outside is also painted white or has white stones. I cannot live without bright colors because I paint canvases in many different styles from floral, scenic, abstract, pastels to impasto yet like to dress in white at times it feels refreshing like the wind. Sometimes it is great to live your life in bright luminous Crayon* (trademark) box colors and revert to the inner child.

You know there is always a small box with a slot for a small donation which is called a tithe. In the Bible it states to give 1/10 of your earnings to help with world hungry, sanitation, medical care, well water, reading, learning, education, churches, charities, widows, orphans, hospital, schools, libraries or other charities. Feed the hungry, give clothing to the cold, give drink to the thirsty and provide shelter to the needy. That is the least we can do as good Christians. A 10% (percent) tithe may seem much yet it isn't. God and Jesus give us so much more abundantly back all the time. They are forever cheerful givers.

I noticed in the three Latin American countries visited many natives have a small alter dedicated to mother Mary in a high corner in their home. Usually a set of rosaries is draped around a statue from eight inches to 1.5 feet high. Other items such as cards, a Bible and cross are placed on a small wooden shelf. Sometimes a Saint Christopher medal or other medallions are placed also. There may be a religious yearly calendar hung for all the saints days and note worthy dates of Mary, angels, apostles, God and Jesus. This is a special place in the house can be in the dining room, living room, a corner of the kitchen or a spare room. Sometimes you will find a concrete statue of Mary bowed down in prayer or angels and fountains in the gardens of many homes. Often times I noticed an altar placed outside surrounded by a dome hand made in cement and seashells as a kind of offering to above.

Ghandi once said he loves God and Jesus just no his followers. Now I realize after thirty-five years what he really meant. That Christians are sometimes too boisterous, direct and proud and at times can be hypocrites. We are flawed and sin often and have many faults. Also the over burdened who force to push their religion on others even when it is not welcomed. Questions like have you been saved yet/today? I think he really meant that instead of a united front many Christians lead solitary lives without others. Not that they do not need others they just choose to live this way. Other believers lead lives of martyrs, suffering and aloneness.

Often times the only real company is their church family. Ghandi meant do not go home and drink, swear and treat your children, relatives, family dishonorably the day after church services. Many are not lonely in their aloneness times. They mediate, watch nature and reflect. Some religions have many problems within their own parishes. Arguments, denial, hidden motives, disputes, dishonesty, favoritism, patronage, pettiness, payoffs are all problems to contend with. What sermons to give and lessons to learn. They have their own children taught catechism or weekly devotion. Ghandi also meant to be open and willing to learn from other people's beliefs/religions and values. In the end what really only matters is love and kindness.

Now this statement will create much controversy. Before I have people accosting me in the streets, all the Rabbi's, teachers, students, reformed, Hasidic and Orthodox or Jewish believers name calling or writing threats please here me out. I'm quoting Jesus' exact words not my own personal opinion. "Jesus is the long awaited predicted Messiah". Jesus told me who in the world do they think the Messiah will be? It is not John the Baptist, Abraham, Moses, David, Jacob, Elijah, or any of the twelve lost tribes named. Jesus said at this point there is no explanation or justification required at all. God indwells in me and I the son in him. Do they not know the first followers of Jesus were Jewish? I was raised as a rabbi/teacher in the Jewish faith by Mary and Joseph with all the education, celebrations and feasts. At the end of the world (date and exact time only God knows), I (Jesus) will arrive in the sky upon the clouds on a white horse (stallion), surrounded by many leagues of angels and it will be written Prince of Peace, King of Kings. Some will not be happy upon my return and try to start war(s)/battles/armies/fights with weapons and all them will lose."

"The truth of the awaited return of the Messiah, the Immaculate Conception, the Baptism, the Crucifixion, The Resurrection, the Ascension, Christmas (my birth), my existence and God living/ indwelling and me and I living in God, and the Holy Spirit (The Trinity), the Revelation will finally be accepted and believed by the entire world population. I'm married to Mary Magdalene in heaven and have a total of six (6) biological children with her. Mary Magdalene was/is the first apostle (female) who followed us all the other apostles for three years providing communication, shelter, food and provided warmth to everyone. Mary is a grand listener, wonderful mother sensitive and sincere. Yes, there was some jealousy during this time period/era in history and those who opposed a woman apostle not I." Jesus stated the name Yahweh is the name of my son and third child. My first child is named John and my second child a daughter is named Sarah-Tamar. Also there is no reason to omit the vowels from the names: Eloi, God, Yahweh or Elohim. I know you find the names too sacred and do this out of respect and beliefs. I am the real light source and life the beginning and the end. My true birth date/birthday is October 25th in the fall. Keep celebrating Christmas on December 25th we and all the angels enjoy seeing such a joyful celebration around the world with singing and wonderful suppers and the beautiful lights." I was not divulged the names of Jesus' other remaining three children.

The heavenly realm states do not gossip, slander, cause defamation of character or judge. I asked legal advice and they stated Nora the commandment states do not bear false witness against thy neighbor. That answered many of my questions. "Comfort ye, comfort ye my people". Always have faith, hope, charity and love. The most important trait and quality being love which roots its good fruit in your fellowmen and neighbor(s). Sort of like the grand oak tree planted and growing from a small acorn. God and Jesus find ingratitude/ ungratefulness one of the worst sins. We must give thanks and appreciate our gifts. Also, do not taunt/bet against God and ask to prove his existence. Jesus finds separateness terrible this is the reason he goes after his lost sheep. God states someone who curses against the Holy Spirit is the unpardonable sin. We need to live today in the here and now. The give me more mantras does not work. The constant requests of: I want, need, desire repeated endlessly in pleading accusations.

These constant demands give of nothing but endless frustration. There is over abundance and God is good. We must have faith with a positive outcome. The intention of the proper outcome will always provide and nothing is impossible with Jesus/God. Yes, Jesus and God want us to persevere and persist yet not be a brat either. Why did I not get what I want and then pout? God and Jesus are pretty slow to answer my prayers. I have been waiting for years now. Why is this happening to me again? It is just not fair. Why was my life spared and not his? Do you hear me? That is not what I asked for? Are you kidding me? I'm really angry right now and disappointed with the outcome. We get anxious and have constant expectations. Do not swear on anyone's grave(s) to prove a point there is no need. You are all blessed. God and Jesus told me you think you are the worst sinner? There are many others.

God and Jesus have forgiven the worst kind of people, sinful, awful. If you plan on holding grudges/vengeance/revenge/ bitterness/ anger all your life you can forget it. When you enter heaven everyone requires to be forgiven in your life as God and Jesus have forgiven you. Every one of your adversaries, enemies, and people you distrust and dislike. They do not like the word hate it is too strong and vile. In order to produce good fruit (us) on the vines (Jesus), branches and roots (God and the Holy Spirit) and to extract God like character takes constant work and re-evaluation of self. God and Jesus can cut off, trim, and shear the branches at any time to prod and chastise us to become better human beings. We must pray sincerely and wholeheartedly and seek their faces (God and Jesus) in order to receive change and the proper decisions from the heavenly realm.

Many place the blame on Jesus and/ or God when events and personal lives are not fulfilled according to our needs. Also much hostility such as: Genocide, killings/murder, rape and the unthinkable losing your entire family or child people are so angry the first reaction is to place blame on one who loves them unconditionally. During the Holocaust when all that after despair and faith all that was left was the word Hope. I learned there was some kind of supply/ storage area where the victims would accumulate things. The storage area was called Canada (Kanada). I think in their dreams to be eventually relieved of the most horrific memories it humbles me to know they wanted to come to the country I was born in. I can go on forever about the injustices done.

The irony is that six million (6,000,000) Jewish people were killed/maimed/gassed/murdered and then buried or incinerated during World War II. Now the total Jewish population 2021 is approximately six (6,000,000). The same number slain has repopulated thanks be to God. There are many genocides and wars in the world where so many lost their lives for hatred, riches, weapons, greed, oil, money, power, corruption and control. What many people do not know at first two million (2,000,000) other people were murdered and killed before the genocide even began who were not Jewish people: gypsies/mentally ill/homosexuals/Polish/Slavic/French/Checkoslovakian/disabled/gypsies/old/mentally challenged/uneducated/or depressed/Homosexuals/Polish/Slavic/French etc.

If they felt threatened and considered you a communist you were ordered to kill others and bury the dead. There were different badges with colors of yellow, pink, blue, red, black, green etc. divided into groups. They went back at least three generations and if one of your great grandparents was Jewish (Juden) and thus you were completely ostracized and hated. This happened to one of the high level prominent SS Gestapo officer. What is important to learn and know is that the massacre happened to innocent victims who thought they were going for good jobs/work.

Not starvation and work to death (slavery) then murdered. All personal possessions in the home (furniture were confiscated), property, contents of businesses, cash/monies (stocks, bonds, certificates, treasury bills, GIC's, securities), rare coins, stamps, antiques, investments, art, jewelry, all clothing, shoes, boots, glasses and even gold teeth, stallions and race horses were all stolen. What I find really gross/disgusting is that human skin was used for soap, and lamp shades.

At this finality of the book I would like to mention various parishes and different religions which exist today globally: Catholic, Roman Catholic. Some titles of the Roman Catholic Church are: Priest (Father), Nun (Sisters), Ministers, Cardinals, Bishops, Deacons, Abbess and of course only one Pope. Protestant, Orange (Orangemen), Pentecostals, Loyalists, Calvinists, Jacobites, Nazarene (Nicine), Methodists, Baptists, Lutheran, Anglican, Presbyterian, United Churches, Quakers, Mennonites, Shakers, Mormons, Moslems (Islamic), Buddhists, Brahma's, Taoists, Hindu, Greek Orthodox, Judaism (Reform, Orthodox, Hassidic etc.). Grey Nuns, Monks, Franciscans, Carmelites, Celtics, also some have the opinion that the Druids (Priests) were Doctors from the East. The old Pioneers and New Englanders (new arrivals) in the U.S.A. were called: Puritans (Purists). Indigenous/Natives: Believe in relationships, gatherings, sharing, loyalty, honor, respect, hope, faith, charity, love, peace, serenity, tranquility, families, nature, (trees, valleys, water, wind/ rain, ocean, lakes, streams, rivers) sacred animals, dream interpretation, prayer, imagery & symbolism, meditating, pondering/reflection, medicinal herbs, and all kinds of art.

Various religious orders started by saints handed down their beliefs. Missionaries, Evangelists are still working around the world. There are presently approximately one thousand five hundred to one thousand eight hundred (1,500-1,800) different organizations/groups of missionaries in the United States of America today who work internationally... There are many religious orders that reside currently in various monasteries which follow strict schedules and regulations to pray/worship/praise/ work/food/clothing/shelter. Some monasteries are located high in the mountains on top of a precipice or on many remote islands with usually all men and/ or all women. With all the wars thousands of monasteries were totally destroyed. A shame to think disciplined people with their unity who wanted just to pray, labor and live in peace would cease for many centuries. In Prince Edward Island (Canada) there is a large group of men and women monks who will be building a new monastery in the near future. They grow their own wheat crops and make homemade wheat buns and bread.

Vikings/Norse (Scandinavian descent) their God was called Odin. They believed in fortune telling of Runes/bones. What I find fascinating is that religion was taught in Latin, Greek, Aramaic and Hebrew for centuries and some were self taught in languages. There was much illiteracy and only one single language spoken in homes. Many people with an English speaking mother tongue could not partake in understanding these languages and it became a great communicative barrier. Approximately in 1600's St. James would translate the Bible into English was no small feat. So if you are going to understand the Bible it is only natural that you would want to read it in the language of your upbringing. It is unfortunate that is the 1500 even until the 1990's many ministers and priests did not want their clergy to completely question nor understand the Bible with its nuances. This would invite debates and challenges. It held people ignorant for centuries. I do not agree that my personal religion could any longer instill fear, abomination nor excommunication. I'm born a Catholic Christian. I have become half barren by twenty-three (23) years old and totally barren at thirty-eight (38) years old due to having Cancer twice in my twenties. Have no fear for the big "C" word. You can get over it with intention; believe me I'm a survivor.

Free Masons have their own secret society/handshakes and meetings in Masonic Lodges worldwide. I do not know if they are a religion/selected private group/

or cult. The Masons are known as the workers/builders of the world (masonry) erecting churches and many other buildings with a corner stone engraved with the year/date of completion and their initials or name. The secrets of masonry are passed down from generation to next generation. Their symbols are compass, rulers and sextant etc. They believe in brotherhood. No one knows what goes on in these meetings because they are sworn to secrecy. From my research there are only two women in the world who were accepted as masons because their father/patriarchal ancestry were known members all their lives. One woman Free Mason was from France. As far as I know the highest level/degree is the number Thirty-Three (33 degrees). Some U.S. Presidents, prominent/elite business men, inventors, authors, writers and Benjamin Franklin were known mason members.

They also had/have been Royal members. I learned that some jobs will not ever grant nor promote to a higher level or pay raise unless you are an accepted mason member patronage at its best. What I discovered in my research is that they do believe in John the Baptist to be the real saviour and not Jesus. This is why you will see many paintings of portraits from Leonard de Vinci with the curly haired blonde male with the index pointing upwards to heaven with the imagery number one or true messiah in their opinion. Leonardo de Vinci was a Mason. You would be surprised at how many famous important people past and present are members of the Free Masons. Free Masons do not give you a list of membership names I already asked. It has something to do with confidentiality. As far as I know there were only two female members in the entire world due to their parentage (father) being long time members into this elite group. One was from France. All male members allowed only. Why? That is a secret too. I'm now joking.

Scientology has got to be the most controversial religion. There are many knowledgeable interesting books and volumes of information which will take you decades to fully read and comprehend. Life is a process. We are all from a main source and are like tendrils Scientology have this fact right. The original CEO person who died started Scientology wrote his own personal biography/book. He was an avid businessman/boatman/worker stated it is a big cult. Who should I believe?

Many people claimed to have stopped/left Scientology and have disappeared from public view. One example is the wife of the present CEO or President the big boss. The lawyers now state she is alive and doing well; we do not hear her audible voice nor see her filmed in a live interview. Why the hiding from the public? She is/was such a strong determined force and enthusiastic chronic supporter for decades. Do people simply disappear without warning alive or dead and no investigation is conducted by agencies or private investigators regarding this topic? Is there no interest or deserved follow-up?

After reading many Scientology books the only few disagreement(s) and personal opinions I have is separating families or breaking-up all families or relationships in order to destroy opinion and communication for the cause. Also duly noted are next to nothing cheap salaries given for free labor of twelve (12) to fourteen (14) hours daily or more. Some only make approximately one hundred and fifty US dollars "150.00 US $"* or a little more per month and are housed, feed and sheltered for free. Depending on your position at a high level you will have an impressive a luxurious apartment/condo/or house very close to your place of work, maid service, cleaners, personal hair stylist, great food and a car or driver every day, privileges and benefits* for free in return for an extremely low salary and long tenuous work hours. This kind of treatment is totally ego driven.

Many are dressed in white and navy, badges, strips and gold brass the whole nine yards in clean ship like uniforms, hats, and polished shoes. Even some women depending on their level and department of work are called "Sir". On a national television channel there was confirmation of genuine stories of parents which are separated from their families and become strangers to their own children. I also read of children doing adult heavy landscape including digging, lifting/moving large rocks work for years with absolutely no monetary compensation.

There is some staff that is hired to manipulate and destroy personal relationships. In Scientology you are extremely encouraged to live for your work. It is such a strong task force I often ask myself is this volunteer or forced due to fear? The money funding issue is strange in many people on average income second mortgaging their homes for new books/knowledge. Also the nepotism is incredible where whole families and relatives join. Now those in Scientology please do not follow me personally, send me legal letters, or jargon this is only my personal view and opinions (freedom of speech).

I have been mocked, laughed at, criticized and ridiculed for many years because of my religious beliefs. I do not take it personally at all. The delicacy arises when some members quit and other family remains.

Everyone is entitled to their views. I would be delighted to speak to the head of Scientology yet for an in person meeting. He seems always unavailable to speak to the public. Perhaps criticism is not everyone's forte and they become naturally defensive. Perhaps he would say I was misinformed, wrong or try to explain the process of their organization. Much may be solved by communication face to face. There is so much negativity concerning this religion which has to be confirmed, answered and justified. No, I do not plan on writing a book about Scientology or grabbing a rare important interview in the future. I'm not an opportunist and have many core values. Notice how I will not write personal names, and do the finger pointing.

Religion is about personal choice. Not everyone will agree with your point of view. I think people should be free to join, quit whenever they chose without worry, apprehension or fear of retaliation. What I want to write about is the large discrepancy between movie stars or famous people treatment and the regular scientology other members. There are differences in preferential treatment for sure. Now I will tell you right now Scientology members are encouraged to stay with their own kind/ types. Does this religion target or want people preferably who are successful, rich and the elite? I cannot comply and answer this question. I do not know or shown enough facts. No religion is far from perfect.

Catholics (Roman Catholics): Many priests had encouraged the rural farming Catholic community families to always procreate it is God's word and way. The priests were celibate and not permitted to marry in my clergy. They were giving advice to women to give birth to at least twelve (12) to twenty-five (25) children in Quebecois household, also Acadian areas and elsewhere. A small family was seven children. The larger families were greatly encouraged to maintain the farms with family members being the new future laborers and workers. What about all the women who were barren and would have to hear all the discussions about all the other mothers with their babies? It is very painful emotionally and mentally to want a child so badly and unable to conceive.

My own mother had troubles after her last 5th (fifth) child was born and was weak for a few months afterwards. She gave birth to her last child my younger sister at forty years old. We are not including still births, crib death, babies dying not long after birth, or miscarriages or death by disease. For example it was not uncommon for a woman to have one (1) to five (5) miscarriages or more between children until she conceived once again. Also it was very common to lose the first child due to lack of hygiene or the mid-wife being late or the mother not being able to reach a hospital in due time.

There is an ongoing feud between the English and French for the last five hundred (500) years besides fur trading. Advancement (lack of) Education for important jobs like: lawyers, doctors, judges, civil work, businessmen which was not inclined ever given to French speaking people. Whereby the rural French farmers were extremely poor, uneducated, with numerous children to support and care for and could never get ahead. Many were illiterate because their children had to work young on the farm to support their parents.

Thus nuns/priests and religions were in collusion with the government and hospitals because they controlled education, hospitals, orphanages even some monasteries. Schools and some colleges/private schools/ universities, paid no taxes and bought lakefront properties to sell later. The Grey Nuns and many other orders would collect spare change door to door from poor families asking for donations for at least one hundred (100) years even though they were worth many millions at the time. How do I know this, my grandmother and mother told me the nuns came knocking on doors with their can offerings to collect for any spare change anyone would provide. This was the instilled guilt and you felt deeply obliged to help/assist others. Who gave the most the poor and we cannot deny to this day. The poorest have the biggest hearts in Quebec. Religion did control the Catholic Church and not many read their Bible nor had opinions or objections to the priests or ministers. To criticize a holy one was just not done. So even if young boys confessed to their parents of priests or nuns wrong doing they would get reprimanded, slapped, denied and called liars. The worst possible feeling would be ostracized from the Church or excommunication was like death from all the shame and guilt. No communication with friends, neighbors, the total community. It was like you were living a death. Even the front pews were paid for by the richest families.

There were thousands of missionaries around the world who worked diligently with the indigenous/native population and overseas. Opportunities were not granted nor warranted for business locales, buildings and grants/bursaries. The nouveau riche or bourgeois has happened for only the last maybe one hundred years at the most not before. The few elite Quebecois families also spoke fluently in both languages or were also educated in English at a young age at private schools some even graduated from Oxford (England). Some privileged rich families such as: Bombardier, Trudeau, Dupont, DuMaurier, Lavelin, etc. were considered rarities and not the norm.

Many did not know that for at least seventy-five (75) years cons from the Maritime Provinces would take advantage of all naive, gullible, good hearted French Acadians and Quebecois. They would try and charm/talk then force their way into your personal homes and completely raid their houses of antiques. Their behavior was very aggressive, pushy and arrogant. They would not even asking permission and just walked into the attics, barns, out buildings, basements looking for expensive antiques to resale at a huge profit. They spoke fast and confused everyone saying you don't use this or that, I will take it off your hands.

Often times offering to clean up the attic and basement and taking away the valuable items and leaving the junk for you to clean up. They would leave a rag to clean or give 5.00 in change for the entire theft, rush to load the truck and drive quickly away oftentimes without a license (to be put on later when they took the ferry). They walked out laughing forever the richer. The French Quebecois and Acadians did not know the monetary value of their antiques/possessions/furniture. Often times the cons would offer a ridiculous price next to nothing for an object worth a few thousand. They would target widows/widowers or people living alone.

They took tools, furniture (slow burning stoves, antique stoves/dressers, old mirrors, milk cans, oil lamps, vanity tables, all collectables/tables/chairs/couches/settees/cabinets/corner tables/card tables/love seats/end tables/large library reading chairs/ wing chairs/built in cabinets/lounge sofas/ bed frames and all floors lamps/chandeliers/small decorative vases/vintage books/dish sets/all glass/ enamel/antique gold/silver and costume jewelry/watches/pocket watches/comics/phones/radios/ retro items/gramophones/old records/small accessories etc.). If you had change or money lying around they would see an opportunity and take it. In the barns they would steal harnesses, ropes, saddles, etc. It was not uncommon to ask to dismantle a large barn piece by piece (rafters, beams, shingles etc) with all its contents and either sell or rebuild the barn elsewhere. They would come with a large van and return with a moving truck if they found a good fish. Also they would clean sweep an area never to return or try until another two to five years later hoping everyone would forget them. They would send relatives of friends in their place not to be recognized.

Don't let me begin to even address and discuss about the deprived Maurice Duplessis (the premier of Canada/Government of Canada) orphan children (approximately 7,000)* who were illegally put in insane asylums. They converted orphanages to asylums and put normal children to live mixed with the insane with no education, books nor games nor motivation. They could neither read nor write. Staring at walls and rocking in chairs all day. Life was a complete blank for them. They were deprived of attention, human touch dignity and love. The excuse no one else wanted to help them at the time. They were starved, tortured, beaten, raped, continual told lies, and some given shock treatment. Some were maimed and killed and chained to their beds for days considered rejected outcasts of society. Many lived with have scars on their faces and elsewhere on their bodies. Whipping on the back and hands was not uncommon. They told some parents their child was dead and in return told the child their parents were dead.

They stated 33%* or one third was not insane. I think the number is much higher and they cheated the families with lies. Doctor's were hired to give tests to the children and they wrote unbelievable diagnosis and given permission to falsify documents. Doesn't this story sound exactly familiar to what happened to the indigenous/Native schools? Why did this happen? Greed, collusion, money, control, power and heartlessness or all combined. An outrage at the time and they worked at least twenty (20) years for their rights. The Church, government, doctors and hospitals denied any wrong doing. Finally the government came forward for a very small settlement. The compensation which I think was only about twenty (20,000 $) per/each individual child of the one thousand five hundred (1,500) orphans who were still alive at the time. It is absolutely deplorable.

It was unheard of to complain about not wanting more children. Aborting a child was non-existent. If you took a chance with an unknown Doctor many women hemorrhaged to death. Some relied on old remedies, herbs and folklore. I heard of stories of a succession of seven sons or daughters and the wife being blamed or was told was her fault. It is the male chromosome that decides the sex of a child period. All this nonsense of always wanting a son and not daughters has got to end. It offsets the balance of nature. You can leave an inheritance and legacy to your daughter. The obsession with sons is only to carry on the family name and more descendents is totally egotistical. A woman does the same just with another family name which is different. I'm hoping we are no longer always thinking like a patriarchal society any longer and getting more evolved. There are countries that are more worried about a dowry than their own child. There are about at least two (2) large countries right now stuck with a huge percentage of males and they cannot now find a wife.

This much I know: An offense by others can become complete turmoil and strife. If you are too sensitive and touchy you remember what someone has said or done and let it fester inside instead of stating for example: "I do not like what you said and you have deeply offended me by your callous words, deeds or acts". This offense turns into dislike, ignoring the person, and deeply rooted resentment. After that in time you learn and play revengeful games in your head and how you want to get the person back and never act on your thoughts. They are just bad thoughts you think. When you see the person you even gravitate towards loathing and eventually hatred. Other sins involved could be covertness, jealously, envy and greed. If someone has a heavy crush on you and is not reciprocated; they are in lust. Our pride does stand in our way.

Have you noticed the most proud people do not even know they are proud? It has to be pointed out many times by others before they even realize their effect on others and their loved ones. Sometimes you will want to walk out of a room in their presence. It is really difficult if you have to work with this person on a daily basis without avoidance. You cannot believe the two faced hypocrites, the constant betrayals, the insults, sarcastic comments and all the drama with the situation. Eventually the person spreads vicious rumours and tries to blame, slander your good name for their own faults. Most people are cowards and cannot face the truth. It becomes a problem or situation to solve.

Do I ignore the person for the rest of my life and pretend nothing bothers me? Will I eventually forgive their wrong doing? Will I harbour so much resentment and vengeance that it will take twenty (20) years or more to give back the same pain? Guess what? The person who has offended you never thinks of you or what they have done because they learned to live in the present moment only.

They are so engrossed in their egos and their selfish acts your time is never appreciated nor respected. So all this wasted energy is sad. Someone told me you might as well dig two graves when you live with revenge on your mind continually which will eliminate and absorb all positive thinking. Some people say drop it and let the pain go. I think the most difficult thing to do is to forgive. When you apologize look into the person's eyes sincerely. State what you did that was wrong, ask for forgiveness, truly repent your wrong doing and pray for aid/assistance. Do not be surprised if the person does not want to forgive you yet. Life is not a movie screen where we always have happy endings. At least you will feel some weight lifted off your shoulders and tried to do your best. No one can be forced to forgive or grant forgiveness. To be continually lied to by someone you trust is extremely painful. Even when confronted they create more lies until the person you love becomes a pathological liar. They lie about everything.

Deception, despair and strife and total frustration may/can lead to murder. If your thoughts always negate constantly 24/7 (day and night) about someone you loathe it warps your personality and mind. Being deceived is no picnic and it takes great maturity to ignore someone's negativity and just move on positively. The expression you cannot touch me rings well. Imagine all that energy you spend and waste on hate and turn it around, into love, release your imagination and generosity, pay it forward and you can indeed change the world. How? The more people perfect their awareness and wake up spiritually then all the matter, auras, energy and we will lift up to higher realms/dimensions. We will all be changed forever to a God-like character to bear good fruit at last.

Another taboo topic hardly anyone one barely discusses is Abortion, the other suicide. The following is only my personal opinion(s). In the animal kingdom such as wolves, the aunt will give milk to the pups until the mother returns with food to eat. The wolf aunt dies a week later starving to save the pups/cubs. A dog will adopt kittens; squirrels even a small monkey as their own and feed them. A dog runs across a highway to put its body on top of a pregnant female dog and he does not even know to protect from oncoming highway traffic. Not one person stopped its car to help. Animals never abandon their offspring. The only time a hard decision is made is either a deer, monkey etc who has twins. There is only enough milk to feed one offspring. The most difficult burden has to be decided for survival. I have seen an Asian monkey's mother carry its three month old dead corpse for three days in her arms, whimpering, crying until she lets it drop to a soft cushion in moss and leaves below a tree. Completely devastated.

Why are human beings killing their babies, life, fetus(es) all over the entire world? There are so many excuses for the fear of life such as: Cost – money as if a baby is a by product or commodity, youth, ignorance, lack of sexual education from the parents/teachers/councillors. Handing out condoms for protection against sexually transmitted diseases and not explaining what they do and that they are not 100% safe. Not a good time and not ready, interfering with education, ruining my youth and I got the whole world in front in me, time and care it takes, my parents will kill me, religion, other addictions. Now the difficult decision which affects a small percentage is pregnancy due to rape or health problems.

I heard of parents beating their children because they are pregnant. Oh yeah that makes lot's of sense when they never spoke, discussed nor communicated how a baby is born and it is always the woman's fault etc. You should know better, I'm ashamed of you, how could you let this happen. Men/teenagers/ boys running away from their responsibilities and some do not. Not one woman I spoke even discussed the abortion with the father. Only the date, cost and time and if they would please be there for support. Perhaps the father wants to raise or keep the child. No one forgets an abortion and always wonder what if...our lives circumstances were different?

Many times the girl/teenager was sent to a house or nunnery to give birth and the child was adopted. There is nothing wrong with adoption. Many await the chance you discard away. It always boils down to the woman's body and I will do what I want with it. Many men pressure/encourage abortion also which is a total cop out and selfish. Just facilitates a way not to embarrass themselves and their families. Class distinction you are not high enough class for me to have a child with you. Arguing back and forth when people think the fetus is now a baby. Did you know there is a huge corporation taking dead aborted fetuses, and body parts in the United States in America under an assumed name that tries to hide and dignify what they are doing? Not in a third world country where they encourage children always. Abortion is not a form of birth control. The pill has to be taken daily to be effective (not a few days skipped).

You think I'm being biased coming from a person who could never conceive because of cancer. I'm barren. My parents never had the birds and the bees talk with me due to religion, shyness, embarrassment. They thought I would learn at school from my friends or teachers. Yes, I'm pro life. In Latin America they felt sorry for me because I was without a child. Some things you do not know: Babies are alive right away after conception. They can feel and hear voices from the womb. If you punch your stomach and reject an unborn child long enough the child will be born very premature and grows with hatred towards its mother. When a mother nourishes her baby with milk and she is irate, angry and screaming, the baby can become very sick. The mother does not feel like giving milk, the baby/child feels rejection and cries more. If you have an addiction to alcohol, drugs then the baby is born with the addiction also. Yes, if you have Aids your child will be born with Aids also. I knew someone who heavily smoked all during pregnancy warned many times for her health. One of her twins died the other survived. All we need is love people.

In closing, I would finally like to sincerely thank the PEI (Prince Edward Island, Canada) islanders and people whom have donated for many years their clothes, books, decorations, shoes, boots and accessories, kitchen items and sometimes even furniture. You may have not known by giving to others is the best gift for years. I have warm coats, and lovely sweaters. All the beautiful dresses that people compliment me on are all because of your warm hearts. Much appreciation and thanks to the church ministry of (West PEI) for the people who still work diligently, give, volunteer their spare time and help serving others. During a time when I moved eight (8) times in three years and lived in motels and rented homes and felt lost. I was one of many of tens of thousands of Canadians who worked hard all their lives and finally lost their personal home due to unforeseen circumstances. You have inspired me through the Holy Spirit that there are people who love and care in this world. United, you have become cheerful givers and we in turn have donated what we could afford at the time. When I was cold you gave me blankets, and warm clothing. When thirsty and hungry you give me spiritual guidance and inspiration to write this book.

Thanks to you God and Jesus and the Holy Spirit for granting me such a precious gift my beautiful twelve (12) year old dog Hallie. My beloved pet dog Hallie has deceased this year on October 27th, 2021 at twelve (12) years old due to lymphatic cancer in the nodes and her breasts. I had to make a choice to euthanize her. The vet told me she would suffer immensely and only had a few weeks to live. I think Hallie was waiting for me to accept her death and held on to the inevitable. She lost movement in one of her back hind legs and had troubles getting up and she could no longer walk. Hallie did not want to go take her favorite daily walks on the beach any longer and would rest in the car for a long time panting; she was exhausted. Her joy was to sit in nature and watch the barn cats, birds, huge old trees, and flowers on the Gallant family homestead farm for hours on the cushion of her seaweed bed on the banks of the house. I love and miss her so much as well as others. She taught me to live with more love in your heart, and charity and to always be a cheerful giver.

Also, it was ok to be depressed and sad at times her comfort so generous. Hallie had given birth to a total of twenty one (21) puppies in three (3) different litters. She was the best mom forever dotting to all her now presently full grown adults of nine (9), seven (7) and five (5) years old all whom have found loving homes. Rest in peace forever my best friend and I positively know and have absolutely no doubt you went on a direct quick flick flash switch straight arrow ticket to heaven.

Many thanks to the Salvation Army staff who provide food and dry products enabling me to continue to feed my many barn cat kittens. They cook and feed lunches to the needy local people five (5) days a week in the small town/city. I was embarrassed and worked most of my life, so it was really difficult to accept assistance from others. When I lost over five large back molars (teeth) from malnutrition it lead me to change my ways. Yes, in this day and age with all the comforts of Canadian society people do still suffer. The fault of obstinacy, charity and stubbornness always gets in the way.

Sometimes you do have to swallow your sin of pride and face the truth. Help is there you just have to grasp and accept it as a gift. Many sincere thanks on behalf of all the others. I pouted and gloated for six (6) months before seeking help. Now I donate clothing, books and kitchen items etc. and give all the time it is contagious. God and Jesus are good and understand. Be a cheerful giver. Remember if your clothing is too small or too large and have not worn the item within the year then give it away to someone else. Make someone else smile today. Do you really need twenty purses, thirty hats and fifty pairs of shoes?

All my love and God blessed be to everyone in the world.

Acknowledgements

I would like to thank God, Jesus, Mother Mary, Mary Magdalene, Saint Joseph, the Holy Spirit and Apostles, Angels for whom this book is made possible. To my parents who were really good. Thank heaven for the abundance of gifts and talents. Commend the Saints and our Guardian and Arch Angels who follow us throughout our lives. To the sixteen (16) Arch Angels: Michael, Raphael, Gabriel, Uriel, Rakiel, Jophiel, Ariel etc. Hi to Chelsea, Garth, Kendall and David (special young child angels). Hello to my twin sister in heaven Nathalie and Brothers Aaron, Zachary, Isaiah and Jean-Mathieu who all died at birth and I have not met in person yet. My younger brother JM (Jean-Marc) also nicknamed as Jimmy. I like to call him Mark. To my niece and nephews (Audrey, Olivier and Tristan) who I see next to never due to the far/long distances we live and no car, you are always on my mind.

To my friends Leonce Gallant, Joseph Gallant (prefers Dennis), Tracy H., Michael P. To my younger sister Chantal and older brother Gilles and Louise. My deceased friends: Clarence Graham, Reg Noonan, Jay Gallant, Art, Leo (Castor), Tony P., Alan MacDonald, William Green, Allen Lecky, Lionel. Hello to my beloved pet three dogs (Chole, Bella, Hallie) and many barn cats that have left this world for a better one: My best companion, friend dog companion Hallie (Black Labrador, Borderline Collie and 1/8th wolf) who had three litters of twenty-one (21) puppies after twelve most cherished beautiful years died this year on October 27, 2021. Chloe (large Labrador Black and White), Bella (long eared beautiful beagle), Caramel (one of the pups who died 7 days after birth), Barn cats: Calico, Sapphire, Ginger, Honey, Blackie Black, Lamb,

Marmalade, Sandy, Rainbow, and Momma. A special thank you to the (West Prince PEI, Canada) Church Ministry and their volunteer staff for supplying clothes, blankets etc. to the needy.

All research for this book was initiated by glory and teachings the Holy Spirit (Holy Ghost). Conversations were all written down in note form in many journals suggested by Mother Mary. The audible voice is God's and Jesus' true word. My friend Cheryl Gallant who is always an inspiration and understands me totally. Through her gave me the idea for this book. It took five (5) years of compiled writings in many journals, notes, poems, conversations, points, prayers and songs etc. The heavenly realm is greater than you can ever imagine. You definitely require an Agent, Editor, Copy Writer, and Proof Reader from a publisher to complete a written book. I am forever grateful to the whole team. Thank you for your assistance, guidance, patience, editing and hard work, correcting drafts etc. to make someone else's dream come true in advance.

Let them help you for they are experienced and do not get upset with their red pen marks with words like stet, edit, delete, omit, redundant, run on sentence, tense, repeat, fragment, what do you mean? Their suggestions and perfectionism is meant to encourage not insult and they just want a polished professional book like you do. Eventually I will get a publicist when the right time arises and if truly needed/required. My dream and legacy is to have this book published in thirty (37) languages. That would make me content and will probably cry. I have included many original prayers from various sources see References section for a detailed list and contact information for their company names, addresses, phone numbers, Email(s), websites when available, cards, pamphlets and/or booklets. I'm hoping you will use this book as a gift for reference to others. Also included is a long recommended list of titles of spiritual books and authors whom inspired me greatly.

Biography

Nora Gravel was a backslider twenty-five years who found her true faith once again. Descendent of French/Irish/Metis Indian and some European, she was raised by a middle class family. Her father was in the Royal Canadian Air Forces (RCAF) for twenty-five (25) years and was pinned personally by Sir Winston Churchill on a rainy day with umbrella and of course his famous cigar. Mother stayed worked at home with her five (5) children and helped manage all the real estate with Dad. My parents owed, opened and operated a small Mom and Pop's restaurant in Longueil (Quebec) in 1958 ran by my mother and Aunt Nora (II) also worked and helped. My father also enjoyed the camaraderie talking to the test pilots and staff of the RCAF by working as a part time bartender after business hours. My mother enjoyed culture, art, dances, concerts and movies. Nora is the middle child and the creative one of the family.

Nora worked for twenty-five years in Quebec (Canada) starting at fifteen (15) in two (2) retail stores. She worked at Mer-Sea Logistics Freight Forwarding, Herzing Institute computer school, and large corporations including Pratt & Whitney Aircraft Ltd., A division of United Technologies USA, temporary at Alcan Aluminium in the Legal Department, Manac-Prenctice Hall (Legal Software) and McGill University as an assistant in (V.P. Physical Resources full time, V.P. Architecture, and Engineering Departments on relocation). Also worked for Collector's Choice Art Company in the Sales Department with the Head Office in New York. Nora assisted in Management Forums, Art Shows and a selling auction only. She was a real estate agent (Realtor) for five (5) years in PEI (Canada). Nora was fortunate enough to enjoy some extensive travelling to Europe (lived for four (4) years on Ramstein base Germany, visited: Luxembourg, Holland, Bavaria at a very young age and much later on her own to three (3) Latin America countries, (Cuba, Guatemala and Mexico), London and Sydney (Australia), New Hampshire, Vermont and Florida in (United States). She enjoyed the cottage style life beside a popular camp on a lake in Val-des-Bois, and the Laurentians (Quebec) with her family and many decades later on in middle age for ten years lived and owned a white (red trim) salt box farm house, extra large Dutch post and beam barn with 11.8 acres sub-divided and remaining with 6.4 acres with water-view of the Northumberland Strait in Cap-Egmont (PEI).

Her true calling is being an author (writer), artist, drawing and painting, making jewelry, writing poetry and lyrics to country songs. Hobbies are: an avid swimmer, enthusiastic flower and herb gardener, reading vintage books, cooking/baking, cycling Nora was in twelve (12) feature films (Montreal), movies and pilots as an extra. She is now often called a loner by neighbors/others. She enjoys nature, trees, birds, flowers, water our element, writing, reflecting, solitude, researching, movies, karaoke singing at times for fun and spending time cooking or making desserts with close friends only. Often you will find her taking long walks or swimming on the beach to collect sea glass shells and drift wood. Her favorite is using an art printer and a tumbler with sand for rocks and sea glass. She will create her own E-commerce personal website for Art/drawing/painting using different mediums etc. Her other hobby is updating her personal Pinterest Pages where you can find pictures of her personal art.

She has resided in Prince Edward Island the smallest Canadian province for the last eighteen (18) years. Nora looks forward to relocating to the beautiful Atlantic Maritime coastal province of Newfoundland in with kind people in the near future for the last few decades remaining of her life. She claims the final stop makes for our real home. My dream is to have a deck/patio overlooking the Atlantic ocean/sea and riding on a Vespa revamped/remodelled scooter. It will be an ideal place for inspiration as an author/writer. Would not mind living in either Italy or France (Europe). She is presently working on her fifth book. You can easily find her imitating other singers and doing various voices.

References

(Servants, Orders, workers, helpers, Bible, Prayers, quotes and religious cards and including Purgatory, Proper way to prayer the Rosary and Novena of the Divine Mercy, Salvation Army Prayers,

The way of the Cross (on Good Friday) by the Pope John Paul II:

The Saint James Bible (Large print my personal favorite with burgundy and gold cover) – Old and New Testaments. Thank you to God and Jesus to whom all four hundred (400) writers and scribes (word for word and counting each word and text) who wrote the greatest book the Bible over thousands of years. For those of you who do not know the Bible language originated in Greek, Aramaic, Hebrew and Latin amongst other languages at the time in history. Therefore it is really difficult to always get the proper right word(s) and meaning(s) in translation. Of course we have David writing Psalms which were really deep prayers, supplications, songs, lyrics and poems composed on his lute/harp while he danced along. There are approximately three thousand (3,000) languages groups of people and their own dialects still waiting to this day to read the Bible (the word) around the world.

The Servants of Mary (The Servite Order founded in 1233), 1439 Harlem Avenue, Berwyn, IL 60402 (708) 795-8885 or (800) 778-4000 Website: www. servitedevelopment.org *Prayer for Strength and Healing, The Use of St. Peregrine Oil

St. Joseph's Workers for Life and Family, P.O. Box 7369 Station Vanier, Ottawa, Ontario (Canada)K1L 8E4 Phone: (613)742-7012, Email: info@sjw.ca, website: www.sjw.ca, follow on Face book at: www.facebook.com/sjw.ca Prayer of Archbishop Fulton J. Sheen, Prayer for the Unborn (Spiritual adoption). Prayers to St. Joseph (Head of the Holy Family, Protector of the Church, Patron Saint of Canada), Prayer to St. Joseph for Our Family, Prayer to St. Joseph for Canada, Nicene Creed, Morning Offering, Act of Faith, Act of Hope, Act of Charity, Act of Contrition, Angel of God, Memo rare, The Seven Sacraments, In God there are Three Divine Persons, The Cardinal Virtues, Seven Capital Sins, Last Things, Theological Virtues, Gifts of the Holy Spirit, Fruits of the Holy Spirit, Spiritual Works of Mercy, Corporal

Association of Marian Helpers (Marians of the Immaculate Conception) Stockbridge, MA 01263 Prayers 1-800-804-3823, marian.org, Orders: 1-800-462-7426, Shop Mercy.org, Prayer to Saint Michael the Archangel, St. Michael Defend Us.

NIHIL OBSTAT, Most Rev. Richard Grecco, Bishop of Charlottetown (PEI) Canada, May 23, 2014, from the Card describing Bernard MacEachem the first Bishop of Charlottetown and missionary work in the Maritimes (Eastern Canada)

Daily Prayer for Priests, Imprimatur (Printer) Robert C. Morlino, Bishop of Madison, 6 September 2018 website: www.CatholicPrayerCards.org 1-888-244-2788 Email: orders@CatholicPrayerCards.org, Card # 714

How to Pray the Rosary properly

Novena to the Divine Mercy – Excerpts taken from the Diary of St. Faustina Kowalska, titled Divine Mercy in my Soul 1987, Congregation of Marians of the Immaculate Conception, Stockbridge MA 01263

The Chaplet of Divine Mercy nine straight days.

Salvation Army Prayers (Given directly to me red and black small booklet), Sowers of Seed, Box 6217 Fort Worth, Texas U.S.A. 76115 "Brethren, pray for us." Personal Bible verses of Comfort, Assurance and Salvation

The Way of the Cross at the Roman Coliseum with Pope John Paul II, presiding on Good Friday, 2004. (Stations of the Cross)

There is More! (The Secret to experiencing God's power to change your life). By: Randy Clark and foreword by Bill Johnson, 2013. Other books: The Essential Guide to Healing by: Bill Johnson and Randy Clark, Healing unplugged (Conversation and insights from Two Veteran Healing leaders by: Bill Johnson and Randy Clark

The Devils Door (How obedience to God can protect you from the bondage of sin). By: John Bevere bestselling author of: The Fear of the Lord and The Bait of Satan. Other books: Bait of Satan (Your response determines your future), Breaking Intimidation (How to Overcome fear and release the gifts of God in your life), Victory in the Wilderness (Growing Strong in Dry Times), The Voice of One Crying (A Prophetic Message for Today!) John Bever Ministries, P.O Box 2002, Apopka, FL 32704-2002, Tel: (407) 889-9617, Fax: (407) 889-2065

The Way of the Cross for the Holy Souls in Purgatory, Edited by Susan Tassone, Our Sunday Visitor Publishing Division, Our Sunday Visitor, Inc., Huntington, Indiana 46750 Periodicals, Books, Tapes, Curricula, Software, Offering Envelopes Website: www.osv.com for a free catalog call 1-800-348-2440, Printed in 2000 Holy Souls Mass Apostolate

Epilogue

After reading this book I hope you will be enlightened of your own spirituality. You can use this book as a reference for the character traits of the apostles and others, properly praying of the rosary etc. Hopefully you can decide yes there is truly higher power and presence in your life. Should you still not believe it possible, read the book once again. Think of a better life with more positive thoughts and outlook. The future is bright and life is a gift so embrace it. We are here to do better for others. Live a life of servitude or teaching, counselling and paying it forward. Listen to the true voice of your calling.

Should you be undecided it is possible to work two jobs before you pick the one which makes you satisfied and content. A job is not a job if you enjoy what you are doing. You will not lack passion. Some people say life is a journey; others say it's a life of suffering, depravity and sadness. It will depend on your outlook, thoughts and personal views. We all have problems and stories. Some people lead impossible lives and come through while others live in torment of the past. Live in the moment of now and let go. I have made lists of many prayers with contact information and references. Also you will find a few religions listed and defined which I have narrowed down to a select few. Finally you will read three (3) of my personal stories and journeys. At the back of the book I have listed a list of recommended reading books which prove beneficial to a spiritual awaking.

You can heal yourself and others through positive intent, living in the now and surrendering the past. The future you have no control over. Just being in the presence (present time the now) not only doing. By accepting and surrendering to your injury/disease and facing your fear(s) directly may increase an eventual healing process. Do not talk and focus all your energies on your sickness all the time to give it any power. Many of our diseases/illnesses are caused by lack of love, fear, loneliness, anxiety, mental issues, deprived pent up emotions of our true selves, caring too much for others and forgetting oneself, selfishness, egotistical pride and unresolved issues of anger.

There are many lessons in life and many people will enter your life for a reason. Do not question everything. Some issues remain a mystery the way God and Jesus have intended. Life is simple: Be kind, truthful, honest, trustworthy, have some integrity, laugh, share, be happy, joyful, cheerful and show your love to everyone. Do not be sad when someone you love dies. Our lives and destinies are pre-planned like a blueprint. Be content for others successes and never laugh at another's demise.

I'm looking forward to heaven and eternal life when my time is destined.

Recommended Reading

(These books will definitely inspire, help and bring messages of peace and love). Perhaps you will get inspired today. I read hundreds of spiritual books of the years and have narrowed down my list to the following:

Daily Light on the Daily Path "Inspirational thoughts for every day of the year. New King James Version dated 1989. Inspirational Press (New York). Published in 1990 by: Inspirational Press, A division of LDAP, Inc. 166 Fifth Avenue, New York, NY 10010 - This beautiful book inspires, makes one contemplate and is addictive. Verses organized according to scripture. I read this book everyday along with my large print King James Bible. A great read.

Roses in December (Mary's Garden of Miracles) by Dom Forker – 2008. A great read. Lovely

Brother Andre – The Wonder Man of Mount Royal – 10th printing 1988 (348,000 copies to 1988)

L'Oratoire St. Joseph (Montreal, Quebec) Canada. The miracle priest/healer/worker cured/helped people from around the world had 2,000,000 million people at his funeral which was duration of two weeks. Highly recommended to read this one. (Paperback book)

Healing the Wounded Soul (Break Free from the pain of the past and live again) by Katie Souza 2014

Charisma House (Spiritual Growth), Facebook.com/CharismaHouse, Twitter:@CharismaHouse, Instagram.com/CharismaHouse, Pinterest.com/CharismaHouse, Modern English Version Bible

www.mevbible.com, Sign up for free at (email): nl.charismamag.com and get topics like Charisma Magazine Newsletter, Charisma Newsletter, SpiritLed Woman, New Man, 3-in-1 Daily Devotionals (Exclusive Content, Inspiring Messages, Encouraging Articles, and Discovering Freedom). I learned many valuable lessons by reading this one book.

The Jesus I Never Knew – by Philip Yancey – 1995. Well written, researched and thorough.

The Secret of Happiness by Billy Graham 2002 – Sermon on the Mount and Beatitudes defined in detail.

Re-Creating Your Self – By the author of Conversations with God author Neale Donald Walsh – 1995. Small book well organized and answers many questions about a self spiritual journey.

Thoughts from the Mount of Blessing by Ellen G. White Edition 1956. Educational.

Come Unto Me – Goodwill Publishers, Inc., Gastonia, North Carolina – 1962 Edition

Power Freedom and Grace (Living from the Source of Lasting Happiness) A lifetime of Wisdom from the International Bestselling Author of The Seven Spiritual Laws of Success by Deepak Chopra

199 Promises of God – 2007 – Prince Edward Island (Canada) Ministry Team: Rev. Paula Hamilton, Chaplain: Rev. Annette Wells, Praise & Worship: Elaine MacLennan and Beverly Beck, 28th Annual Women's Retreat Sept. 28-30, 2012, Rodd Mill River Resort, Standing on the Promises (1 Peter 1:25) – (Small booklet)

Psalm 23 – The Song of a Passionate Heart, Hope and Rest from the Shepherd by David Roper. Well written. Thick cover. Makes you think

Worship by Robert L. Dickie (What the Bible Teaches about...Adoration, God Centered, Preaching, Praise, Focused on Christ, Liturgical, Music) – 2007 – I enjoyed reading this book.

Fresh Wind Fresh Fire (What Happens When God's Spirit Invades the Heart's of His people) by Jim Cymbala with Dean Merrill – 1997

What the Bible Says about Angels (Powerful Guardians A Mysterious Presence God's Messengers) by Dr. David Jeremiah – 1996

The Wisdom of the Celts, Compiled and introduced by David Adam – 1996 (Small book) Unexpected.

The Expected One a Novel by Kathleen McGowan – 2006

A Tale of the Tardy Oxcart by Charles R. Swindoll – 1998 Edition. Thoughtful spiritual tales/stories. I constantly re-read this book many times. Witty full of wisdom and truth.

All Things Are Possible Through Prayer by Charles L. Allen (From one of America's most beloved inspirational writers, the Bestselling Author of God's

Psychiatry) The faith-filled guidebook that can change your life! I like all books about praying.

The Wonders of God by William MacDonald (Christian Living – Gospel Folio Press)

Soul Speak the Language of Your Body (How our higher selves deliver messages to us through our physical bodies to keep us on our chosen paths of development) by Julia Cannon

Secrets of the Vine for Teens by Bruce Wilkinson with David Kopp – 2003. Small book and Interesting.

The Tender Farewell of Jesus (Meditations on Chapter 17 of John's Gospel) by Adrian van Kaam with a Foreword by Susan Muto – 1996. Well planned collaboration. Answered many questions.

Be Not Afraid by Jean Vanier "All of us are captives of our fear", "Love seems impossibly distant and people are afraid", "Our political and economic structures reflect our inner fears" 1975 Edition

Prayers for Lent Easter and Pentecost by Donna E. Schaper – 2005. Informative

Why Jesus? Millennium Edition by Nicky Gumbel – 2000 (booklet). Easy to comprehend.

Prayers at a High Altar by Charles Frederick Boyle, Book of War Poems – 1942 (booklet) Nice write up.

The Birth of Christ (Catholic Know-Your-Bible Program), Sponsored by the Benedictine Monks of Belmont Abbey by Katherine Burton – 1958 with plates/images/prints/illustrations. Simply beautiful.

The Christmas Story as given in the Edgar Cayce Readings – 1956 (booklet) A fast read.

Jesus Taught Me to Cast out Devils by Norvel Hayes, 3rd print over 20,000 copies (booklet). Surprising.

He Loves Me! – By Wayne Jacobsen (Learning to live in the father's affection) – 2007. A book to give as a gift.

The Power of Transforming Prayer (the classic work by: J. Oswald Sanders) – 2019. A keeper.

The Grace of God by Williams MacDonald – 1960 Fundamental Baptist Church, 200 MacEwen Road

Summerside, PEI (C1N 2P6) www.fbcsummerside.org (booklet)

The Laws of Spirit (A Tale of Transformation, Powerful Truths for Making Life Work) by the Author of Way of the Peaceful Warrior by Dan Millman – 1995

Earth the Toughest Boot Camp in the Universe (A thought-provoking guide to navigating the realms of Past Life Regression) by Elizabeth Taylor-Wey. Wow, I had no idea you should read this one.

The Tender Farewell of Jesus (Meditations on Chapter 17 of John's Gospel) by Adrian van Kaam with a foreword by Susan Muto – 1996. Well done.

Soul Speak (The Language of Your Body) How our higher selves deliver messages to us through our physical bodies to keep us on our chosen paths of development by Julia Cannon. Truthful, enjoyable mentions most ailments.

Be Not Afraid "All of us are captives of our fear" "Love seems impossibly distant and people are afraid" "Our political and economic structures reflect our inner fears" by Jean Vanier – 1975

Stand (Core Truths you must know for an unshakable faith) by Alex McFarland – 2005

Transforming the Inner Man (God's powerful principles for inner healing and lasting life change) The Transformation Series by John Loen and Paula Sandford

Heal Your Body – The bestselling author of You Can Heal Your Life by Louise L. Hay, The Mental Causes for Physical Illness and the Metaphysical Way to Overcome Them. Thoughtful I like this one.

Finding Meaning in the Lord's Supper by The Rev. Herman Kyle Nagel – 1958. Oldie but goodie.

The Secret of the Rosary – St. Louis De Montfort 28th Printing 1995. 4,600,000 printed of this Edition since 1965 to 1995. Newer editions available. (Small book) Millions of people cannot be wrong.

L'image de Jesus dans l'Histoire et dans l'Art avec deux cent (200) illustrations et deux (2) planches en couleurs hors texte preface du Prof. S. Ricci – Jean H. Meille, Agence Generale de Librairie et publication,

Paris (7ieme) – 7, rue de lille, Librairie JU. H. Jeheber Geneve, 20, rue du marche. In French lovely drawings/images/illustrations and pictures of various artists who portrayed Jesus around the world.

The Applause of Heaven by Max Lucado, 1995

Epic Battles of the Last Days by: Rick Joyner (MorningStar Publications, 16000 Lancaster Highway, Charlotte, NC 28277 Toll Free: 1-800-542-0278

The True History of God's True Church (and Its 2,000-Year war with the great false church) by: Gerald Flurry. Canada: Philadelphia Church of God, P.O. Box 400. Campbellville, ON L0P 1B0, Facebook: facebook.com/ PhiladelphiaChurchofGod, Google+:plus.google.com/+PcogOrg, Twitter: @ PCG_News

This one is not about religion yet really enjoyed reading because I'm a child of creativity. Title: The Courage to create by: Rollo May (author of Love and Will) 1975. Other books by same author: The Discovery of Being, Psychology and the Human Dilemma, The Meaning of Anxiety, Power and Innocence, Freedom and Destiny

Printed in the United States
by Baker & Taylor Publisher Services

Printed in the United States
by Baker & Taylor Publisher Services